The Un-Civil War:

BLACKS vs NIGGERS

Taleeb Starkes

<u>To My Mother:</u> *Although dysfunction and crime saturated our public housing landscape, and the typical excuses for failure were embraced by the average resident, you never subscribed to that victimization mentality. Instead, you became a motivating example where none existed. My love, gratitude, and respect for you are eternal.*

<u>To My Boys and Candy Girls:</u> *Troy, Mal, Malik, Ike Jr, Najee, Muff, Shug, and Tootsie. Despite any of my preventative measures, undoubtedly, you will encounter the NIGGER subculture. When it occurs, I hope that you'll be able to recognize that their illusory, short-term delights are loaded with real, long-term, and sometimes irreversible consequences. More importantly, I simply want you to maximize your potential and not make the same mistakes as me. Remember,* ***"The two most important days in your life are the day you were born and the day you find out why."*** – Mark Twain

Read Before Proceeding

1. *I am* ***not*** *advising, advocating, or otherwise condoning engagement of any act that would be in violation of local, state, or federal law.*

2. *This book excessively uses the word 'NIGGER' and its many derivatives. Advisedly, if you're a person who is easily offended by its usage, you'll really be pissed!*

3. *The news headlines referenced throughout this book are actual, unadulterated, headlines. In many instances, my comments are noted underneath the headlines [in bold parenthesis] to emphasize a point. In the online version of the book, the headlines are hyperlinked.*

4. *This book may contain copyrighted material in which the copyright owner may not have specifically authorized usage. Such usage is permitted under the "Fair Use" provisions located in the Copyright Act of 1976, which permits usage* ***"for purposes such as criticism, comment, news reporting, teaching (including multiple copies for classroom use), scholarship, or research."***

***

This book is dedicated to the memory of those innocent souls whose premature demise was NIGGER-inflicted.

Foreword

A *multi-generational clash continues between two oppositional cultures within the African-American community... BLACKS and NIGGERS. This uninterrupted animosity stems from the NIGGER subculture's self-defeating, anti-society, values conflicting with the forward-thinking, pro-society values of BLACKS. As evidenced by the unparalleled amounts of homicides, violence, and mayhem occurring in the African-American community, this battle is essentially an Un-Civil War.*

Over generations, many people (from all races) have sacrificed their time, careers, money, and even lives, so that African-Americans could have equal footing in this mosaic of a country called America. However, as evidenced by their entitlement mentality, the NIGGER subculture chooses to selfishly reap the benefits obtained through the Civil Rights struggle, while ignoring the associated responsibilities that accompany those rights.

The dysfunctional NIGGER subculture is determined to commandeer the African-American image, and re-shape it into their counterproductive image and likeness. Moreover, their lack of positive achievement is devaluing historic BLACK achievements. Therefore, as BLACKS, exposing and isolating this defectively mutated segment from the African-American community must become our highest priority. Failure to aggressively act has exacerbated our dire predicament, and continued stagnation only furthers their destructive agenda. Today is the tomorrow that we should have prepared for yesterday.

"It's some shit going on with Black People right now. It's like a civil war going on with Black people and its two sides. It's Black People and there's Niggers...and Niggers have got to go!" - **Chris Rock**

Table of Contents

*Taleeb's Definitionary

The listed definitions are the opinions of the author and are necessary for content clarity.

African-Americans – A general, politically correct, and encompassing term that consists of three separate groups; BLACKS, NIGGERS, and blacks with NIGGER tendencies a.k.a blacks (W.N.T). Generally, a quick observation of an African-American's dress, mannerisms, and vocabulary, is a strong indicator to which group an Af-Am individual most likely belongs.

***Anti-NIGGER* -** Any person, place, or thing that serves as a repellent or turn-off to NIGGERS and their subculture.

BLACKS – The most diverse and upwardly mobile segment of African-Americans. The term is capitalized throughout the book to differentiate them from the other two African-American segments (blacks [W.N.T] and NIGGERS). BLACKS are a minority group within the African-American community.

blacks (W.N.T) – The largest segment within the African-American community. They are blacks (lower-cased) with NIGGER tendencies who have embraced certain aspects of both the NIGGER and BLACK lifestyles.

Euro-Americans – A general term used when speaking of WHITES, wiggers, and White Trash as a single entity. WHITES, wiggers, and White Trash are the three distinct European tribes native to America.

HNCUs **–** An acronym for Historically NIGGER Correctional Universities. They specialize in providing an alternate form of education to the NIGGER segment of African-Americans. Similar to Historically BLACK Colleges and Universities

(HBCUs), HNCUs have campuses spread throughout the country, and are funded by state, federal, or private sectors.

HNCU Semester **–** One calendar year

HoG – An acronym meaning "Hood or Ghetto." A physical place of limbo and stagnation where Obsessive Nigger Disorder (O.N.D) and its destructive elements manifest. It is essentially ground zero for NIGGERtivity.

Homey-cide – The homicide of a NIGGER.

JuviNIGGERS – A fusion of the words "Juvenile" and "NIGGERS." The term includes pre-teens, adolescents, and young adult NIGGERS.

NIGative – A fusion of the words "NIGGER" and "Negative."

NIGGERS – Also called BLACK trash, are the lowest, most dysfunctional, and violent segment of African-Americans. The term is primarily used throughout the book to describe males, but at times, describes the entire parasitic subculture. Like BLACKS, this rogue splinter group is also a minority within the African-American population. NIGGER is also an acronym for Negro Individual Generating Grief Everywhere Routinely.

NIGfestation – A fusion of the words "NIGGER" and "Infestation" that describes the clustering of NIGGERS in a place or event, usually to the detriment of others. Also, it can be any place or event that has been overrun or lost to NIGGERS.

NIGGERfilia – The act of justifying NIGGER behavior; usually by sympathizers and apologists. Also, any impenetrable excuse-making for NIGGERtivity and/or their dysfunctional subculture. NIGGERfiliacs are essentially sheep protecting wolves.

NIGflation – A fusion of the words "NIGGER" and "Inflation," which describes the unintended, indirect, and associated costs (mental and/or physical) caused by NIGGERS when doing business within the African-American community or with African-Americans as a group.

NIGGERgeddon - A fusion of the words "NIGGER" and "Armageddon," which describes the collective NIGGER reaction (usually chaotic) to a situation that does not benefit them. *[Example: Reaction to the "Not Guilty" verdict in the Rodney King trial].*

NIGGERnomics - A fusion of the words "NIGGER" and "Economics," which describes NIGGERS' monetary affairs (Budgeting, Investments, Expenditures, Income, etc.)

NIGGERtivity –A fusion of the words "NIGGER" and "Activity," which describes the typical turmoil and violence caused by NIGGERS. It ranges from simple assault, murder, and all crimes in between. *[Authors note: The full range and impact of NIGGERtivity is incalculable].*

NIGvana – It is a fusion of the words "NIGGER" and "Nirvana," which describes the blissful reaction after receiving welfare benefits.

NIGvasion – a NIGGER invasion.

O.N.D – An acronym for Obsessive NIGGER Disorder. A condition in which a person simply enjoys being a NIGGER

Quadruplers – Baby Mamas whose lifestyles are subsidized by taxpayers at least four different ways. *Ex: Subsidized housing, daycare, food stamps, cash, medical etc.*

Sugar Daddy – The taxpayer funded entity that subsidizes the NIGGER subculture. Also known as the government.

WHITES – Capitalized throughout the book to differentiate this diverse, and upwardly mobile class from the other two segments (wiggers and White Trash) within the Euro-American community. Unlike BLACKS, who are a minority within the African-American populace, WHITES are the majority amongst Euro-Americans.

White Trash – Also called trailer park trash, are a minority segment within the Euro-American populace. Oftentimes, popular culture stereotypes them as rednecks.

wiggers – A fusion of the words "WHITE" and "NIGGER." They are lower cased whites who are essentially whites with NIGGER tendencies, abbreviated as white (W.N.T). Similar to blacks (W.N.T), wiggers have embraced certain aspects of the NIGGER subculture. However, unlike blacks (W.N.T) who are a majority amongst the African-American populace, wiggers are a minority within the Euro-American populace.

Urban Terrorist – A NIGGER who has committed a violent crime(s) or act(s) against a non-NIGGER citizen/civilian(s).

XeNIGphobia – The fear of NIGGERS

Introduction

Why Write This Book?

"I'm for the truth, no matter who tells it. I'm for justice, no matter who it is for or against. I'm a human being, first and foremost, and as such I'm for whoever and whatever benefits humanity as a whole." – Malcolm X

First and foremost, I must disclose that I'm not a novelist by profession. I am simply a BLACK man who possesses multi-layered animosity towards a dysfunctional and sociopathic subculture that openly exists within the African-American community. My abhorrence runs so deeply that I'm committed to combatting this subculture on any accessible platform. Secondly, I'm no aristocratic, BLACK elitist that has "made it," and subsequently decided to condemn other African-Americans from my ivory tower. Nope, this is an honest and direct assessment recorded from an ugly front line; it's void of political correctness and happy endings. My meager academic credentials consist of a public high school diploma and an incomplete HBCU experience; thus, my viewpoint isn't that of a scholar, intellectual giant, or wordsmith. Instead, it's shaped from my experience as a father-husband- son- brother- uncle- cousin- friend, and neighbor living in a modest row home in a "working poor" area of a NIGfested city. Overall, I'm just a fed-up citizen who's venting about the impact of a dysfunctional and bloodthirsty minority within a minority. Despite the reoccurring fear that my thoughts wouldn't effectively transfer into words, continued frustration and anxiety superseded all hindrances, and has resulted in a form of spontaneous combustion that I didn't foresee... this book.

(The Book)

As an individual, I felt powerless against a subculture that was seemingly dictating terms in most major cities. So, for more than a decade, mentorship has been my primary, combative weapon against them. However, my efforts haven't kept pace with their unending lawlessness that's dilapidating communities and cities.

Subsequently, writing became my therapeutic method to convert bottled frustration into effective action. During this writing process, I went through a range of emotions that ultimately made their way into this manuscript: angriness, happiness, somberness, liveliness, pessimism, optimism, sadness, lightheartedness, conservatism, extremism, liberalism, and even sarcasm. Moreover, I found that formal and informal conversational tones were both necessary forms of expression. Predictably, NIGGERfiliacs will interpret my analysis as "self-hating," and likely dismiss this book as another *"Afristocracy versus Ghettocracy"* attack. In other words, the Huxtables attacking HoG residents. Actually, this work is the opposite of self-hating; it's self-loving. The BLACKS versus NIGGERS culture clash shouldn't be confused with the universal conflict between the *"haves"* versus the *"have nots" (My most recent bank statement confirms my enduring membership in the "have nots").* Please understand that NIGGERS aren't the ***"have nots,"*** instead, they're the ***"rather nots"***! Why do I call them the ***"rather nots"***? Because they ***"rather not"*** productively contribute to society, they ***"rather not"*** cease NIGGERtivity, they ***"rather not"*** accept responsibility for their actions, they ***"rather not"*** (feel free to fill in the blank).

(All in Vain)

Emphasis must be placed on the fact that this book wasn't written as a rehabilitation instrument for NIGGERS; if books such as the Holy Bible, Holy Qur'an, Torah, Message to the Blackman etc. don't influence them to constructively change, then what book can? Moreover, countless well-intentioned books have been written by concerned BLACK people to address, guide, and reform the NIGGER subculture. Nevertheless, NIGGERS enjoy being NIGGERS, so all benevolent attempts of outreach or reformation have generally been futile. Even the historic and groundbreaking accomplishment of having a BLACK First Family has had minimal transformative effect in the HoG. Arguably, NIGGERtivity has worsened under *"Hope and Change."*

Member of 'Obama Boyz' gang charged in St. Louis shootings

stltoday.com

(The Reality)

Although this book exposes the continuing class warfare (those "with class" battling those without), I realize that this unconventional endeavor will not be unilaterally supported by BLACKS. Regardless, I will continue to speak on behalf of those BLACKS who've exhausted their empathy for the NIGGER subculture. Nature decrees that the young bury the old, but in the African-American community, NIGGERS ensure that the opposite is practiced; the old are burying the young. Statistics confirm that NIGGERS don't subscribe to the open-minded mantra of *"live and let live."* For that reason, our self-preservation depends on removing or isolating the NIGGER virus from its African-American host, or the host will perish. (Sigh) I'm truly TIRED of premature funerals... I'm truly TIRED of parents burying their children... I'm truly TIRED of candlelight prayer vigils, and makeshift stuffed animal memorials... I'm truly TIRED of "R.I.P" tee shirts, and murals of victims... I'm truly TIRED of the cycle of violence and dysfunction engineered by Urban Terrorists! I'm truly tired of being tired; therefore, the NIGGER subculture had to be confronted.

(Denial 101)

During a 2009 speech commemorating Black History month, U.S Attorney General Eric Holder took America to task for its inability ***"to have frank conversations about the racial matters that continue to divide us."*** He professed, ***"Though the nation has proudly thought of itself as an ethnic melting pot, in things racial we have always been and continue to be, in too many ways, essentially a nation of cowards."*** He also concluded (in part), ***"we, average Americans, simply do not talk enough with each other about race."*** While many African-Americans applauded Attorney General Holder's interpretation of national affairs, I found it extremely disingenuous to expect a national, interracial dialogue when we (African-Americans) refuse to internally dialogue about the destructive subculture residing within our race! Grandmomma Starkes always said, ***"When pointing your finger, realize that there are three more fingers pointing back at you."*** So, Mr. Holder, remember that three are pointing back at you. Understandably, other races typically avoid such calls for honest, interracial discourse with African-Americans because of the assured accusations of racism. As a result, no true dialogue can commence, especially when not-so-flattering facts cannot be included into the ***"frank conversations."*** Pertinent truths such as the disproportionate amounts of crime, murder, and societal dysfunction that are consistently perpetrated by an African-American subculture are summarily dismissed as racist statistics; thus, excluded from the discussion. The African-American community frequently utilizes finger pointing as an alternative to honest dialogues without acknowledging that three fingers are pointing back. We bury our garbage (the NIGGER subculture) in our backyard, and then get upset when others complain about the smell. Instead of using his BLACK history speech to chastise America, Attorney General Holder should have emphasized the cleaning of our backyard. Sadly, by playing the blame game, the highest cop in the land was essentially contributing to the denial, and code of silence mentality that's destroying our communities.

(Pledging Allegiance)

Undoubtedly, this book will be unpopular in many circles because it exposes an inconvenient truth. Furthermore, venting publically about the NIGGER nuisance will make me a pariah to some, and sell-out to others. Nevertheless, unlike NIGGERfiliacs, I've abandoned the habit of rationalizing for a subculture that embraces irresponsibility, promotes ignorance over information, and when all else fails (as it usually does), plays the victimization card. Simply stated, my allegiance is to the like-minded.

In summary, this critique is an attempt to capture all aspects of the NIGGER subculture. However, with the seemingly endless amount of NIGGERtivity, this book (even if it were as large as the original King James Bible) is merely a drop in the ocean. Even so, regardless of impact, my uncensored delivery is meant to convey a stark reality while confronting the NIGGER subculture. The Un-Civil War: BLACKS vs NIGGERS wasn't written to make Oprah's Book Club. Instead, this literary endeavor is my unapologetic *"Declaration of Independence."*

(Definitions of the Word)

The definition and history of the word *"Nigger"* is extremely interesting because it clearly means different things to different people. Its usage varies from a term of endearment (commonly spelled and pronounced as "Nigga") to the most venomous racial slur. The *freedictionary.com's* base definition of *"Nigger"* is, ***"a disparaging term for a Black person."*** I really like this definition because it boldly assigns "NIGGER" to a specific race, unlike *Dictionary.com's* definition, which offers a politically correct, race-neutral, sanitized definition. *Nigger* is primarily defined as, ***"Extremely Disparaging and Offensive. A person of any race or origin regarded as contemptible, inferior, ignorant, etc."*** Unsurprisingly, NIGGERfiliacs prefer *Dictionary.com's* definition. Many believe that anyone of any race can essentially be a Nigger because "Nigger" is supposedly based on the content of one's character, and not skin color. I partly agree. Sure, others can be *Nigger-ish* (wiggers), but in real life, Nigger is exclusive to blacks. This is why Euro-Americans have been culturally conditioned to avoid using the word (despite intended application) or any similar, phonetically sounding words for that matter (refer to headline).

Aide in 'Niggardly' Flap to Be Rehired / New D.C. mayor admits he acted too hastily

sfgate.com

[Author's Note: A BLACK mayor fired his WHITE aide for audaciously using the non-racial term "Niggardly" in the presence of African-Americans. Soon after the aide used this "N-word", the overly-sensitive African-Americans (apparently ignorant of its definition) reacted with a collective, "Oh, no he didn't!!"]

(Examining the PC definition)

Let's test the legitimacy of *Dictionary.com*'s "one size fits all" definition of *'Nigger'* in real world scenarios. If a WHITE teacher (working in a racially diverse school) tells an ***"extremely disparaging and offensive"*** WHITE student to stop behaving like a *"Nigger,"* would she face reprisals even though she used *"Nigger"* in the color-blind, character-based, context (as defined by *Dictionary.com)*? Yes, she would face swift reprisals, and possibly court martial lol. Another scenario: While in a grocery store's express line, which had a ten-item maximum, an African-American woman got behind me with a cart of items that clearly exceeded the ten-item limit. The cashier (who happened to be Euro-American) pointed to the posted *"10 item maximum"* sign and kindly informed the Af-Am woman that the express line couldn't service her numerous items. The Af-Am woman repeatedly tried to convince the cashier to break the rules for her, but when the cashier wouldn't, the Af-Am woman launched a verbal assault against her. I watched her tirade anticipating the moment when the cashier would be accused of racism (it's a typical ploy). I eventually realized that the race-card couldn't be easily played because my presence negated it. So, she initiated plan B; bait the cashier into exchanging racial epithets. Presumably, this alternate strategy would demonstrate that the cashier is inherently racist. She began to antagonistically call the cashier *"White Bitch"* and *"White Trash"* (purposely emphasizing race). Although the African-American woman was aggressively hurling racial slurs, the cashier stayed professional, and did an amazing job of internalizing her true feelings. Suddenly, I realized the existence of a lop-sided dynamic; at any moment, African-Americans can freely use racial epithets towards others, yet it's considered racist or taboo when others do the same (even in this instance). If this Euro-American cashier would've told this ***"contemptible, inferior, ignorant"*** verbal assaulter to cease the NIGGER-like behavior (using *Dictionary.com*'s definition), would she be reprimanded, even though the context wasn't racially based? Certainly, and may even lose her job if sensitivity/diversity training isn't mandated. Since *"Nigger"* is an indictment of character as deemed by *Dictionary.com*, why is it taboo to use whenever someone is actually being a NIGGER? Well, because the real world actually identifies with *freedictionary.com's* definition of NIGGER, which is ***"a derogatory name for a black person."*** Despite the varying definitions of NIGGER, the African-American community (and NIGGERfiliacs) will generally interpret any usage of the word (regardless of context or intended application) by anyone outside of the African-American community as racist. I've created my own definition of NIGGER because the definitions from *Dictionary.com* and *freedictionary.com* still don't sufficiently describe the degenerative subculture that I disdain.

(My Definition)

As a teenaged NIGGERfiliac, I simply viewed "Nigger" as a racial epithet that demeaned African-Americans. In spite of the massive amounts of atrocities, and violent crime that a certain type of African-American committed in the community, I still believed that calling them NIGGERS was worst. Now, experience and statistics confirm that "Nigger" isn't simply a racial slur... it's a physical entity that personifies the African-American community's dark side. In short, the word that I formerly dismissed as a superficial racial slur is actually ***"a feral black person with sociopathic tendencies."*** Additionally, it's a ***(N)***egro ***(I)***ndividual ***(G)***enerating ***(G)***rief ***(E)***verwhere ***(R)***outinely. I'm amazed by the amount of people who agree with my overall perspective about the NIGGER subculture, but take issue with me calling them NIGGERS. So, I always ask for "Nigger" synonyms, and the same generic words are presented: thugs, hoodlums, criminals, ruffian, hooligan etc. Understandably, people misconstrue words such as thugs, hoodlums, criminals, ruffian, hooligan, etc. as synonyms because the NIGGER subculture has purposely aligned themselves with those terms. However, although these are all Nigger attributes, they're race-neutral, and lack the racial element contained in the word "Nigger." See, "Nigger" is unique because it encapsulates the racial dimension along with their negative, self-defeating attributes. Finding a cure for death is more probable than finding an accurate synonym. Oh, and for those who say I shouldn't call other African-Americans NIGGERS because that word was created to degrade and dehumanize an entire race of people, Ok, I promise to stop calling them NIGGERS... as soon as they stop being NIGGERS! Feel free to use whatever descriptive term tickles your fancy, but predictably, as NIGGERtivity continues to thrive, average people like you or someone you know will be victimized. And once you've been impacted by NIGGERtivity, I'm certain that whatever politically correct, alternative term you've adopted will quickly revert to "Nigger!" Advisedly, if you *"bleeding hearts"* don't correctly label and acknowledge these domestic terrorists, you'll literally have *"bleeding hearts."* It bears repeating that NIGGERS are ***feral blacks with sociopathic tendencies***. They should be recognized and treated as such! By the end of this book, the analogous behavior exhibited by NIGGERS and sociopaths will not only be evident, but undeniable. Below is a partial list of sociopathic traits from the checklist of *H. Cleckley* and *R. Hare*; these traits parallel the NIGGER subculture.

- **Lack of Remorse, Shame, or Guilt**
- **Shallow Emotions**
- **Need for Stimulation**
- **Callousness/Lack of Empathy**
- **Poor Behavioral Controls/Impulsive Nature**
- **Early Behavior Problems/Juvenile Delinquency**
- **Irresponsibility/Unreliability**
- **Promiscuous Sexual Behavior/Infidelity**
- **Lack of Realistic Life Plan/Parasitic Lifestyle**
- **Criminal or Entrepreneurial Versatility**
- **Contemptuous of those who seek to understand them**
- **Does not perceive that anything is wrong with them**
- **Seeks out situations where their tyrannical behavior will be tolerated, condoned, or admired**
- **Has an emotional need to justify their crimes and therefore needs their victim's affirmation (respect, gratitude and love)**
- **Ultimate goal is the creation of a willing victim**
- **Incapable of real human attachment to another**
- **Narcissism, grandiosity (self-importance not based on achievements)**
- **Manipulative and Conning**

Chicago Running Out of Euphemisms
frontpagemag.com

(A Lil Honesty Please!!!)

Many BLACKS share my view of NIGGERS, yet will not openly express this feeling because of another misguided notion... *"It makes us all look bad."* With that flawed logic, I guess that men shouldn't report male pedophilia or rape because it'll make us men look bad. Kudos to John Ridley (a stand up Black man, and race-realist) for writing a necessary article titled, *"The Manifesto of Ascendancy for the Modern American Nigger."* In it, he stated profound truths that are visible to anyone with eyes. He wrote, ***"LET ME TELL YOU SOMETHING ABOUT NIGGERS** [sic]**, the***

oppressed minority within our minority. Always down. Always out. Always complaining that they can't catch a break. Notoriously poor about doing for themselves. Constantly in need of a leader but unable to follow in any direction that's navigated by hard work, self-reliance. And though they spliff and drink and procreate their way onto welfare doles and WIC lines, niggers will tell you their state of being is no fault of their own." Predictably, if Mr. Ridley, who is also the Oscar-Winning Screenwriter of *"12 Years a Slave"* and Co-Writer of the Tuskegee Airmen inspired film *"Red Tails,"* had written this article demonizing the WHITE man, he'd be a household name in the HoG. But since he administered truth serum to a ***"minority within a minority,"*** he remains relatively unknown in the HoG, despite his achievements.

(Proper Perspective)

One day, after reading about another Urban Terrorist's attack on civilians, my disgusted wife slammed the newspaper onto the ground and yelled, ***"What kind of animals are these that would stick a gun into a three-year old child's mouth!"*** Equally angered, I responded, ***"First of all, they're not animals, they're NIGGERS! Secondly, please don't insult the animal kingdom by including NIGGERS into their kind. People understand why animals behave the way that they do... but NIGGER behavior is inexplicable! It's time to put their wretched behavior into the proper perspective."*** Indeed, NIGGERS appear to act like animals, but unlike animals, their (NIGGERS) misbehavior is choice-based. They're a rusted link on the African-American evolutionary chain manifesting as a mutated version of BLACKS. Some observers have referred to them as the "Black underclass," "low achieving Blacks," or "dysfunctional Blacks." But judging by the mosaic of terror and dysfunction that they've imposed, I think that "human underclass" is more appropriate. Furthermore, they're an "underworld" or better yet, "undeveloped world" that purposely disregard opportunities afforded them to become productive citizens. This trash heap would rather take refuge in the African-American community where it can cultivate its despicable lifestyle, making it difficult for others to separate BLACKS from NIGGERS. Once upon a time, when political correctness didn't have a chokehold on

America, comedian Red Foxx stated (without reprisal), ***"See, I talk about Niggers...you know what I mean... because Niggers are holding Black people back. I know that's confusing to you white friends, but there is a difference."*** In 1987, the Oprah Winfrey show aired a segment from a town-hall meeting in Forsyth County, Georgia, where an African-American person hadn't lived in 75 years. During the meeting, a local citizen named Dennis made an astute and accurate observation. He stated, ***"You have blacks and you have niggers. Black people don't want to cause any trouble. ... A nigger ... wants to come up here and cause trouble all the time. That's the difference."*** In his memoir, *All Souls,* Michael Patrick MacDonald describes how several Euro-American residents of the Old Colony housing project in South Boston used the word (NIGGER). He wrote, ***"Of course, no one considered himself a nigger. It was always something you called someone who could be considered anything less than you. I soon found out there were a few black families living in Old Colony. They'd lived there for years and everyone said that they were okay, that they weren't niggers but just black. It felt good to all of us to not be as bad as the hopeless people in D Street or, God forbid, the ones in Columbia Point, who were both black and niggers."*** Scenarios that contrast BLACKS and NIGGERS really disappoint NIGGERfilacs because it deviates from their narrative, which categorically denies the existence of this dysfunctional and criminal subculture within the African-American community.

(Other Characteristics)

From the HoG, the outside world is realized through a narrow lens. It's a place where their (NIGGERS) immediate, present day surroundings are the extent of their concern. As a result, this lack of horizon impairs their ability to meaningfully connect with others outside of their bubble. Moreover, environmental or social issues like climate change (whether it's real or fake), recycling, conservationism, etc. which affects our bubble (Earth) is deemed inconsequential. Seemingly, they know there's no future in being a NIGGER, so their lives are structured around instant gratification. While some NIGGERS are oblivious of their social branding as such, others embrace the lifestyle. Even so, there's no difference between the two. Gangs, for example, annually account for thousands of homey-cides because of their supposed differences; however, under close inspection, they share the same Ebonic speech, gangster hip-hop, style of dress (only different colors), and taxpayer-dependent existence. Although they appear to be rivals, culturally, they're all NIGGERS. Actually, there are more similarities than differences between these so-called rivals/gangs. Remember, they are two sides of the same, worthless coin. Don't be fooled.

(Stating the Obvious)

This subculture willingly clinches onto a sadistic, violent lifestyle that eventually bleeds into civilization. They have a hair-trigger temper, and are extremely quick to take offense to any minor altercation or disagreement *(refer to headlines*). Since they display predictable patterns of negative behavior and childlike propensities, fierce confrontations over trivialities is standard operating procedure. A simple web search will confirm the seemingly infinite amount of senseless shootings and/or assaults stemming from "someone staring at someone" or "someone disrespecting someone." To them, life is a cheap commodity. Statistically, the extremities of NIGGERtivity manifest as murder and rape, yet NIGGERfiliacs will quickly state that other races murder and rape, even though FBI data consistently reveal the NIGGER minority as most dangerous. Resorting to violence to resolve any conflict is a patented, predictable attribute of the NIGGER subculture, and its effects are felt nationwide. In an article titled, *"Black Man's Burden: Those Who Make Them Victims"*, Larry Elder wrote, ***"Jesse Jackson once told an interviewer that when hearing footsteps behind him while walking down a street a night, he is relieved if he turns to see the sound is coming from white feet. Michelle Obama, when asked whether she worried about the safety of her then presidential candidate husband, said, 'I don't lose sleep over it, because the realities are that, you know, as a black man, you know, Barack can get shot going to the gas station."*** Mr. Jackson and Mrs. Obama's quotes are direct indictments of the NIGGER subculture, and the realities associated with co-existence.

Prosecutors: Dispute over hat led to slaying
chicagotribune.com

Police: New Castle Man Slain After Yelling 'Slow Down'
wpxi.com

[Author's Note: Telling a NIGGER to slow down from driving 70-80 mph in a resulted with the advice-giver being fatally shot.]

Man shot dead in row over dripping air conditioning unit
dailymail.co.uk

Man accused of gouging relative's eye over TV remote
chicagotribune.com

[Author's Note: Fortunately "Exulam" won't have access to the remote at the HNCU.]

Detroit pastor, father killed after asking neighbors to quiet down
clickondetroit.com

[Author's Note: The Pastor was shot and killed for simply requesting that the music be lowered.]

'That's what I do to people that don't listen'
dailymail.co.uk

[Article's Quote: "Newark gang banger brags about shooting dead rural cab driver for 'taking the long way'"]

(No Love)

Since this subculture suffers from self-inflicted wounds and conditions, I honestly have no sympathy for them. Perhaps that sounds inhumane, but my feeling is a result of this splinter group's intentional decadence. As validated by the various referenced newspaper headlines throughout this book, NIGGERS have an insatiable appetite for destruction, and the impact of (NIGGERtivity) isn't limited to African-Americans; NIGGERtivity touches all races. Therefore, it's amusing to hear NIGGERfiliacs yell racism when WHITES, ASIANS, LATINOS, and others publically condemn this subculture. I argue that condemnation of NIGGERtivity in any form is actually the opposite of racism; it is humanism. The fact is, all races have an underclass, but contrary to the underclasses of other races, the NIGGER minority has successfully re-defined and re-shaped the African-American community; no race should be defined by its exceptions! The unseen benefit of NIGGERtivity is that NIGGERS are their own worst enemies, and if left to their devices will self-destruct. We simply have to get out of their way so that their destinies can be fulfilled. NIGGERS are the gremlins of the African-American community, intentionally lacking any basic progressive outlook. This deliberate lack of quality makes them a detriment to our race... the human race.

(OND)

People are generally baffled as to why NIGGERS do what they do. Oftentimes, their misbehavior is thought to be symptomatic of deeper issues; it isn't. They've happily embraced a condition that I call *"Obsessive NIGGER Disorder,"* abbreviated as O.N.D. Despite spending gazillions of taxpayer dollars on various social, outreach, and prevention programs, O.N.D remains in heavy rotation. NIGGERfiliacs dismiss O.N.D as P.T.S.D (Post Traumatic Slavery Disorder), but the truth is that NIGGERS are simply being NIGGERS. Again, don't over think the reasons for NIGGERtivity. In fact, comedian Louis CK hilariously paralleled my sentiment regarding NIGGERS when he wisecracked, ***"Do you know how the word "NIGGER" started? There was some Black guy being a NIGGER, so they called him a NIGGER... He was being a real NIGGER, so they said; What a NIGGER!"*** To my point, acting like a NIGGER will rightfully have one labeled as such. Comedian Chris Rock also commented on their distinctively warped mind state. He observed, ***"You know the worst thing about niggers? Niggers always want credit for some shit they supposed to do. A nigger will brag about some shit a normal man just does. A nigger will say some shit like, 'I take care of my kids.' You're supposed to, you dumb motherfucker! What kind of ignorant shit is that? 'I ain't never been to jail!' What do you want, a cookie?! You're not supposed to go to jail, you low-expectation-having motherfucker!"*** O.N.D distorts their sense of self-perception, and has them dress, talk, act in ways that are detriments to any non-NIGGER environment or personality. O.N.D is also the reason why NIGGERS never leave the sanctity of the HoG. Also, O.N.D will transform any environment it encounters into a HoG; their parasitic subculture replicates horrid conditions wherever it exists. In other words, *"A NIGGER can be taken out the HoG, but the HoG can't be taken out the NIGGER."* Therefore, it is, and will continue to be a waste of taxpayer money, time, and resources in attempt to assimilate NIGGERS into society.

(Summary)

Remember, NIGGERS as I define them, are ***feral blacks with sociopathic tendencies***. Inexplicably, their lack of self-awareness somehow inflates their self-esteem. In reality, this artificial self-image is simply a coping mechanism for their inability to effectively assimilate into a merit-based society. Since image and bravado are essential in the HoG, this false self-image obstructs their view of society's reality outside the HoG. Through the eyes of a drug user, the world may seem drugged; through the eyes of a drunkard, the world may seem drunk. However, through the eyes of a NIGGER...ummm...I'm lost as to what's seen.

Chapter I

JuviNIGGERS

"Little children, headache; big children heartache"

-Italian proverb

It's said that a tree is judged by the fruit it bears; well, JuviNIGGERS are the rotten fruit yielded from the NIGGER tree. Just like NIGGER adults aren't typical adults, JuviNIGGERS aren't typical teenagers. Their behavior is best explained as delinquency on steroids. Individually, JuviNIGGERS are menaces; but when united with other JuviNIGGERS, a state of excited delirium occurs, and they morph into Flashfloods. Since their troublesome ways exponentially increase when in numbers, these Flashfloods, mistakenly called "flash mobs" are to be avoided like a pandemic. Again, these aren't flash mobs! Historically, flash mobs were groups of people staging impromptu performances (dancing, singing) to the onlooker's delight; not committing random felony assaults, robberies, hate crimes, and other NIGGERtivity to the onlooker's dismay. "Flash mob" is another term that the NIGGER subculture is attempting to redefine into their image, and after their likeness.

Philly Mayor Says Flash Mobbing Teens Are "Damaging The Race"
newsone.com

Teen Arrested In Wisc. Flash Mob Attack; City Blames Black Families
newsone.com

(Typical Adolescence)

As a parent, I understand the reality of teenagers behaving like teenagers; rebellion is typically a prerequisite of the adolescent experience. In fact, it's generally accepted that teens usually reject wise parental advice, violate household rules, and make questionable decisions. Even still, most teens eventually mature past that rebellious phase, assimilate into society, and periodically reflect on their carefree adolescent life of yesteryear. Ultimately, those experiences, lessons, and values are passed onto their children as the cycle of life renews itself. Contrarily, in the NIGGER subculture, NIGGERS never evolve from that adolescent phase, and their offspring stand as testaments. NIGGERfiliacs rationalize the destructive, soul-less energy that fuels JuviNIGGERS by blaming society instead of indicting the parents. Certainly, it's possible for a JuviNIGGER to come from a "good" household just as it's possible for a Euro-American to have sickle cell; but that's not the norm. The fact is that JuviNIGGER behavior is usually enabled at home.

The young and the reckless are wreaking havoc on Philly's streets
philly.com

(The Study)

Familyfusion.org explains the typical teenage brain and its development: ***"The prefrontal cortex is the brain's executive center, responsible for planning ahead, considering consequences and managing emotional impulses."*** Elaborating further, ***"It appears that the prefrontal cortex begins growing again just before puberty, and is then pruned back during the entire period of adolescence. Clearly, this region of the brain is not yet fully wired in teens. Knowing this helps us better understand the risk taking, disorganization, distractibility, conflict seeking and lack of impulse control that teens can experience. In fact, the prefrontal cortex – the "smart" part of the brain, is the last part of the brain to reach cognitive maturity."*** Soooooo, if the typical teenage brain goes through this transformative process, why do JuviNIGGERS exhibit atypical and extreme behavior? Moreover, why do JuviNIGGERS have a uniquely different reputation than their counterparts, and seemingly never outgrow this behavior? Oh yeah, that's right... I almost forgot the NIGGERfiliac's default answers: slavery, racism, and poverty.

Mobs Attack on City Buses: Police
nbcchicago.com

Police: Teens Leave Church Picnic To Riot In East Liberty
wpxi.com

(JuviNIGGERS' Pastimes)

NIGGERfiliacs misleadingly claim that JuviNIGGERtivity results from the lack of structured activities/outlets and boredom. However, neither are the real reason; the elementary truth is that JuviNIGGERS chose to be JuviNIGGERS. In adolescence, managing boredom and other setbacks are part of the maturation process, so instead of blaming society, perhaps NIGGERfiliacs should investigate how "bored" teenagers from other ethnicities manage to refrain from destructive, criminal behavior. Whenever bored during adolescence, I indulged in a variety of recreational (not wreck-creational) activities such as sports, and teenage love. JuviNIGGERS, on the other hand, purposely avoid the classic adolescent pastimes; choosing instead to indulge in sadistic, violence-centered games like *"Polar Bear Hunting" (assaulting Euro-Americans), "Knockout King," "Catching Wreak,"* and *"Apple Picking"* (assaulting people for Apple products). Depending on region, the game's name may differ, but the theme remains the same; defenseless, unsuspecting strangers are preyed upon for sport. Although JuviNIGGERS consider them games, they're nothing less than physical assaults, robbery, hate crimes, and even murder in the guise of recreation (wreck-creation). A simple web search will easily confirm that these so-called "games" have resulted in murders, comas, and mental/physical disabilities.

Surveillance Video Captures Teens Beating 73-Year-Old Elderly Man
foxnews.com

Teenage gang charged under lynching law after 'savage attack on 18-year-old student'
dailymail.co.uk

(Knockout King)

A *River Front Times* article (6/9/11) described the heartlessness of the 'Knockout King' game: ***"A lead attacker is chosen from among a group of boys, usually young adolescents. Next a target is picked out. Then the attacker either charges the unsuspecting victim or motions for his attention. When the target turns or lifts his head, the attacker strikes. If the victim is felled by the punch, the group usually scatters. But if the target withstands the blow, other members of the group may follow up with their***

fists to finish the job." Although this article intentionally neglected to mention the perpetrators' race, and instead, generically label them ***"young adolescents,"*** they were actually JuviNIGGERS.

Knockout King: The sickening 'game' claiming lives across the country as youths beat up the vulnerable 'for attention'
dailymail.co.uk

[Author's Note: Is it coincidental that this so-called "game" seemingly thrives in cities with gun bans?]

BLACK MOBS' KNOCKOUT GAME RAISING ALARMS
wnd.com

UPDATE: Police Reveal Sick Game in Beating Death of Immigrant
stlouis.cbslocal.com

(I'm not Surprised)

In Philadelphia, where flash flooding has been a familiar occurrence, the mayor attempted to provide an outlet for teens called *"Teen Night."* Naturally, most teens viewed this event as a festive time to socialize and unwind with peers, but not JuviNIGGERS; this was another opportunity to get attention. As reported by *foxnews.com (8/15/11)*, ***"The 'Teen Night' event at the bowling alley, where Mayor Michael Nutter bowled with teenagers in an effort to stop the violence, had just ended when several hundred teenagers were released in groups before heading home."*** Whenever that many urban African-American teenagers are left to their own devices, especially after leaving a late night party, JuviNIGGERS will definitely capitalize. During one 16-year-old girl's walk to the bus stop with friends, she was lustfully approached by a JuviNIGGER. After ignoring his repeated advances, the JuviNIGGER reacted in a typical sociopathic fashion...he stabbed her. *[Author's Note to JuviNIGGERS: A way to a girl's heart isn't by stabbing them.]*

Philly Hosts Teen Bowling to Curb Violence; One Person Stabbed
nation.foxnews.com

(School)

School provides children with more than just an academic learning experience. Coupled with the curriculum, it's a place to broaden horizons, develop appropriate social behavior, and learn positive interaction skills. The importance of schools cannot be overstated. W.E.B Dubois correctly surmised, ***"Education is that whole system of human training within and without the school house walls, which molds and develops men."*** Sadly, many inner-city schools have yielded to JuviNIGGERtivity because NIGGER parents simply view school as daycare. Consequently, driven students suffer as the academic atmosphere and educational standards are relaxed to accommodate JuviNIGGERS. In other words, academic criteria decreases while security standards increases. Rampant JuviNIGfestation of urban schools is why most of them are academically low-performing, and repeat offenders on the *"persistently dangerous"* list (as defined by the *No Child Left Behind Act)*. To the NIGGERfiliac's chagrin, this is why Oprah Winfrey really "kept it real" by building her $40 million dollar school far away from the HoG. Speaking to Newsweek magazine (1/8/07 issue), Oprah confessed, ***"I became so frustrated with visiting inner-city schools that I just stopped going. The sense that you need to learn just isn't there. If you ask the kids what they want or need, they will say an iPod or some sneakers. In South Africa, they don't ask for money or toys. They ask for uniforms so they can go to school."*** Translation: This perceptive investor has recognized that the NIGGER subculture has commandeered inner-city schools, and thus, wisely invested in a foreign entity that would yield a noticeable return. Despite her foreign investment, Oprah still contributes to many inner-city, American magnet schools, a.k.a Anti-NIGGER schools.

(Proposal)

JuviNIGGERS don't give a damn about the BLACK patriots who reversed the stereotypical misperceptions of BLACK Americans, and paved a path of opportunity for all African-Americans (including NIGGERS) to walk. Their carelessness exists because entitlement and defiance are proudly worn on their sleeves. Therefore, if a school that's named after a prominent BLACK person becomes JuviNIGfested, and no longer represents the principles for which that particular BLACK leader stood, it should be renamed. Surely, JuviNIGfestation in any school is repugnant, but these BLACK patriot-named schools should be ground zero for this type of revolutionary change. After all, they were intentionally named after BLACK leaders to instill pride and inspire African-American pupils. Essentially, schools are brands, and JuviNIGGERS are tarnishing these brands. It's agonizing to see a school honorably named after Reverend Dr. Martin Luther King, who sacrificed his life for equality, justice, and peace, be desecrated by JuviNIGGERtivity. Dr. King said to judge by *"content of character."* JuviNIGGER behavior proves that they're the antithesis of the principles that these schools' namesake represented, and so, they should be renamed! The students of Medgar Evers' School shouldn't be impacted by the JuviNIGGERS' disdain for learning. Instead, they should be inspired from the fact that Medgar Evers travelled twelve miles to an ill-equipped, shanty-like school designated for African-Americans. Honorable BLACK trailblazers like Harriet Tubman, Marcus Garvey, and Benjamin Banneker, (just to name a few) are probably turning in their graves as BLACKS allow NIGGERS to spit on their legacies. When real racism (not the pseudo-racism that NIGGERS yell as an excuse for failure) was pervasive, BLACK patriots relentlessly overcame racist barriers. Again, I recommend that BLACK people demand that BLACK patriot-named schools maintain a collective standard of excellence in exchange for the continued usage of BLACK trailblazers' names. Admittedly, it's a challenging task because establishing Anti-NIGGER learning environments entails removing JuviNIGGERS, and abolishing NIGGERfilia. Even so, such battles are nothing compared to those fought by our forefathers.

Shooting at Martin Luther King Jr. High School Forces Lockdown

KeysToSaferSchools.com

[Article's Quote: "Two students were shot inside Martin Luther King Jr. High School in Manhattan today, forcing officials to lock down the building on the nonviolent activist's birthday." Surely, this incident was a huge misunderstanding...it was simply people exhibiting the "content of their character" as a salutation to Dr. King.]

(Starting in Baltimore)

Even though the JuviNIGGERS' trend of academic apathy occurs nationally, the city of Baltimore comes to mind as a place to immediately implement my revolutionary proposal. According to the 2010 census, Baltimore's sixty-four percent (63.7%) African-American population is the fifth largest percentage of U.S cities with at least 100,000 people. Also, the Baltimore City school district has an eighty-nine percent African-American student body, and is home to many schools named after BLACK trailblazers.

SIXTEEN BALTIMORE SCHOOLS ARE CITED FOR DANGEROUS CONDITIONS

msde.maryland.gov

[Author's Note: At the time of this press release (8/2004), no other school district in Maryland's twenty-three district system was on this shameful list.]

Dr. W.E.B DuBois, the first BLACK to earn a Ph.D. from Harvard University (1895), and a pioneer in the study of race and crime in the United States, has a Baltimore high school named in his honor that was labeled *"persistently dangerous"* for three consecutive years (2006-2009).

Thurgood Marshall, who argued the landmark Supreme Court case of Brown vs. Board of Education, and later became a Chief Justice, has a Baltimore middle and high school named in his honor. The middle school was labeled persistently dangerous for four consecutive years (2005-2009), and its closure probably prevented it from reaching a fifth. Determined to further degrade Chief Justice Marshal's legacy, Thurgood Marshall High went from *"probationary status"* in 2008, to full-blown *"persistently dangerous"* in 2009. *(Author's Note: There is also a Thurgood Marshall high school in San Francisco, which in 2008-2009, had only three African-Americans graduate).*

Thurgood Marshall's high dropout rate studied

Only three black boys graduated from Thurgood Marshall Academic High School last year

sfexaminer.com

[Author's Note: This lack of achievement wasn't due to a scarcity of African-American students.]

(Mr. Douglass)

Another disrespected trailblazer is ***Frederick Douglass***. Although born enslaved, he stood as a counter-example to society's point of view that enslaved African-Americans lacked the intellectual aptitude to function as self-determining citizens. During his era, learning to read and write was a criminal offense for enslaved African-Americans, and the repercussions were severe. Regardless, through self-determination, he transcended physical and mental enslavement, and as a Republican, became the first African-American to be nominated for Vice-President of the United States. Now, fast forward to the twenty-first century, where a Baltimore high school (named in his honor) stands in stark contrast to his legacy. This JuviNIGfested high school, which was annually labeled *"persistently dangerous"* and *"low performing,"* was also the subject of a documentary *(Hard Times at Douglass High*) that highlighted the self-inflicted issues plaguing it, including the widespread rejection for learning. Additionally, it once ranked #26 on *neighborhoodscout.com's "100 Worst Performing Public Schools in the U.S" list.* Apparently, Douglass High students decided against being inspired by the fact that Douglass himself overcame worst societal and economic conditions without the Civil Rights legislation, affirmative action, or welfare programs. Unlike Douglass High's students, Douglass himself didn't invest in excuses. Instead, he turned a tragic start into a triumphant ending.

(Mr. B.T. Washington)

Educator, author, orator, and political leader, ***Booker T. Washington*** believed that with self-help, people could go from poverty to success in America. He was confident that African-Americans would eventually gain full participation in society by showing themselves to be responsible and reliable citizens. However, judging by the multi-year *"persistently dangerous"* label of the middle school (99% Af-Am) that's named in his honor, the school wasn't producing responsible and reliable American citizens. Instead, JuviNIGGERS were produced. The proper respect must be paid to these patriots by renaming all schools that have succumbed to the NIGGER subculture's tenets.

(From L to R) Dubois, Douglass, Marshall, King, Washington

(Alternative Schools)

Many school districts have confronted JuviNIGfestation by transferring JuviNIGGERS to JuviNIGGER-ready learning environments called *"Alternative schools."* "Alternative schools" are politically correct, NIGGERfiliac endorsed, names given to last resort schools. These *"Alternative schools"* are essentially miniature holding facilities where bad apples are placed in a barrel with other bad apples. Enrollment in these schools means that a student has consistently failed to adhere to the basic, courteous, behavioral functions in a traditional school. Without even acknowledging that their child corrupts normal learning environments, NIGGER parents always complain that placement in *"Alternative schools"* prohibits their child from acquiring a proper public education. Yet, lost upon them is the fact that their JuviNIGGER is only in this predicament because he/she behaviorally opted out of attaining such education under normal circumstances.

Court Hears Testimony After Teacher Pummeled At Alternative Philadelphia School

philadelphia.cbslocal.com

[Author's Note: Two JuviNIGGER students aged 19 and 20 were charged. At ages 19-20, their education should've occurred at an HNCU.]

(My Alternative School)

My version of "alternative schools" would be called "Menace Academies." These academies would operate like military boot camps, placing strong emphasis on structure, discipline, rules, and accountability. In order to effectively guide the outcast's development (pupils would be called "outcasts" until graduation), enrollment would be court ordered, with the instructors having full access to their criminal and mental history. The outcasts will face indefinite enrollment (in Menace Academy) until they demonstrate a thorough understanding of the specialized curriculum, and prove fit for societal integration. Moreover, graduation will not be based on social promotions (age) and/or a "maxing out" scenario. Graduates will be allowed to re-assimilate into society with all the rights and privileges guaranteed to American citizens by the U.S Constitution. If a menace prematurely drops out of the academy, a warrant would be issued for their immediate detainment, and he/she will be required to further their education at the local HNCU campus.

(What to Name Them?)

I'm not duped by fancy school names; seemingly, the more elaborate the school's name, the more NIGfestation. However, in Baltimore, there used to be a school whose name was intriguing, admirable and most importantly, honest. It was named, "Homeland Security High." Judging by its student body (the usual suspects), and 2009 label as *"persistently dangerous,"* its given name was extremely fitting. This was an excellent name for a JuviNIGfested school, yet schools with straightforward names (such as this) are extremely rare. I sincerely hope that JuviNIGfested BLACK patriot-named schools adopt appropriate monikers such as this. In fact, all JuviNIGfested schools should have catchy, embraceable names such as *"Ghetto Tech"*, *"Hood High"* or even *"Keep it Real Institute"* (acronym is K.I.R.I). Trust me... there's nothing to lose. These names will be embraced by the NIGGER subculture, and perhaps instill a sense of school pride. Yes, it would be a warped sense of school pride, but even so, it's school pride. Another option is to re-name these schools after its geographic location or region, i.e. Southside High School, South Central High School, and East Side High School etc. Oh wait, this option is already utilized lol. I favor this idea because the property values in these JuviNIGfested schools' vicinity have probably eroded, so renaming them after the region would serve as another warning sign to potential homebuyers. This correlation is explained in a *prospect.org* article (12/6/10) by Steven Hawkins titled, *"Education vs. Incarceration,"* which states, ***"NAACP research shows that matching zip codes to high rates of incarceration also reveals how low performing schools, as measured by math proficiency, tend to cluster. The lowest performing schools tend to be in the areas where incarceration rates are the highest."*** In other words, low performing HoG schools equals high performing HNCUs. JuviNIGfested schools are nothing more than feeder schools to prisons. It should be noted that the NIGGER subculture willingly maintains this relationship.

(Reinforcement)

Again, I maintain that if BLACK patriot named schools aren't reclaimed and restored, then they must be renamed after antagonists from the NIGGER subculture, or the school's region! Curiously, if JuviNIGfested schools were actually named after prominent NIGGERS, who would be considered? As ridiculous as my proposal may seem, a fictional diploma obtained from these fictionally NIGGER-named schools is still as valuable as a real diploma from today's NIGfested schools.

(Parents of JuviNIGGERS)

During school hours, Baby Mamas spend the entire day at home updating social network statuses, tweeting, posting pictures on Instagram, and/or watching television. Surely, teachers easily recognize NIGGER parents because they talk, dress, and act like teens, and picking up report cards/school participation isn't a high priority. Also, they'll generally respond with threats of violence or obscenities if their child is reprimanded. Despite the accepted societal fact that the least educated are especially prone to poverty, NIGGERS believe that classroom-setting learning is an inconvenient sidebar of life. To them, street knowledge is superior to formal education. Moreover, NIGGERnomics teaches that school doesn't have to be tolerated because the financial future is sports, entertainment, government handouts, and NIGGERtivity. Ultimately, NIGGER parents will blame their child's academic shortcomings and misconduct on everything/everyone (teacher, school's environment, curriculums etc.) except the obvious...themselves. As a parent, I understand that there are circumstances involving the children that we cannot control; even so, we must still provide the necessary tools to help them maximize their potential.

Parents Arrested in Beating of 73-Year-Old Crossing Guard
aolnews.com

Parents Brawl At Preschool Graduation: Weemes Elementary School Ceremony Ends In Fight (VIDEO)
huffingtonpost.com

Student's MOTHER leaves teacher unconscious in school hall after 'kicking and strangling' her to the ground - as other kids piled in
dailymail.co.uk

("Free" Civil Rights?)

Ironically, NIGGERS will zealously jump for anything that's free, except education. They're unconcerned with the history regarding this "free" public school education, which in actuality, wasn't obtained freely. In fact, while being physically assaulted, pelted with rocks, bitten by dogs, sprayed with fire hoses, and indiscriminately arrested, a racially diverse citizenry paid for these "rights" through blood, sweat, and tears. Nevertheless, the NIGGER subculture expects to enjoy these "rights" without accepting any of the attached responsibilities. Those who don't care that "rights" are accompanied with responsibility should be denied those rights. In other words, Civil Rights shouldn't be extended to those intentionally, lacking civility. Ironically, in the not too distant past, African-Americans had to be escorted ***'to'*** schools; presently, JuviNIGGERS are being escorted ***'from'*** schools. Go figure.

(Failure is an Option)

NIGGER parents don't mind if their children fail to adjust to society's measures of success because they inherently believe that America is rigged by WHITES for African-Americans to fail. In the NIGGER subculture, failure is always an option because of their belief that racism is so pervasive that no amount of individual effort will overcome it. Furthermore, failure is routinely embraced because it navigates their kids toward that reliable path of government handouts, which generationally has been the financial pillar of their subculture (Refer to ***NIGGERnomics*** chapter). Oklahoma State representative, Sally Kern (R), expressed similar sentiment regarding the subculture's outlook by stating, ***"We have a high percentage of blacks in prison, and that's tragic, but are they in prison just because they are black or because they don't want to study as hard in school? I've taught school, and I saw a lot of people of color who didn't study hard because they said the government would take care of them."*** Although she makes the common mistake of mis-labeling NIGGERS as BLACKS, her observation is spot-on.

Republican: Blacks Are In Prison Because They Don't Want To Study

newsone.com

(The Facts)

The Manhattan Institute released a study in 2006 that surveyed the 100 largest school districts in the United States. It found that only 48 percent of African-American males earn a high school diploma, which was 11 percent less than African-American females. Additionally, 1 in 4 Af-Am males who drop out of high school end up incarcerated. Even though Euro-Americans are 63.4% of the U.S population, and African-Americans are only 13%, the U.S. Department of Education documented that in 2007, not one state had a Euro-American high school student dropout rate higher than the African-American dropout rate. Additionally that same year, there were twenty-one states where the dropout rate for African-American high school students was at least double that of Euro-American high school students. As documented in a *prospect.org* article by Mark Kleiman (12/6/10) titled, "*Smarter punishment, Less Crime*", ***"Nearly a million Black Americans are behind bars, a black male high school dropout has a better than even chance of serving prison time before age 30."*** The National Center for Education Statistics (NCES) reveals, ***"Dropouts also make up disproportionately higher percentages of the nation's prison and death row inmates. Comparing those who drop out of high school with those who complete high school, the average high school dropout is associated with costs to the economy of approximately $240,000 over his or her lifetime in terms of lower tax contributions, higher reliance on Medicaid and Medicare, higher rates of criminal activity, and higher reliance on welfare."*** Citing a U.S study, *Reuters* stated (12/7/11), ***"High school dropouts on average receive $1,500 a year more from government than they pay in taxes because they are more likely to get benefits or to be in prison***." It continued, ***"And yet over a dropout's entire working life, he or she receives $71,000 more on average in cash and in-kind benefits than paid in taxes. The societal costs may include imprisonment, government-paid medical insurance and food stamps."*** Maybe I should hand out this information at the next Flashflood occurrence.

Black Male High School Dropouts Headed to Prison
rollingout.com

(JuviNIGGER's Contempt for School)

The corrosive mindset of NIGGER parents undoubtedly manifests in their seed's behavior; subsequently, JuviNIGGERS don't respect the teachers, curriculum, school environment, or authority figures. Like oil and water, education and NIGGERS simply don't mix; they refuse to see the world outside of the HoG, and lack any desire to escape. Chicago Tribune's article *"School discipline tougher on African-Americans" (9/25/07) explains,* ***"In every state but Idaho, a Tribune analysis of the data shows, black students are being suspended in numbers greater than would be expected from their proportion of the student population. In 21 states—Illinois among them—that disproportionality is so pronounced that the percentage of black suspensions is more than double their percentage of the student body. And on average across the nation, black students are suspended and expelled at nearly three times the rate of white students."*** At the end of the day, detention and suspensions don't bother a subculture that admires and aspires to be HNCU enrollees. The NIGGERfiliacs argue that these numbers are reflective of a racist conspiracy, but apparently, they haven't attended school with JuviNIGGERS.

School discipline tougher on African-Americans
chicagotribune.com

In Washington area, African-American students suspended and expelled two to five times as often as whites
washingtonpost.com

[Article's Quote: "The problems extend beyond the Washington area to school districts across the country and are among a host of concerns about school discipline that sparked a joint effort by the U.S Justice and Education departments in July to look into reforms." Coincidentally, this pattern of expulsion resembles the national imprisonment rates between African-Americans and Euro-Americans, but I'm sure that it's coincidental (wink-wink).]

(Dumbing the Curriculum)

One would think that the continuous dumbing and streamlining of today's public education curriculum would be advantageous to the NIGGER subculture. Because of the massive pressure on teachers to push JuviNIGGERS through the curriculum, their (JuviNIGGERS) minimal academic effort, and below average attendance is still typically sufficient for a social promotion.

Diplomas once symbolized the successful comprehension of basic knowledge (the three R's), but these easily obtained diplomas from NIGfested cesspools are nothing more than consolation prizes. This *"cater to the lowest denominator"* system places pressure on school administrators to redirect educational resources from students likely to demonstrate proficiency, towards those who are below proficiency. In other words, the capable children are short-changed in order to raise the scores of the slackers. Although this backsliding approach benefits JuviNIGGERS, the other students aren't being prepared for a meritocracy. Society should stop wasting resources in attempt to convert a subculture that prefers ignorance to education, and instead focus on those who appreciate education.

Florida Passes Plan For Racially-Based Academic Goals

tampa.cbs.local.com

[Author's Note: Florida's Board of Education passed a revised strategic plan to have 90 percent of Asian students, 88 percent of white students, 81 percent of Hispanics, and 74 percent of Black students to be reading at or above grade level by year 2018. For math, the goals are 92 percent of Asian kids to be proficient, Whites at 86 percent, Hispanics at 80 percent, and Blacks at 74 percent.]

Firestorm Erupts Over Virginia's Education Goals

npr.org

[Article's Quote: "Here's what the Virginia state board of education actually did. It looked at students' test scores in reading and math and then proposed new passing rates. In math it set an acceptable passing rate at 82 percent for Asian students, 68 percent for whites, 52 percent for Latinos, 45 percent for blacks and 33 percent for kids with disabilities."]

(Sympathy for Teachers)

I pity the teachers employed in HoG schools because their safety is always jeopardized. Even though most states keep crime and arrest records of students confidential, teachers should still be privy to such pertinent information. In these schools, which are typically scarcely controlled juvenile-holding facilities, teachers double as correctional officers, and should know as much as possible about their students to develop a customized approach. They regularly juggle the tasks of teaching, parenting, disciplining, counseling, and are sometimes physically assaulted for merely doing a thankless job. Any schoolteacher working in a HoG school already knows that JuviNIGGER students have a completely altered view of education and the learning process. The high turnover rate at HoG schools supports the growing sentiment that any teacher that willingly braves these elements should receive combat pay. Though, as not to offend the NIGGERfiliacs or HoG natives, this "combat pay" should be given a politically correct name such as "Durability Pay." Additionally, like soldiers returning from war, these teachers should be monitored for Post-Traumatic Stress Disorder (P.T.S.D). Teachers can't effectively perform their job in JuviNIGfested classrooms when they first have to get the JuviNIGGER's attention, keep their attention, and then ultimately teach. Successful confiscation of cell phones, IPods, MP3 players, etc. without a physical retaliation, requires educators to be equally skilled in behavior modification and de-escalation techniques.

The school from hell (VIDEO)
Teachers fear for lives as students run amok
nypost.com

"Two teens assault teacher after he confiscates one's iPod"
engadet.com

[Author's Note: The 60-year-old teacher's neck was broken in two places]

(Shhh... Don't Mention the Truth)

Echoing my *"teachers double as correctional officers"* observation was a first-grade teacher in Paterson, New Jersey who stated on her Facebook page, ***"I'm not a teacher – I'm a warden of future criminals."*** Eventually, her comment went viral, and the African-American community (the school is predominately African-American) was outraged that she voiced those feelings. Consequently, the teacher was placed on administrative leave, and ultimately fired, after a judge ruled that her conduct was ***"inexcusable."*** Amazingly, despite the atrocities, assaults, or disruptions that routinely occur in NIGfested classrooms, teachers are unrealistically expected to internalize these realities or face a politically-based expulsion. This particular teacher, like anyone (even entertainers) that says something interpreted as "racially insensitive," are either crucified, or forced to attend "sensitivity" training followed by an apology tour. In this teacher's case, it's statistically true that some of her students will indeed be future criminals. It's also probable that many will be future gardeners on the welfare plantation. Even so, never, ever, ever, ever mention the truth, regardless of its statistical relevancy. Fortunately, I attended grade school prior to all this political correctness, and can still remember my WHITE middle school teacher issuing an ominous prediction to the class regarding our consistently disruptive JuviNIGGER classmates. Without hesitation, he'd say, ***"Take a good look, and laugh with them while you can because tomorrow they will be behind bars."*** Although we dismissed his words in the typical pre-teen fashion, I can confirm that his prophesy has been fulfilled several times; those JuviNIGGERS students continued their higher learning at HNCUs. So, how did he know that prison would be their fate? Chicago Tribune's *Howard Witt*_noted (9/25/07), ***"Studies show that a history of school suspensions or expulsions is a strong predictor of future trouble with the law—and the first step on what civil rights leaders have described as a "school-to-prison pipeline" for black youths, who represent 16 percent of U.S. adolescents but 38 percent of those incarcerated in youth prisons."*** Even though the numbers don't lie, observant people such as this former Paterson teacher will always be ostracized for acknowledging them.

NJ 1st-Grade Teacher Suspended Over Facebook Posts
nbcphiladelphia.com

(Lean on Me)

This isn't the first time that the national spotlight has highlighted the educational complications in Paterson's HoG schools. The movie "***Lean on Me***" was based on Principal Joe Clark's unconventional and controversial disciplinary measures utilized to turn around the notorious Eastside High school (named after region lol). Principal Clark, identified the JuviNIGGERS, marginalized their presence, and then established an Anti-NIGGER learning environment. Of course, the NIGGERfiliacs vilified Clark and his Anti-NIGGER actions, but because he was BLACK, he didn't face the same reprisal as this WHITE teacher who worked under similar conditions.

(Teacher & Parent Collaboration???)

When it comes to assessing children, teachers have a unique vantage point because they're with the kids five days a week, several hours per day, nine months a year. They typically see characteristics that may not be obvious to parents. Therefore, a partnership between parents and teachers is essential; my grade school teachers had parent-supported muscle. This open line of communication made me fear any spontaneous parent-teacher conferences or phone calls resulting from bad behavior. However, collaborating with a NIGGER parent about anything that's school-related is an exercise in futility, unless, it's regarding food voucher submission. The parental disconnect is so pervasive that some HoG schools are actually bribing parents to pick up report cards. In my city, I personally know of a HoG elementary school that pays parents ten dollars (cash) for picking up their child's report card. Similarly, a HoG high school offers an automatic "A" grade (used at the student's discretion) on any quiz, as an incentive for parents to pick up report cards. Perhaps these schools should also consider issuing "parent" report cards that grade parental involvement (amongst other things).

Chicago plans to pay parents $25 to pick up their children's report cards and go to parent-teacher conferences

dailymail.co.uk

(BLACK Parents' Mindset)

BLACK parents are intimately familiar with the NIGGER subculture's asinine custom of ridiculing any BLACK that exhibits intellectual prowess. NIGGERS don't care that self-improvement is an eternal endeavor, and thus, collectively perceive eloquent or academically attentive BLACKS as "WHITE" wannabes or "Oreos." As a result, studious and articulate BLACK students can't excel or maximize their potential in a JuviNIGfested learning environment. The disorderly learning environments combined with the constant threat of violence is demoralizing. Arguably, allowing a youngster to reside in a JuviNIGfested environment is a form of child abuse, or constitutes cruel and unusual punishment. Therefore, BLACK parents will do whatever it takes to get their children into "better schools"; some may even resort to illegal or controversial measures. One debatable act is the usage of a relative or friend's address to transfer/register their children into "better schools." Essentially, such desperation is a result of trying to avoid or escape JuviNIGfestation.

"Black Mother Jailed For Sending Kids to White School District"

blackeconomicdevelopment.com

[Author's Note: This "Jailing" strategy prevents NIGfestation in primarily Euro-American schools districts.]

A Disturbing New Trend: Jailing Poor Black Mothers for Trying to Educate Their Children

aclu.org

("Better Schools")

Of course, "better schools" is often a code phrase for predominately Euro-American schools or school districts. Even if it (the Euro-American district) isn't highly ranked academically, cultural conditioning still places the Euro-American school district over African-American school districts. I've never heard of incidences where Euro-American parents took similar drastic measures (as the BLACK parents) to enroll their kids into predominately African-American school districts. Why is that? Do they know something that BLACKS don't? Never mind, don't answer. Anyway, the solid academic image that WHITES have built is strong enough to give credibility to all Euro-American school districts, regardless of their educational rank. On the other hand, BLACKS, being the minority in the African-American community, simply don't have the numbers or support to turn around entire school districts. Thus, diplomas from African-American schools (especially JuviNIGfested schools) are negatively stereotyped, irrespective of strong student achievement or academic support system. There's a dearth of "good" African-American school districts because JuviNIGGERS are coddled and embraced, instead of coldshouldered. At the very least, Euro-American school districts seem to strategically maintain an agreeable learning atmosphere by marginalizing deliberate underachievers, and maintaining a zero tolerance policy for NIGGERtivity (whether it's from wiggers, White Trash, NIGGERS, or blacks W.N.T). In turn, this key attribute gives them the opposite reputation of their African-American counterpart. NIGGERfiliacs argue that Euro-American districts excel because they have "better resources." I agree. Of course, my interpretation of "better resources" is "better parental involvement," "better expectations," and "better ways to prevent NIGfestation." In other words, more money doesn't necessarily mean more academic success.

Kansas City Public Schools Faces Lawsuit From Suburban Districts Over Transfers

huffingtonpost.com

[Author's Note: Five suburban school districts have filed suit to stop student transfers from Kansas City Public schools to their districts until various issues like costs, and student eligibility are resolved. Translation: these five suburban school districts are trying to prevent a JuviNIGfestation.]

(Charter School Options)

In the inner-city, reputable charter schools have become viable alternatives to JuviNIGfested schools, but their few numbers limit their acceptance spaces. So, in attempt to provide an equal chance of acceptance, charters are legally required to use a lottery system when there are more applicants than space, thus unintentionally creating a loophole for JuviNIGfiltration. As a result, several charter schools are suffering from the similar JuviNIGGER created conditions as HoG public schools. NIGGERfiliac politicians and self-appointed NIGGERfiliac leaders are keenly aware of JuviNIGfestation at inner-city schools, yet will disingenuously claim that these schools are safe. Meanwhile, their children attend private schools.

'Public school mom' and education reformer Michelle Rhee accused of sending eldest daughter to $22,000 elite private school
dailymail.co.uk

(Microsoft's School of the Future)

In 2009, *eschoolnews.com* gave a three-year progress report of Microsoft's School of the Future, which exists in the HoG. Upon SOF's inception, I, like many, had assumed that it would beat the odds and thrive as one of the few Anti-NIGGER schools in the city. But, it turned out to be fool's gold. ***"When it opened its doors in 2006, Philadelphia's School of the Future (SOF) was touted as a high school that would revolutionize education: It would teach at-risk students critical 21st-century skills needed for college and the work force by emphasizing project-based learning, technology, and community involvement. But three years, three superintendents, four principals, and countless problems later, experts at a May 28 panel discussion hosted by the American Enterprise Institute (AEI) agreed: The Microsoft-inspired project has been a failure so far."*** In a calculated effort to avoid offending the group that it was built to serve, the ***"experts"*** blamed SOF's failure on many factors while ignoring the most obvious one

(JuviNIGGERS). Although this futuristic school's vision was to ***"invest human capital and expertise into a newly built LEED-certified school,"*** and provide alternative school hours with laptops, the NIGGER subculture exploited SOF's naiveté. In fact, a former member of the SOF Curriculum Planning Committee confirmed the regression by stating, ***"We naively thought, I guess, that by providing a beautiful building and great resources, these things would automatically yield change. They didn't."*** Hey Bill Gates, perhaps you should've first consulted with Oprah about building an inner-city school. Moving forward, if acceptance standards aren't based on Anti-NIGGER principles, "School of the Future" will become "School of the Past."

School of the Future: Lessons in failure
How Microsoft's and Philadelphia's innovative school became an example of what not to do
eschoolnews.com

(Ethnic Intimidation & Gangs)

Another problem with JuviNIGfested schools is ethnic intimidation. Whether it occurs in schools or the streets, JuviNIGGERS intimidate and bully (especially other ethnicities) for wreck-creation. As a result, students from other ethnicities that can't escape JuviNIGfested schools are victimized. For example, South Philadelphia high school (70% Af-Am & 18% Asian-American), which was labeled by the state as "persistently dangerous," was once ground zero for the amounts of systematic JuviNIGGER attacks against Asian students. For political reasons, the rampant abuse/harassment/violence experienced by Asian students was routinely ignored and dismissed by school officials. Walter Williams's *Townhall.com* article *"America's New Racists"* (6/22/11) explains: ***"Asian students report that black students routinely pelt them with food and beat, punch and kick them in school hallways and bathrooms as they hurl racial epithets such as 'Hey, Chinese!' and 'Yo, Dragon Ball!' The Asian American Legal Defense and Education Fund charged the School District of Philadelphia with 'deliberate indifference' toward black victimization of Asian students."*** Following one particularly massive assault, which sent several Asians to the emergency room, Asian students boycotted the school, and refused to attend class until their concerns were seriously addressed. The Asians should've taken things further by temporarily shutting their businesses in the HoG. Just think of the collective outrage that would've occurred if African-American students (including NIGGERS) were treated this way in a majority Euro-American school. Undoubtedly, the NAACP would stage an "Occupy Wall Street" type protest. In fact, even a simple vandalistic act of writing KKK on a locker room wall usually warrants a full-scale investigation into ethnic-intimidation. How soon African-Americans forget that less than a century ago, during school desegregation, we (African–Americans) were subjugated to similar hostilities. Nevertheless, the African-American community exhibited no empathy, and didn't unite with the Asian community against NIGGERS.

Attacked Asian Students Afraid To Go to School
nbcphiladelphia.com

13-Year-Old Nadin Khoury Violently Attacked by 'Teen Wolf Pack' While Community's M.I.A.
bvblackspin.com

[Author's Note: JuviNIGGER students videotaped their assault on a Liberian student.]

Asian Students were routinely attacked by JuviNIGGER students

(Attending High School Sporting Events)

Before, during, and especially after inner-city high school games, JuviNIGGERtivity poses a real threat to public safety. During the game, the atmosphere is usually volatile, and highly combustible. I understand the intensity associated with competitive sports, but JuviNIGGERS are always looking to be the main event; which is why attending high school games at inner-city, Af-Am schools are typically "attend at your own risk" endeavors. Although JuviNIGGERtivity can disrupt at any inner-city high school sporting event, basketball games are particularly high-hazard events because of the confined space and limited exits. As a result, many schools utilize Transportation Safety Authority (TSA) inspired pat downs, and courthouse-type metal detectors before entry. Actually, these security measures are an extension of the safety protocol utilized during normal HoG school hours. As reported by *edweek.org*, ***"Minority students in a high-poverty neighborhood are more likely to pass through a metal detector on the way to class than their better-off and white peers are, even if the schools are equally safe, according to new research."*** The research further suggested, ***"Security measures adopted from the criminal-justice arena—from metal detectors and surveillance cameras to full-time guards and drug-sniffing dogs—have proliferated in the past decade or so, particularly in secondary schools. Yet, even after accounting for the levels of crime on schools' campuses and in the surrounding neighborhoods, the researchers found that high-poverty schools were disproportionately likely to use such security mechanisms, and that the racial makeup of the student enrollment was a powerful predictor of whether the school would use metal detectors."*** I have nephews who played varsity basketball at inner-city schools, and while sitting in the bleachers, I spent just as much time watching my surroundings as I did watching their actual games. At any time, a hard foul or exchange of words (trash talk), could easily (and I mean easily) turn into a melee. Even if violence didn't occur, the relentless cursing, unsportsmanlike behavior (sometimes from players themselves), and overall unruliness, prevented me from bringing my youngest daughters to spectate. It is a common occurrence for inner-city schools to sometimes prohibit spectators from games entirely, or limit the viewership to just parents. By preventing their own students from attending games, these schools are essentially acknowledging the problems posed by JuviNIGGERS.

Study Finds Metal Detectors More Common in High-Minority Schools

edweek.org

[Author's Note: Which "High-Minority schools" could this article be referring to? Hint... it's not the Asians.]

"Five teens shot after bullets fly following high school basketball game in Brooklyn"

nydailynews.com

[Author's Note: The shooting occurred outside of "Christ The King" high school over a Louis Vuitton knit cap.]

(Ebonics)

JuviNIGGER students severely affect schools in two areas: safety and academics. Regarding safety, school districts throughout America have become increasingly adept at installing safety measures to prevent/punish JuviNIGGERtivity within their walls; however, forcing them to actually learn is a less successful endeavor. In attempt to address this academic shortcoming, a few school districts have even proposed incorporating Ebonics into their curriculum. Defining Ebonics, John R. Rickford, from *Linguisticsociety.org* wrote, ***"At its most literal level, Ebonics simply means 'black speech' (a blend of the words ebony 'black' and phonics 'sounds'). The term was created in 1973 by a group of black scholars who disliked the negative connotations of terms like 'Nonstandard Negro English' that had been coined in the 1960s when the first modern large-scale linguistic studies of African-American speech-communities began. However, the term Ebonics never caught on among linguists, much less among the general public."*** Although Ebonics is identified as ***"Black speech,"*** it must be clarified that Ebonics is actually the manner of speech preferred by NIGGERS, and is the HoG's official language. BLACKS like me have shunned Ebonics in favor of learning a language (Standard English) that would serve outside the HoG (I guess that makes me bi-lingual). Amusingly, the NIGGER subculture interprets the usage of Basic English as talking "white." Surely, the English would disagree that Americanized English is proper. Although English enunciation generally varies between geographical locations, Ebonics is simply lazy speech embraced by the NIGGER subculture. Ironically, NIGGERS make fun of the broken English spoken by immigrants (despite the fact that many own businesses in HoG) not realizing that English is usually their (immigrants) second or third language, whereas English is the NIGGERS' only language, but it's spoken as if it isn't! NIGGERS actually speak English in the manner that they text and tweet. When texting or tweeting, I understand that character limitations require shorthand script, but

NIGGERS really speak that way! The NIGGERfiliacs say that Ebonics is a dialect resulting from hundreds of years of forced illiteracy. But come on... there's no excuse for self-imposed ignorance in this era of free public education and the internet! Both are intentionally misused by the NIGGER subculture. Certainly, a formerly enslaved person such as Frederick Douglas would be highly insulted that the *"slavery did this to me"* excuse is still being hustled in today's age of information and technology. Geesh, even he didn't use that excuse during his lifetime when it was actually applicable.

(Usefulness of Ebonics)

It's truly an act of desperate outreach to integrate the NIGGER subculture's manner of speech into certain curriculums. Sure, Ebonics has its benefits and usefulness in certain environments like HNCUs or the HoG, but in the real world, the marketplace requires standardized speech. In other words, advancement opportunities are greater for those that speak standardized English than urbanized English (Ebonics). Philadelphia mayor Michael Nutter rightly stated to the youth, ***"Keep your butts in school. And why don't you work in extending your English vocabulary from these grunts and mumbles that no one can understand?"*** Educated BLACKS will never allow their children to speak this inferior and demeaning second-class scrap called Ebonics. It's not a language of productivity. Additionally, it severely limits the chances of being gainfully employed or attaining a position of power (Professional athletes and entertainers are notable exceptions). In today's world, Ebonics is associated with counterproductive, non-achievers who likely have HNCU resumes and HoG affiliations. On the flip side, employment opportunities are readily available for "bi-lingual" African-Americans. In fact, the Justice Department was looking for "bi-lingual" African-Americans to assist with NIGGERtivity investigations. As reported by *thesmokinggun.com,* ***"The Department of Justice is seeking to hire linguists fluent in Ebonics to help monitor, translate, and transcribe the secretly recorded conversations of subjects of narcotics investigations, according to federal records."*** Clearly, this job opportunity isn't for NIGGERS because they wouldn't be able to translate the recorded Ebonics into decipherable English.

Justice Department Seeks Ebonics Experts
DEA to hire nine "Black English" linguists
thesmokinggun.com

(A Moment of Clarity)

Since the NIGGER subculture has consistently demonstrated the inability to grasp the fundamentals of English, Ebonics manifested to supplement their handicap. But here's the truth... their assumed speech impediment is actually an embraced and encouraged attribute of their subculture. During his 2004 Ghettoesburg address, Bill Cosby highlighted this aspect of the NIGGER subculture, and correctly surmised: ***"It's standing on the corner. It can't speak English. It doesn't want to speak English. I can't even talk the way these people talk. "Why you ain't where you is go, ra," I don't know who these people are. And I blamed the kid until I heard the mother talk. Then I heard the father talk. This is all in the house. You used to talk a certain way on the corner and you got into the house and switched to English. Everybody knows it's important to speak English except these knuckleheads. You can't land a plane with "why you ain't..." You can't be a doctor with that kind of crap coming out of your mouth. There is no Bible that has that kind of language. Where did these people get the idea that they're moving ahead on this. Well, they know they're not, they're just hanging out in the same place, five or six generations sitting in the projects when you're just supposed to stay there long enough to get a job and move out."*** Naturally, Dr. Cosby was vilified for telling the truth. Even when schools try to break this barrier, NIGGER parents obstruct those efforts because correct speech is an Anti-NIGGER attribute.

Chapter II

BLACKS -vs- blacks with NIGGER Tendencies

"People pay for what they have allowed themselves to become. And they pay for it very simply; by the lives they lead." – James Baldwin

After reading a rough copy of this manuscript, my wife asked, *"Who is winning this intra-racial war between BLACKS and NIGGERS?"* I candidly informed her that the NIGGERS are winning. Why do I believe that the NIGGERS are winning? Well, their advantage stems from the continued NIGGERfiliac support, tolerance from non-confrontational BLACKS, and ambivalence from another segment of the African-American community, whom I refer to as blacks with NIGGER tendencies. Comparable to swing voters, this black (WNT) segment, which I believe is the largest (numerically) African-American segment, has the ability to tip the scale in one direction. Seemingly, they have shifted the scale of power towards the NIGGER subculture. Although this book spends a lot of time dissecting and condemning the NIGGER subculture, I'm also disappointed with blacks (WNT) because they deliberately maintain neutrality in this Un-Civil War. People struggle with the fact that African-Americans (like other American ethnic groups) are comprised of multiple segments. This reality challenges America's traditional ethnic classifications, so understanding that several types of African-Americans exist, may ignite an honest race dialogue.

(Three of a Kind)

Within the African-American populace, BLACKS and NIGGERS will forever be oppositional segments. BLACKS are the cream of the crop, upwardly mobile, productive, taxpaying, law-abiding, assets to society who characteristically don't subscribe to the NIGGER subculture. Whereas, NIGGERS are the dysfunctional, counterproductive, non-contributing, law-breaking, liabilities to society, who personify the negative stereotypes that plague the entire African-American community. Existing as the "gray area," are the blacks that embody principles of both BLACK and NIGGER segments. They're generally law-abiding (but criminally opportunistic) taxpayers, usually employed at menial jobs, yet, embrace the NIGGER subculture in a limited way. They are blacks (WNT).

(BLACK Person)

"BLACK" (as used in this book) is an autonomous term. I'm not insinuating that this segment is perfect or flawless; BLACKS are flawed in manners consistent amongst all races. In fact, many BLACKS (like many WHITES) are NIGGERfiliacs, and will likely denounce this book. Quite simply, this minority segment is comprised of non-NIGGERS. Though the professional, political, religious, and financial statuses (amongst other things) vary, BLACKS are fundamentally united by their Anti-NIGGER characteristics. For instance, BLACKS altruistically provide charity and perform community service, whereas, NIGGERS consider court-ordered restitution as charity, and court-mandated community service as "giving back." Overall, the BLACK segment continues to yield W.E.B Dubois' prophesized *"talented tenth."*

(To Each, His Own)

Contrary to the monolithic NIGGER segment, BLACKS are a mixed bag of ideologies, political affiliations, occupations, and incomes. The lifestyle and philosophical variation amongst BLACKS frequently clashes with NIGGERS and blacks (WNT). BLACKS typically think, live, and act independently of the crabs in a barrel (HoG) mentality. Because BLACKS are a minority within the African-American populace, they've formed organizations where like-minded BLACKS could network and socialize. Not to be outdone, NIGGERS have also formed organizations where like-minded NIGGERS could network and socialize... they're called gangs.

(Only BLACKS Lend a Hand)

Historically, the NIGGER subculture wasn't as prominent as it is presently; once upon a time, the African-American underclass mainly consisted of blacks (WNT). This was when African-

American communities were based on common-unity, low illegitimacy rates, and children respecting adults. Moreover, "black on black" homicides were anomalies. Even though blacks (WNT) were the general problem, they weren't today's NIGGER. BLACK trailblazers such as Booker T. Washington and W.E.B Dubois were often at philosophical odds regarding the catalysts for blacks (WNT) behavior, and appropriate remedy. Generations later, the debate continued amongst new leaders such as Malcolm X, Dr. MLK, and others. Point being, BLACKS have always tried to reform the other segments of the African-American populace; some blamed racism while others cited shiftlessness. In fact, BLACK entrepreneur Nannie Burroughs actually wrote a self-help plan to guide blacks (WNT). Although this plan is still valid for blacks (WNT), it's pointless for those who have chosen to be NIGGERS.

*12 Things The Negro Must Do For Himself by Nannie Helen Burroughs

(Circa Early 1900's)

1. The Negro Must Learn To Put First Things First. The First Things Are: Education; Development of Character Traits; A Trade and Home Ownership.

The Negro puts too much of his earning in clothes, in food, in show and in having what he calls "a good time." The Dr. Kelly Miller said, "The Negro buys what he WANTS and begs for what he Needs." Too true!

2. The Negro Must Stop Expecting God and White Folk To Do For Him What He Can Do For Himself.

It is the "Divine Plan" that the strong shall help the weak, but even God does not do for man what man can do for himself. The Negro will have to do exactly what Jesus told the man (in John 5:8) to do—Carry his own load—"Take up your bed and walk."

3. The Negro Must Keep Himself, His Children And His Home Clean And Make The Surroundings In Which He Lives Comfortable and Attractive.

He must learn to "run his community up"—not down. We can segregate by law, we integrate only by living. Civilization is not a matter of race, it is a matter of standards. Believe it or not—some day, some race is going to outdo the Anglo-Saxon, completely. It can be the Negro race, if the Negro gets sense enough. Civilization goes up and down that way.

4. The Negro Must Learn To Dress More Appropriately For Work And For Leisure.

Knowing what to wear—how to wear it—when to wear it and where to wear it, are earmarks of common sense, culture and also an index to character.

5. The Negro Must Make His Religion An Everyday Practice And Not Just A Sunday-Go-To-Meeting Emotional Affair.

6. The Negro Must Highly Resolve To Wipe Out Mass Ignorance.

The leaders of the race must teach and inspire the masses to become eager and determined to improve mentally, morally and spiritually, and to meet the basic requirements of good citizenship.

We should initiate an intensive literacy campaign in America, as well as in Africa. Ignorance—***satisfied ignorance***—is a millstone abut [sic] the neck of the race. It is democracy's greatest burden.

Social integration is a relationship attained as a result of the cultivation of kindred social ideals, interests and standards.

It is a blending process that requires time, understanding and kindred purposes to achieve. Likes alone and not laws can do it.

7. The Negro Must Stop Charging His Failures Up To His "Color" And To White People's Attitude.

The truth of the matter is that good service and conduct will make senseless race prejudice fade like mist before the rising sun.

God never intended that a man's color shall be anything other than a ***badge of distinction***. It is high time that all races were learning that fact. The Negro must first **QUALIFY** for whatever position he wants. Purpose, initiative, ingenuity and industry are the keys that all men use to get what they want. The Negro will have to do the same. He must make himself a workman who is too skilled not to be wanted, and too **DEPENDABLE** not to be on the job, according to promise or plan. He will never become a vital factor in industry until he learns to put into his work the vitalizing force of initiative, skill and dependability. He has gone **"RIGHTS"** mad and **"DUTY"** dumb.

8. The Negro Must Overcome His Bad Job Habits.

He must make a brand new reputation for himself in the world of labor. His bad job habits are absenteeism, funerals to attend, or a little business to look after. The Negro runs an off and on business. He also has a bad reputation for conduct on the job—such as petty quarrelling with other help, incessant loud talking about nothing; loafing, carelessness, due to lack of job pride; insolence, gum chewing and—too often—liquor drinking. Just plain bad job habits!

9. He Must Improve His Conduct In Public Places.

Taken as a whole, he is entirely too loud and too ill-mannered.

There is much talk about wiping out racial segregation and also much talk about achieving integration.

Segregation is a physical arrangement by which people are separated in various services.
It is definitely up to the Negro to wipe out the apparent justification or excuse for segregation.

The only effective way to do it is to clean up and keep clean. By practice, cleanliness will become a habit and habit becomes character.

10. The Negro Must Learn How To Operate Business For People—Not For Negro People, Only.

To do business, he will have to remove all typical "earmarks," business principles; measure up to accepted standards and meet stimulating competition, graciously—in fact, he must learn to welcome competition.

11. The Average So-Called Educated Negro Will Have To Come Down Out Of The Air. He Is Too Inflated Over Nothing. He Needs An Experience Similar To The One That Ezekiel Had--(Ezekiel 3:14-19). And He Must Do What Ezekiel Did

Otherwise, through indifference, as to the plight of the masses, the Negro, who thinks that he has escaped, will lose his own soul. It will do all leaders good to read Hebrew 13:3, and the first Thirty-seven Chapters of Ezekiel.

A race transformation itself through its own leaders and its sensible "common people." A race rises on its own wings, or is held down by its own weight. True leaders are never "things apart from the people." They are the masses. They simply got to the front ahead of them. Their only business at the front is to inspire to masses by hard work and noble example and challenge them to "Come on!" Dante stated a fact when he said, "Show the people the light and they will find the way!"

There must arise within the Negro race a leadership that is not out hunting bargains for itself. A noble example is found in the men and women of the Negro race, who, in the early days, laid down their lives for the people. Their invaluable contributions have not been appraised by the "latter-day leaders." In many cases, their names would never be recorded, among the unsung heroes of the world, but for the fact that white friends have written them there.

"Lord, God of Hosts, Be with us yet."

The Negro of today does not realize that, but, for these exhibits A's, that certainly show the innate possibilities of members of their own race, white people would not have been moved to make such princely investments in lives and money, as they have made, for the establishment of schools and for the on-going of the race.

12. The Negro Must Stop Forgetting His Friends. "Remember."

Read Deuteronomy 24:18. Deuteronomy rings the big bell of gratitude. Why? Because an ingrate is an abomination in the sight of God. God is constantly telling us that ***"I the Lord thy God delivered you"***—through human instrumentalities.

The American Negro has had and still has friends—in the North and in the South. These friends not only pray, speak, write, influence others, but make unbelievable, unpublished sacrifices and contributions for the advancement of the race—for their brothers in bonds.

The noblest thing that the Negro can do is to so live and labor that these benefactors will not have given in vain. The Negro must make his heart warm with gratitude, his lips sweet with thanks and his heart and mind resolute with purpose to justify the sacrifices and stand on his feet and go forward—***"God is no respector of persons. In every nation, he that feareth him and worketh righteousness is"*** sure to win out. Get to work! That's the answer to everything that hurts us. We talk too much about nothing instead of redeeming the time by working.

R-E-M-E-M-B-E-R

In spite of race prejudice, America is brim full of opportunities. Go after them!

Nannie Helen Burroughs (1879-1961) was an educator, orator, religious leader and businesswoman who moved to Washington, D.C., as a young woman to take advantage of the city's superior educational opportunities. While living in Washington she decided to open a school for African-American girls to prepare them for a productive adult life. Burroughs was an active member of her church, where she organized a women's club that conducted evening classes in useful skills such as typewriting, bookkeeping, cooking, and sewing. Her responsibilities within the church increased when she became secretary of the Women's Auxiliary of the National Baptist Convention, which supported missionary work and educational societies in Baptist churches throughout the nation. Burroughs's lifelong dream was realized when she opened the National Training School for Women and Girls in Washington, D.C., in 1909.

Source:** ***BlackMenInAmerica.com

(blacks WNT)

Growing up as a black (WNT), I'm intimately familiar with their mindset, and know that the ability to change exists. For that reason, I'm increasingly displeased with their neutrality in this Un-Civil War. Blacks (WNT) are a major reason why the NIGGER culture appears to define the African-American culture. Although they're on the cusp between BLACKS and NIGGERS, a closer bond actually exists between NIGGERS and blacks (WNT). This connection exists because being a NIGGER is easier than being a BLACK. NIGGERS are to blacks (WNT) what rats are to mice.

(Who is Who?)

In a variety of areas, blacks (WNT) and NIGGERS behave similarly. The manner in which they walk lock step is pathetic; it's truly the blind leading the blind. The dress, speech, interests, and overall character, sometimes make it difficult to differentiate between them. However, one key separating characteristic is that blacks (WNT) usually aren't violent menaces to society. Even still, this close black (WNT) and NIGGER correlation is the reason that African-Americans are statistical tops in most negative categories.

(Politics)

As far as politics, this segment uncritically and in zombie-like fashion, votes Democrat with no interest of exploring other platforms. Consequently, the Democrat party has learned to repeatedly exploit them. Even Malcolm X noticed this trance-like allegiance. He declared, ***"Anytime you throw your weight behind a political party that controls two-thirds of the government and that party can't keep the promise that it made to you at election time and you are dumb enough to walk around continuing to identify yourself with that party, you not only are a chump, but you're a traitor to your race."*** Author Robert Heinlein explained this phenomenon allegorically, ***"Once the monkeys learn they can vote themselves bananas, they'll never climb another tree."*** By the way race-peddlers, Heinlein's comment was based on realism, not racism.

(Help or Not?)

Unlike NIGGERS, who refuse to be civilized, blacks (WNT) aren't entirely lost causes; they are typically capable of reformation. I stand as a testament that blacks (WNT) can evolve. They don't shun education to the extent that NIGGERS do, but any higher education is preferably obtained at HBCUs or community colleges. Like NIGGERS, they prefer any environment where African-Americans are the obvious majority. Since blacks (WNT) are commonly identity lacking, generic, African-Americans with misplaced priorities, the military is a perfect environment for them to develop character. For NIGGERS, however, this military option isn't appropriate because guns and NIGGERS are a toxic brew. Moreover, the military training and developed skills would most certainly be parlayed into urban terrorism. Besides, the only manner in which NIGGERS care to "serve" their country is by "serving" HNCU time. Although blacks (WNT) are able to lawfully function in society, they suffer from an inferiority complex, and sometimes exhibit attention-seeking behavior (like NIGGERS). They're usually in denial about their NIGGER affliction, which is advantageous to the seductive NIGGER subculture. Even though blacks (WNT) are capable of violence, and sometimes indulge in NIGGERtivity, extreme violent acts such as homicides, rapes, brutal assaults, etc. are characteristically the NIGGERS' domain. Simply put, while blacks (WNT) embrace certain aspects of the NIGGER subculture, the NIGGERS' consistent willingness and desire to commit extreme violence is a major dividing factor.

(Employment)

Blacks (WNT) are over-represented in minimum wage, service, and unskilled jobs sector. Yes, you know them; the employee with the bad attitude that makes one wonder how they obtained a customer service job in the first place. They're the ones that received certifications from fly by night accreditation schools for quick fix occupations that don't require a lot of specialized schooling. They are the HoG residents that complain about the neighborhood/city conditions, yet know not the name of their city council person, district ward leader, or state representative to petition. Many entertainers and athletes could also be categorized as blacks (WNT).

McDonald's Manager Punches Customer for Bringing in a Service Dog

gawker.com

[Author's Note: This manager was likely a black (WNT) because NIGGERS don't work.]

(Public Transportation)

According to *urbanhabitat.org*, ***"African-Americans are almost six times more likely to ride mass transit than whites, while Hispanics are three times more likely to use transit to get around. In urban areas, African-Americans and Latinos comprise over 54 percent of transit users-62 percent of the bus riders, 35 percent of subway riders, and 29 percent of commuter rail riders."*** Essentially, this study is warning citizens of a likely encounter with the NIGGER subculture or those with NIGGER tendencies on public transportation. I sometimes take public transportation, and the most frustrating part of the commute is enduring the disrespectful conduct of the teenagers with NIGGER tendencies. Sometimes the commute feels like self-inflicted cruelty. The passengers are routinely subjected to profanity-laced dialogues, and the unwelcomed content of openly conducted cell phone conversations. These kids never have their phones on vibrate because of the desired attention received from blasting vulgar, and expletive laced ringtones. I understand and appreciate Amtrak and other local regional rail lines for establishing "quiet cars." These "quiet cars" are essentially "Anti-NIGGER" environments that provide a refuge from their annoying mannerisms and lack of courtesy. Still, a primary NIGGER tendency is to always circumvent rules because rules are clearly for everyone else. As reported by the Daily Mail, ***"Police said the 39-year-old became aggressive and was involved in a 'verbal altercation' when asked to be quiet during the journey from Oakland, California to Salem, Oregon."*** In summary, this non-compliant, black (WNT) was charged with "disorderly conduct" after refusing to abide by the primary, quiet car rule. Her arrest exemplifies the extreme measures necessary to keep civility in public places. Of course, after her detainment, racism, not her behavior was alleged, thus establishing grounds for a frivolous lawsuit. I labeled her as a black (WNT) because this story wouldn't have been violence-free if she were a NIGGER. In fact, compare this 'confrontation' on public transportation to the following story of 'confrontation,' and the NIGGER/black (WNT) difference is obvious.

Woman arrested on train for talking loudly on phone for 16 HOURS! (And she was in the quiet carriage)
dailymail.co.uk

(The NIGGER Response)

How many of us board public transportation equipped with a survival plan? How many of us ride the bus thinking that domestic terrorism could occur? Well, if NIGGERS are daily passengers, then it's wise to be prepared. Oh, I'm not simply talking about guarding valuables; I'm talking about guarding your life. For example, on a bus in Philadelphia, a Baby Mama had gotten upset with another passenger because he criticized her for spanking her young child. By "threatening" to report her to the authorities for child abuse, the concerned passenger, who happened to be African-American, disregarded the rules of NIGGER engagement. Feeling "threatened" and disrespected, the Baby Mama made a phone call to acquaintances that would remedy the situation in typical NIGGER fashion. As the bus approached her stop, NIGGERS were waiting in plain sight, anxious to confront the passenger for being a child advocate. While exiting from the rear of bus, the Baby Mama held open the door so that her NIGGER accomplices could step aboard. After she identified the child advocate, the NIGGERS pulled out assault rifles, and commenced to indiscriminately shoot. In a panic, the other unsuspecting passengers hit the floor, while some clustered in the driver's stairwell. Stuck like a deer in headlights, an eighty-year-old senior was the only passenger that remained standing during most of the shooting. Miraculously, the shooting spree yielded no serious injuries, and the Urban Terrorists were apprehended.

Dramatic Video Shows Gunmen Firing Into Philadelphia City Bus
foxnews.com

(Other Races with NIGGER Tendencies)

NIGGER tendencies aren't exclusive to African-Americans, they can manifest in other races. Regardless of race, any family living in the HoG is at a higher risk of their children developing NIGGER tendencies than those living outside the HoG. Whenever I see teenagers of other races exhibiting NIGGER attributes, I think of Jesus' words found in Luke 23:34, ***"Father forgive them, for they know not what they do."*** Sometimes, these impressionable teenagers (with NIGGER tendencies) deserve more pity than scorn. And though I *"pity the fool"* who wants to emulate the NIGGER subculture, fools are constitutionally protected to do so. I particularly empathize with their parents because most forward-thinking people know that there's no future in being a NIGGER. Meanwhile, their children are under the NIGGER subculture's dangerous spell unconcerned with the associated costs.

(Wiggers)

Euro-Americans who grow up around the NIGGER subculture will rebuke it, embrace it in a limited way, develop a tolerance, or become wiggers. But, if they leave the HoG and surround themselves with WHITES, they usually learn that being white with NIGGER tendencies is self-sabotage. This is why I liken wiggers to blacks (W.N.T) because blacks (WNT) need to surround themselves with non-NIGGERS to help break the spell. After or during an HNCU experience, wiggers usually realize that they were playing for the wrong team, and then will seek refuge amongst Euro-Americans. The suburban WHITE kid that embraces wiggertivity usually does it as a means of rebellion or identity-purposes, not because they necessarily want to be a wigger. As they age, they usually grow to understand that being a wigger stifles societal advancement and subsequently shed that wigger identity. Unfortunately, black kids (WNT) aren't so quick to do the same.

(The NIGGER Frat)

The ridiculousness of the NIGGER subculture becomes evident when other races emulate them. The imitated dress, Ebonics, and artificial swag, provides a synopsis for a comedy flick. Once, I suggested to a Filipino teenager who had NIGGER tendencies (talk, dress, mannerisms) that he surrender the regressive, NIGGER-inspired lifestyle, and alternatively maximize the privileges (as immigrants) that America has extended to him. Regrettably, it usually takes a tragedy to make the NIGGER wannabe realize that he/she should've embraced their heritage and left the NIGGERtivity to the professionals. In fact, the only way NIGGERS truly embrace and respect NIGGER wannabes is if that NIGGER wannabe does something extremely senseless. It's like being initiated into a fraternity. The wannabe has to exhibit worthiness to become a member, and the NIGGER fraternity only accepts members who are unruly, menacing, violent, and criminal. Additionally, murder, rape, assaults, shootings, uncivilized behavior, and other forms of NIGGERtivity are all pre-requisites of membership, which is finalized by an oath to always "keep it real," regardless of how self-defeating it is. Thus, in order for the non-Af-Am neophyte to be accepted and respected by the NIGGER subculture, the NIGGER wannabe has to exhibit all these attributes (times two). Quite simply, the NIGGER wannabe has to be a super NIGGER to prove that he isn't a poser.

Chapter III

Actually, it's not "BLACK on BLACK" Violence

"The cause of violence is not ignorance. It is self-interest. Only reverence can restrain violence – reverence for human life and the environment." - **William Sloan**

While researching, I encountered a sentiment echoed throughout cyberspace; African-Americans seemingly don't care about *"BLACK on BLACK"* violence. Admittedly, the outrage from BLACKS regarding this continual intra-racial genocide and associated impact is not noticeable. In fact, I address that very issue in ***Memo to BLACKS***. Somehow, the African-American community has developed a tolerance for a violent and dysfunctional subculture that other communities would not, but I digress; this chapter isn't about NIGGERfilia. This chapter addresses the misperception associated with the terminology *"BLACK on BLACK"* crime. The term *"Black on Black"* is a misnomer that indicts all African-Americans, while not accurately assigning blame to the proper perpetrators (usually NIGGERS). Furthermore, it perpetuates the notion that BLACKS are committing crimes against BLACKS, even though the NIGGERS are actually committing crimes against everyone. Understand that NIGGERS and BLACKS have different cultural outlooks, and *"Black on Black"* is only accurate regarding skin color not culture. Outside of skin color, little commonalities exist between the two groups. One day, I hope that society would officially distinguish BLACKS from NIGGERS, until then, ***BLACKSvsNIGGERS.com*** will keep the record straight.

(My Public Relations Firm)

If I were to start a consulting firm, I'd advise the media, government, and law enforcement, to use these five categories to accurately catalogue African-American crime and victimization statistics. Since NIGGERS (mislabeled as BLACKS) are the perpetrators and victims of disproportionate amounts of crime, they (NIGGERS) need an independent system of record keeping. This way, the media and law enforcement could convey to society the clear and present danger posed by this subculture without indicting the entire African-American populace. The following five categories are listed in the order of probable occurrence.

Category **N/N**: ***NIGGER ON NIGGER CRIME***

The ***N/N*** category would be reserved for NIGGERS who commit crimes against other NIGGERS. Because they commit the bulk of violent crimes inside and outside the African-American community, and are overrepresented as victims, this category would be the most active. NIGGER on NIGGER ***(N/N)*** crime is essentially a form of ethnic cleansing, and because ***N/N*** incidences are easily recognized (no specialized skill is required), police labor, and taxpayer money shouldn't be wasted on lengthy ***N/N*** investigations or homey-cides. In fact, due to Chicago's lack of manpower and other factors, only 129 of their 506 murders (2012) were solved. Even still, these limited resources should be reserved for circumstances where NIGGERtivity affects civilians; i.e. ***NIGGER on BLACK*** **(N/B)** or ***NIGGER on Euro/Asian/Latino/Other*** **(NEALO) crimes**.

Gang Violence Smolders On Hot Chicago Streets
npr.org

(Homey-cide Sentencing)

After a long, thorough analysis, I've concluded that the death penalty should **not** be utilized for ***N/N*** homey-cides. As an alternative, punishment for ***(N/N)*** homey-cides should be mandatory life sentence of hard mental and physical labor. My recommendation is based on simple math. Ultimately, society benefits best from imposing a life sentence to the homey-cide perpetrator because a two (NIGGERS) for one deal is netted; one societal threat is dead, and the other menace is removed from society to start his/her perpetual HNCU classes. Since taxpayers pay the HNCU tuition, which includes room, board, and meal plan, the perp will spend the rest of his/her natural life-repaying taxpayers in any beneficial capacity.

(Repaying Taxpayers)

Undoubtedly, society should profit from these massive HNCU investments, but the return doesn't necessarily have to be monetary. For example, in addition to the enrollee's intensive physical labor performed at the HNCU, he/she could be subjugated to experiments and clinical trials that aid in the advancement of science and medicine. Once the HNCU enrollee loses his/her usefulness, he/she should be put down and the corpse used in other capacities. Replacing artificial crash test dummies with cadavers is an area where the usage of authentic flesh and bone could potentially lead to innovated safety features. Additionally, the bodies can be used to test safety equipment such as bulletproof vests, helmets, minesweeper footwear, etc. for the military or law enforcement. Finally, the cremated remains can be used as filler for firework displays. Face it; NIGGERS inherently know that their fate is centered on two boxes... the prison box or casket.

(The War on Terror)

After 9/11, the Patriot Act was quickly passed, and the War on Terror commenced. Although the Patriot Act addresses domestic terrorism, somehow, Urban Terrorists unfairly escaped the intent of this legislation. Currently, they aren't even charged or tried under the Patriot Act; this contradiction needs to be addressed. Urban Terrorists should face the same consequences as any "terrorist." Moreover, a military tribunal should serve as judge and jury over Urban Terrorists' cases, and their incarceration should be limited to military installations (not HNCUs) such as Guantanamo Bay. Urban Terrorists fearlessly indulge in NIGGERtivity because they know that the worst outcome is mandatory semesters at their local HNCU. They've become accustomed to attending HNCUs where campus life is good; consequently, the HNCU recidivism rate is as high the national debt *(Refer to the **HNCU** chapter).* I guarantee that urban terrorism would decline if Urban Terrorists were court martialed as enemy combatants in the "War on Terror." Again, civilian courts shouldn't hold judicial proceedings for Urban Terrorists because they aren't equipped to consistently render the appropriate justice. Furthermore, Urban Terrorists have an advantage in civilian courts because blacks (WNT) or

NIGGERfiliacs may potentially serve on the jury, which enhances the probability of a soft verdict or acquittal. On the other hand, at a military tribunal, any excuse-making for NIGGERtivity, such as the usual narrative of a poverty-stricken, rough childhood with no male role model, would be ignored. Due to their criminal nature, and lack of an innate moral compass, NIGGERS need strong deterrents to NIGGERtivity, so let's utilize laws that already exist such as the Patriot Act.

Tearful apology from repeat offender 'falls on deaf ears,' judge says

pulsejournal.com

[Author's Note: NIGGERtivity would wane if this type of intolerant judge presided over every NIGGER case. Judges like this epitomizes my vision of a tribunal for Urban Terrorists.]

Category **N/B**: ***NIGGER ON BLACK CRIME***

This ***N/B*** category is reserved for crimes committed by NIGGERS that directly or indirectly target or affect BLACKS. In African-American communities across the country, NIGGER crossfire, and other forms of NIGGERtivity, has continually resulted in BLACK collateral damage. Basically, the high rate of ***N/B*** crimes is the result of the NIGGER virus continuously feeding from its African-American host.

(Sentencing for Urban Terrorists)

It should be considered a crime against humanity whenever an Urban Terrorist commits a violent crime against a non-NIGGER (civilian). The *"content of character"* factor (as preached by Dr. MLK) has led me to presume that Urban Terrorists are always guilty until proven innocent. Therefore, if a civilian is murdered by an Urban Terrorist, (whether the crime was premeditated or not) the appropriate punishment for this crime(s) against humanity would be death. Furthermore, if the evidence is indisputable, the standard appeal process should be nullified, and the plea bargain option for a lesser, life-sparing sentence is negated. After all, the Urban Terrorist stripped that (plea deal) option from the victim(s), so it damn sure shouldn't exist for the victimizer! Also, the death penalty has to occur in a timely fashion. Since a speedy trial is constitutionally guaranteed, why not a speedy execution? Nowadays, even if high definition video conclusively shows a person committing a crime, while leaving DNA, and eyewitnesses, the crime is still considered "alleged." In other words, even though undeniable evidence is present, "due process" usually takes too long to get "dude processed." Yes, I understand that all legal avenues must be explored to ensure that an innocent person is not put to death, but an innocent Urban Terrorist is an oxymoron. Anyway, until the Urban Terrorist's date with death, he/she will work in some capacity to pay restitution to all impacted parties for any damage caused by their NIGGERtivity, including but not limited to funeral/medical expenses plus pain and suffering.

(No Lethal Injection)

Urban Terrorists would **not** be allowed to die by lethal injection. First of all, that prolonged process consists of treating the Urban Terrorist to dinner of his choice (the last meal), while providing time to bid farewell to family/ friends. Then, after being strapped (tucked) in, society gives him/her the long-awaited figurative farewell kiss, which usually comes in the form of a sedative. Give me a break, the only thing missing from that process is a teddy bear and Snuggie blanket. Secondly, HNCUs unfairly provides rights and privileges to the criminal as if he/she are the true victims. In fact, a Euro-American death row inmate named Danny Hembree validated my sentiment regarding the extreme pandering of death row inmates at taxpayer's expense. He wrote a letter that highlighted several troublesome truths about so-called "punishment" in the penal system. These are his unedited words: ***"My name is Danny Hembree. I was tried in Gaston Co. by twelve of its fine citizens. I was found guilty of 1st degree capitol murder and sentenced to death by Judge Beverly Beal on Nov, 18, 2011. The Great State of North Carolinas Dept. of Corr. was ordered to carry out my murder, or was it, or is it just another piece of the politition political money pie. I wonder if the public is aware that the cost of my first trial was a half a million dollars. Are they aware that the State has in place a system that automatically delays my lawful murder for years so that pieces of the money pie can continue to be passed around. Is the public aware that the chances of my lawful murder taking place in the next 20 years if ever are very***

slim. Is the public aware that I am a gentlemen of leisure, watching color tv in the A.C, reading takeing naps at will, eating three well balanced hot meals a day. I'm housed in a building that connects to the new 55 million dollar hospital with round the clock free medical care 24/7. There are a lot of good citizens who bloges on various web sites stating their opinions about me and the punishment that I deserve. Most of the blogs were made by anonymous cowards, but not all. I laugh at you self rightous clowns and I spit in the face of your so called justice system. The State of North Carolina has sentenced me to death but it's not real. You citizens of Gaston Co. should petition the State and force them to carry out my murder sentence instead of blindly taking it up the ### from the State or are you to stupid to proceed. I am a man who is ready to except his unjust punishment and face God almighty with a clear conscience unlike you cowards and your cowardly system. Kill me if you can suckers. Ha! Ha! Ha!" Many argue that *"an eye for an eye and tooth for a tooth"* punishment will leave this country blind and toothless. I vehemently disagree; the statistics have shown that one hundred percent of murderers/rapists that were executed by the state didn't commit another violent crime (or any crime for that manner). I like those odds.

(Death Penalty Specs)

If conditions permit, the death penalty should be executed utilizing the same method that the Urban Terrorist used to victimize the civilian. For example, if the weapon was a knife, then he/she (Urban Terrorist) must die by a similar or same knife. If the weapon was a gun, then they should also die from lead poisoning (if possible, from the same type of gun). If a rape conviction accompanies a murder conviction, then his penis would also be considered a weapon, and the death penalty decree should include castration without anesthesia. Following all executions, any salvageable body part or organ should be donated to the appropriate medical or research organization. If circumstances prevent the Urban Terrorist from being executed as specified by these guidelines, then an alternate form of cruel or unusual punishment shall be utilized as determined by the tribunal (being dropped into a volcano is my recommendation). Although the Eight Amendment protects United States citizens from **"cruel and unusual punishment,"** Urban Terrorists shouldn't be constitutionally protected since their actions are that of enemy combatants. Besides, it's not fair that they be protected from ***"cruel and unusual punishment,"*** when their victim(s) weren't.

(Parole)

A HNCU enrollee should never be paroled after committing a violent N/B or NEALO crime (which currently happens too frequently), but if it occurs, he/she should be registered as a certified threat to society. Moreover, the community should be alerted in the same manner as Megan's Law deems for sex offenders, and the parolee should be sterilized to ensure that he/she doesn't further burden taxpayers. If the parolee commits another violent crime, the parole board that granted the release should be subjected to civil litigation.

Police chief blames shootings on 'violent chronic offenders'
daytondailynews.com

(Headlines)

The following headlines represent N/B crime. These headlines are only morsels of the daily urban terrorism. While I personally don't know any of these victims, their stories are still personal. The shared thread between these tragic stories is that these souls had their earthly time and inherent right to live stripped from them by Urban Terrorists. Each tragedy (and the thousands like them) should have been the necessary catalysts for BLACKS to declare war against NIGGERS. Needless to say, it hasn't occurred. Without hesitation, I would exchange the lives of all NIGGERS that have ever existed to bring back one of these innocent victim lost too soon via urban terrorism. Some of these stories are lesser known than others, so I encourage the reader to web search them for details.

Sleeping six-year-old dead after early morning drive-by shooting in Eclectic"
prattville.wsfa.com

Assault bullets from an Urban Terrorist drive-by killed Kenyetta Kendrick while sleeping

[Author's Note: "Stalandous" and two other Urban Terrorists were charged with capital murder and other offenses. Death is the only acceptable punishment for these Urban Terrorists.]

Shooting over $60 kills 6-year-old Jonaries Holden; police still searching for suspected killer

mlive.com

While sleeping with his twin brother in the backseat of his parent's car, an Urban Terrorist walked up and fired into the car

[Author's Note: The suspect "Davontrae" was said to have an altercation with Holden's father over a $60 debt. The irony of this situation is that Davontrae's debt to society is considerably more than sixty-dollars, so perhaps we should vindictively shoot him for that outstanding debt.]

2 more wanted in alleged carjacking killing girl

chron.com

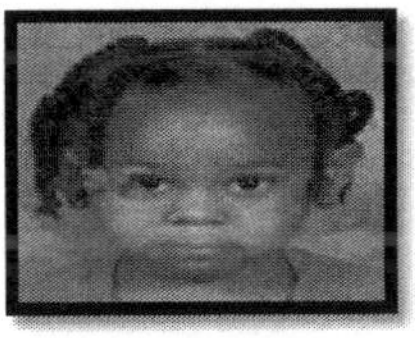

Urban Terrorists armed with an AK-47 murdered Charissa Powell

[Author's Note: Her 1-year-old brother was also wounded by the bullet fragments from the AK-47. I bet that these Urban Terrorists can't even spell AK-47.]

Bobby Tillman, Randomly Murdered, Had Just Seen Play on Bullying

abcnews.go.com

While being stomped, Bobby died after a broken rib punctured his heart

[Author's Note: "Quantez" was one of the three Juvi-Urban Terrorists charged with Bobby's death. In order to impress a girl at a party, they decided to jump the next person they saw, which happened to be Bobby. Bobby's injuries were comparable to those sustained in automobile accidents.]

Chilling details emerge in 9th Ward massacre of four family members

nola.com

Angela Davis-25, her children Joseph Davis-4, Jamaria Ross-7, and sister, Malekia Davis-17, were N/B victims

[Author's Note: This case exemplifies why Urban Terrorists need to be tried as domestic terrorists under the Patriot Act. Instead of being dropped into a volcano, the judge alternatively enrolled (sentenced) this Urban Terrorist into an HNCU for eighty semesters (80 years). That verdict, not only forces taxpayers to pay for this terrorist's tuition, which includes, room, board, and meal plan for the next 80 semesters, but provides him (for at least 80 years) the privilege of breathing the very oxygen that he snuffed from the victims.]

Chicago Honor Student Who Participated in Inauguration Shot Dead

bet.com

An Urban Terrorist murdered Hadiya Pendleton for being in the right place at the wrong time

(Burying a Child)

A childhood friend, who was raised in the same HoG, recently buried his eldest teenage son. His son was shot in the typical inner-city manner to which society has become desensitized. At the funeral, I couldn't help to notice my friend's calm composure and demeanor. Actually, I was in awe, yet puzzled as to why he wasn't hysterical. After all, this was his first-born, and I knew how mentally unstable I would be if I saw my child in a casket. Even as I write this, my hands tremble at the notion of burying my child. I presumed that his resilient demeanor was an intentional show of strength for the family. After the funeral, I (once again) expressed condolences, and subsequently inquired about his noble ability to maintain his composure. I gently asked, ***"How are you able to hold up so well?"*** His response shocked me as much as his demeanor. ***"Taleeb,"*** he said softly before carefully selecting his words, ***"I recently found out that my son was in a gang."*** I stood in disbelief because as a young man, my friend was a black (WNT) and had walked that dead end path, only to escape and evolve into a quality, productive member of society. Forcefully this time, he repeated, ***"Taleeb, my son was in a gang!"*** I stood in silence, while shaking my head in disbelief. He continued, ***"After I found out about his gang affiliation, I tried to reinforce to him the most likely outcomes of that lifestyle, which is usually prison or death. I let him know that I was lucky to beat the odds, but now look, he still chose to gamble, and lost."*** With nothing to add to his comments, I agreeably nodded my head as a testament to his words. I remember him sharing with his son the endless stories of near death experiences, HNCU stints, and other bad decisions hoping they'd serve as deterrents. Following our brief exchange, I immediately understood why he wasn't an emotional wreck. His demeanor wasn't based on emotion; it was the result of a prophecy being fulfilled. His grieving process started as soon as he learned about his son's gang affiliation, and thus, was mentally prepared when the inevitable news manifested. He was able to maintain his composure because of repeated, wholehearted attempts to prevent his son from being seduced by the NIGGER subculture; yet, those candid and preventative talks didn't deter the kid from NIGGERtivity. Although my friend grieved, he admirably made no excuses for this outcome. I shared with him one of my favorite poems written by Khalil Gibran titled:

"Your Children Are Not Your Children"

Your children are not your children.
They are the sons and daughters of Life's longing for itself.
They come through you but not from you,
And though they are with you yet they belong not to you.
You may give them your love but not your thoughts,
For they have their own thoughts.
You may house their bodies but not their souls,
For their souls dwell in the house of tomorrow,
which you cannot visit, not even in your dreams.
You may strive to be like them,
but seek not to make them like you.
For life goes not backward nor tarries with yesterday.
You are the bows from which your children
as living arrows are sent forth.
The archer sees the mark upon the path of the infinite,
and He bends you with His might
that His arrows may go swift and far.
Let your bending in the archer's hand be for gladness;
For even as He loves the arrow that flies,
so He loves also the bow that is stable.

Category **B/B**: ***BLACK ON BLACK CRIME***

This category is reserved for crimes that are committed by BLACKS. More than likely, this category will be dominated by non-violent blacks (WNT). If the perpetrator's criminal history is that of non-violent offenses, then the ***B/B*** case can be held in normal civilian court. However, because NIGGER tendencies are vast, the judge needs to recognize if this type of perpetrator is a potential NIGGER, and sentence accordingly. Without the lopsided levels of NIGGER crime, the true ***B/B*** crime rate would be on par with other minority communities.

Category N/E/A/L/O: NIGGER on EURO/ASIAN/LATINO/OTHER CRIME

This category is designated for crimes that NIGGERS or Urban Terrorists commit against other races. Due to political pandering, most of these crimes are underreported by the media/police departments, and aren't labeled as "Hate crimes." Conversely, if Euro-Americans committed these kinds of crimes (referenced in the headlines) against NIGGERS, NIGGERgeddon would ensue with the full support of NIGGERfiliac organizations. According to 2011 Uniform Crime Report, Af-Americans killed more than twice the amount of Euro-Americans (448) than the amount of African-Americans (193) murdered by Euro-Americans. Since NIGGERtivity is colorblind, and continues to impact citizens without prejudice, these individual ethnicities (Euro, Asian, Latino, Other) could actually have individual categories; unfortunately, space constraints forced me to cluster these ethnicities into a single category. Overall, ***(N/E/A/L/O)*** acts are crimes against humanity, and the appropriate punishment has already been duly documented.

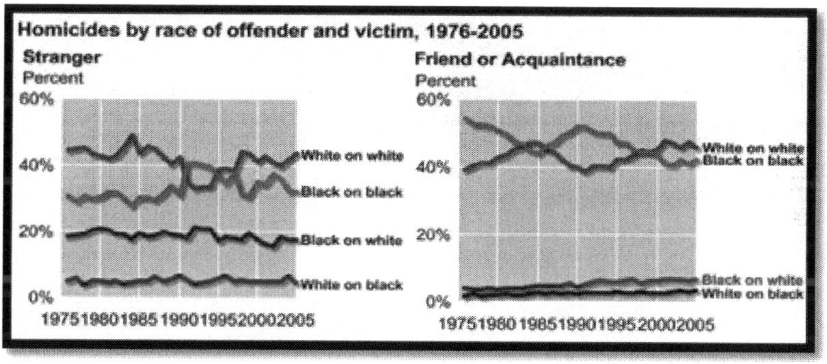

***Source: Bureau of Justice Statistics**

[Author's Note: On the "Stranger" graph, notice the difference between the percentages of Black on White homicides versus White on Black homicides. NIGGERfilacs hate these statistics because it doesn't support their race-baiting narrative.]

Black-on-white link in Minneapolis violence

wnd.com

Dirty secret of black-on-Asian violence is out

sfgate.com

(The American Salad)

The often-used metaphor of America being a melting pot is inaccurate; it's more comparable to a tossed salad with the individual ethnic groups represented as distinct vegetables in an American bowl. I've often wondered how NIGGERS symbolically fit into this multi-cultured American dish. Hmmm... Let's see. Well of course, they can't be vegetables, because each vegetable (in the American melting pot) provides a unique, tasty, and healthy flavor, whereas NIGGERS provide nothing of the sort (except their "uniquely" dysfunctional subculture). Furthermore, based on their natural ability to spoil events, schools, neighborhoods, etc. their obvious representation (in this American tossed salad analogy) would best be described as E. coli or Salmonella bacteria; their existence taints and ultimately destroys the salad. In fact, NIGGERtivity has touched each vegetable (ethnic group) in this symbolic salad, and these referenced ***NEALO*** headlines serve as tiny testaments.

Suspect Accused of Taunting Parents With Text Messages After Killing Teen

foxnews.com

14 yr. old Kelli O'Laughlin was murdered by an HNCU parolee

[Article's Quote: "Even the most experienced investigators and prosecutors have been brought to tears by the very facts of this case and the chilling nature of this case."- Cook county State Attorney]

'Let's pray together': The heart-breaking plea by kidnapped college student to her captors- just minutes before they executed her

dailymail.co.uk

The former UNC student body president was abducted, robbed, then murdered

[Author's Note: "Demario" and accomplice (who was also connected to the January 2008 murder of a Duke University engineering student) shot Eve Carson five times; including the final shot from a sawed-off 12 gauge shotgun as she tried to shield herself. Even when victims such as Eve Carson comply, they're still murdered. Urban Terrorists have no honor! Initially, my recommended verdict for these particular Urban Terrorists was death in the same method they used on Eve Carson, but that isn't adequate. I would like to see these two Urban Terrorists handcuffed together and then slowly lowered into an active volcano.]

Four suspects charged with murder in Knoxville double slaying

wate.com

Channon Christian & Christopher Newsom were carjacked, tortured, raped, & then murdered by Urban Terrorists

[Author's Note: "Lemaricus," "Letalvis," (not typos) and 2 others were charged for this heinous act called the Knoxville Horror. These Urban Terrorists should experience 10 times the trauma they inflicted on Channon and Chris. Then they should be handcuffed together and slowly fed to Mt. St. Helen volcano.]

Jury Calls for Death in 5 Kansas Murders

latimes.com

Heather Muller, Brad Heyka, Aaron Sander, Jason Befert, Ann Walenta

[Author's Note: The Wichita Massacre, also known as The Wichita Horror, was murder/assault/rape/robbery spree perpetrated in the winter of 2000 by Urban Terrorists (who were also brothers) Reginald and Jonathan Carr in Wichita, Kansas. The brothers were convicted of forcing victims to engage in sex acts before shooting them on a snowy field. Overall, the Urban Terrorists killed five people and a dog. They were sentenced to death in October 2002. However, through the lengthy appeals process, and the fact that the state of Kansas hasn't executed anyone in 44 years, I doubt that true justice will be served for the victims.]

Georgia boys face murder charges after cold-blooded killing of infant being strolled by mother

nydailynews.com

Antonio Santiago enjoyed life for 13 months

[Author's Note: During a robbery, the Urban Terrorist asked, "Do you want me to kill your baby?" before shooting the toddler in the head.]

Teens accused of beating elderly man to death appear in court

bakersfield.com

Ezequiel Jimenez Perez, 81, was pummeled by Juvi-Urban Terrorists as he collected cans

[Author's Note: Mr. Perez was voluntarily performing community service when he was fatally assaulted. I hope that the judicial system will also perform a service to the community by sending these Juvi-Urban Terrorists to the Lake of Fire.]

Tian Sheng Yu Dies After Vicious Daylight Assault in Oakland

zimbio.com

A victim of NIGGER on Asian crime

[Author's Note: "Lavonte" and fellow Juvi-Urban Terrorist fatally assaulted and robbed the 59-year-old Chinese immigrant in front of his wife.]

Prosecutors: Man killed nurse, stole her rings, then used them to propose

chicagotribune.com

An HNCU parolee killed Virginia Perillo, 73, a civilian nurse

[Author's Note: This Urban Terrorist was paroled after being convicted of breaking into a Chicago woman's home, raping her, cutting her neck, and beating her for several hours before setting multiple fires to her home in 1997. Only three weeks prior to that attack, he had been released from prison for a 1993 armed robbery, vehicular invasion, and burglary charge. In my opinion, the parole board needs to be held liable for their dreadful decision to shorten his HNCU semester! Had the Urban Terrorist been sent to the lake of fire (per my recommendation) for his initial violent crime against humanity, Virginia Perillo would still be alive enjoying her golden years.]

Category ***C/N***: ***CITIZEN(s) or Civilian(s) on NIGGER crime***

This ***C/N*** category is reserved for citizens or civilians (regardless of race) that allegedly commit crimes against NIGGERS. Actually, these circumstances aren't crimes; instead, they're mostly retaliatory or self-defense scenarios. I believe that these scenarios vindicate the citizen/civilian because self-preservation is the first rule of survival. However, in these politically-correct times, the criminals seemingly receive more protection under the law against citizens/civilians than citizens/civilians receive against the criminals. Self-defense and property protection are the most likely ***C/N*** scenarios, and sometimes, may result in a homey-cide. In reality, any homey-cide that occurs because a citizen was protecting him/herself, property, or loved one(s), ultimately saves tax dollars. Perhaps, a fund should be created to reward ***C/N*** citizens for saving tax dollars. For starters, the fund could include rebates on property taxes or discounts on homeowner's insurance. There are many tax saving benefits of ***C/N*** homey-cides, and I've listed a few:

1. No expensive trial and/or numerous appeals at taxpayers' expense. It's mind-boggling that NIGGERS commit crimes against the taxpaying public, but then are appointed taxpayer-funded attorneys.

2. No taxpayer money spent on expensive HNCU room and board.

3. No hospital care at taxpayer expense.

4. Zero percent HNCU recidivism rates.

5. One less burden on society.

The following examples of ***C/N*** cases will become more common as national austerity measures disrupt the flow of NIGGERnomics.

Police: Homeowner Shoots Intruder To Death In East Islip
newyork.cbslocal.com

Murder Suspect Killed In Another Home Invasion
wftv.com

Woman fatally shoots home invasion suspect
wbtv.com

(Classic "C/N" Case)

In the mid-nineteen eighties, New York City's violent crime rate had more than tripled, and was over seventy-percent (70%) higher than the rest of the country. So, when subway passenger Bernhard Goetz (Euro-American) shot four JuviNIGGERS who tried to rob him on a train, he had the public's empathy. Although he had the public's support, he was still criminally charged with attempted murder, assault, reckless endangerment, and several firearms offenses. Adding insult to injury, one of the injured JuviNIGGERS filed a civil suit against Goetz, and the NIGGERfiliac–filled jury found Goetz guilty of inflicting emotional distress. The wounded JuviNIGGER was awarded forty-three ($43) million dollars (18 million dollars for pain/suffering and 25 million dollars in punitive damages). See, this is why the NIGGER subculture believes that crime does indeed pay.

(Pop Quiz)

Following their near-death experience and favorable verdict, which was capped with a substantial monetary judgment, what was the likelihood that these JuviNIGGERS (turned victims) denounced NIGGERtivity to become productive members of society? Oh, I forgot to mention that one of the four was forced to take a permanent sabbatical from NIGGERtivity because a Goetz-fired bullet paralyzed him. So, what about the other three? Well, after the Goetz incident, JuviNIGGER#1 committed two known robberies. One of them was a chain snatching in the elevator of the building where he lived. This robbery brought him a sentence of up to four years for probation violation. JuviNIGGER#2 held the gun while an associate raped, sodomized and robbed a pregnant eighteen-year-old woman on the rooftop of the Bronx building where he lived, and in 1986 was sentenced to 8⅓ to 25 semesters at an HNCU. There was nothing to report about JuviNIGGER#3 except that he was ordered to undergo treatment at a rehabilitation center. So, did you actually think that these JuviNIGGERS would abandon their sociopathic existence and became productive citizens? If so, are you interested in buying a unicorn that I have for sale? Trust me... this unicorn isn't a horse with a horn glued to its head.

(Past vs Present)

After this ordeal, Goetz was dubbed the "Subway Vigilante," and rightfully found not guilty of all criminal charges except an illegal firearms possession count. He served eight months of a one-year sentence. As evidenced by the following story, ***C/N*** scenarios now come at an even heavier price, which only citizens are unfairly forced to pay.

(The Pharmacist)

As reported by msnbc.com, ***"An Oklahoma pharmacist has been sentenced to life in prison with the possibility of parole for first-degree murder in the shooting death of a teenager who tried to rob the south Oklahoma City pharmacy where he worked."*** In other words, the Urban Terrorist came to the pharmacy for non-medicinal reasons, and the pharmacist gave him lethal dosages of a lead-filled prescription. While being confronted by the two perps, the pharmacist ***"pulled a gun, shot one of them in the head and chased the other away. Then, in a scene recorded by the drugstore's security camera, he went behind the counter, got another gun, and pumped five more bullets into Parker as he lay on the floor unconscious."*** This is another classic ***C/N*** case where the citizen was found guilty for doing the right thing. Of course, NIGGERfiliacs are happy that the pharmacist is going to prison for first-degree murder. They believe that the Urban Terrorist shouldn't have been shot five additional times. Astonishingly, they refuse to acknowledge the fact that he wouldn't have died from lead poisoning had he not tried to rob the pharmacy. As with most ***C/N*** scenarios, if this Urban Terrorist had survived, he most certainly would've sued the pharmacist for violating his civil rights, and probably awarded a monetary judgment. The *"criminal justice system"* has routinely lived up to its namesake by consistently providing *"justice to criminals"* (especially repeat offenders). Society needs to restructure the *"criminal justice"* system so that it becomes the *"victim justice"* system. Maybe this way, criminals will know that the system serves its victims, not its criminals.

Oklahoma pharmacist sentenced to life for killing would-be robber
Fifty-nine-year-old calls his sentence 'an injustice of a monumental proportion'
msn.com

FAMILY OF MAN SHOT WHILE ROBBING A WAFFLE HOUSE CALLS FOR STRICTER GUN LAWS
Breitbart.com

Pizza worker who shot 2 was former deputy, had been robbed twice
wbtv.com
[Author's Note: More businesses will serve this type of "Take-out" to NIGGERS.]

Sheriff: Dead motel robber was going to rape clerk
wxix.com
[Author's Note: I love when bad people are referenced in past tense.]

(NIGGERS vs. KKK)

I find it odd that taxpayer money is sent overseas to combat terrorism and other violent entities, while Americans are being terrorized by HoG grown terrorists. The domestic effort to eradicate Urban Terrorists is minimal (at best). Although the Ku Klux Klan has been the historical enemy to African-Americans, and a Tuskegee Institute study shows that 3,446 African-Americans were lynched during an 86-year span, NIGGERS actually murder the same amount of African-Americans roughly every six months. The KKK has unknowingly outsourced the murdering of African-Americans to NIGGERS, specifically JuviNIGGERS. In fact, a twenty-eight year (1980 to 2008), Bureau of Justice Statistics study, documented that young adult African-American males were the highest homicide-offenders (rate wise) compared to offenders in other racial and sex categories. Moreover, while these young Af-Am males have accounted for about 1% of the population from 1980 to 2008, they have made up an increasing proportion of homicide victims, going from 9% of all homicide victims in 1980 to 18% in 1994. After 1994, their proportion of homicide victims has remained relatively stable at about 16%. The percentage of young Af-Am male homicide offenders also increased rapidly from the mid-1980s to the early 1990s, going from 17% in 1985 to 35% by 1993 before declining. By 2008, young Af-Am males made up about a quarter of all homicide offenders (27%). Undeniably, NIGGERS are the updated and deadlier version of the Ku Klux Klan; white tees have replaced white sheets. Their (NIGGERS) embedded penchant for violence coupled with the insatiable taste for street credibility has statistically made NIGGERS a more effective killing machine than the combination of the Ku Klux Klan and foreign combatants! Even scarier is the fact that these astounding homicide numbers are dwarfed when juxtaposed to the daily NIGGERtivity incidents.

(For the Record)

To be clear, I don't mind the NIGGER herd thinning itself via homey-cides, but the resulting collateral damage is concerning. During a nearly three decades-long Bureau of Justice Statistics study *(1980-2008),* African-Americans made up almost half of the national homicide victims *(47.4%)* and more than half of the offenders *(52.4%).* Honestly, if the entire *47.4%* of African-American victims were from the NIGGER segment, I wouldn't lose an ounce of sleep, but unfortunately, such wasn't the case. Even still, considering the reality that African-Americans are only 13% of the total U.S population, the NIGGER threat is undeniable. So, who is killing African-American males? Here's a hint... it isn't the Ku Klux Klan or George Zimmerman types. It's the NIGGERman types.

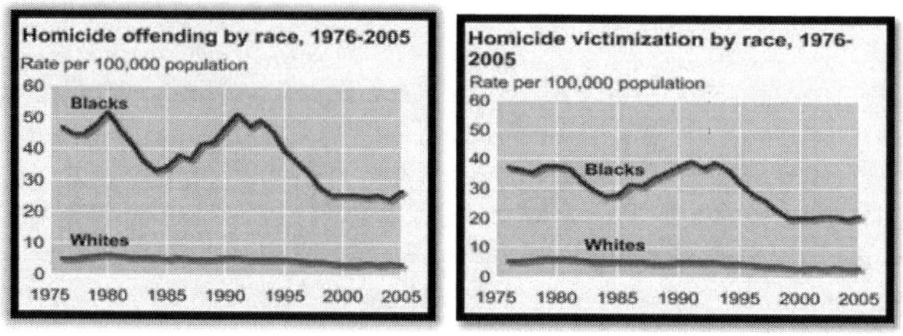

Three decades of NIGGERtivity perpetrated by a tiny subculture

(NIGGERS need BLACKS)

Across America, a correlation can easily be seen between places with a substantial African-American populace and violent crime. Part of the reason why NIGGERtivity flourishes is because of their subculture's parasitic ability to exist in the African-American community. The other part is the African-American communities' inability or unwillingness to properly dispose of this garbage. For example, in New York City, NIGGERtivity thrives because NYC numerically has the largest African-American population in America, which supposedly bodes well for the image of diversity. But, the unspoken, yet statistically confirmed costs associated with such diversity (that won't appear in the official NYC brochures) are the overwhelming occurrences of violent crimes perpetrated by the NIGGER minority.

(NYC)

Despite being a quarter (25%) of New York City's population, African-Americans accounted for sixty-seven percent (67%) of the 536 murder victims in 2010. A 2010 analysis from the New York Police Department documented that African-American males between the ages of fifteen to twenty-nine were most likely to be killed. Astoundingly, this tiny 15-29 age segment makes up less than three percent (3%) of the city's population, yet in 2010, represented thirty-three percent (33%) of all homicide victims. Hey NIGGERfiliacs, if you have the guts, research 2011 and 2012.

(The Categories)

Although the NYPD's 2010 Crime and Enforcement Activity report illustrated that African-Americans accounted for the majority of victims (67%), suspects (60.9), and arrests (54.5%), in the category of Murder and Non-Negligent Manslaughter, it's important to note that NIGGERtivity isn't limited to homicides and homey-cides. Here are the other aspects of NIGGERtivity that demonized the entire African-American populace. In the category of Rape, Af-Ams accounted for the majority of arrestees (48.2%). In the category of Robbery, Af-Ams were (61.6%) of the arrestees. In the category of Felonious assaults, Af-Ams were (51.5%) of the arrestees. In the category of Misdemeanor assaults, Af-Ams placed first in arrestees (47.8). Wait, I'm just getting warm. These are the other categories in which NIGGERS (under the guise of African-Americans) claimed first place: Grand Larceny (50.9%) arrestees, Petit Larceny arrestees (48.9%), the Drug Felony Arrest population were most frequently Af-Ams (45.7%). Unsurprisingly, the Firearm Arrests were most frequently Af-Ams (69.3%). Drug Allegations most frequently identified Af-Ams (46.4%). The Drug Misdemeanor Arrest population was most frequently Af-Ams (52.8%). The Misdemeanor Criminal Mischief arrestees were most frequently Af-Ams (38.2%). Even the juvenile arrest (based on Felony and Misdemeanor Complaint Records with Identified Juvenile Victims, Suspects, and Arrestees) population was most frequently Af-Ams (57.1%). The Felony Stolen Property Arrest population was most frequently Af-Ams (53.3%). The Misdemeanor Stolen Property Arrest population was most frequently Af-Ams (47.4%). The most frequently occurring race/ethnic group within the Violent Felony suspects was Af-Ams accounting for (66%). Overall, this tiny NIGGER tribe has made the entire African-American populace the most frequent suspects in all the above referenced categories. In the ***"Mistaken Identity and NIGGER Tax"*** chapter, I elaborate on NIGGERtivity affecting BLACKS.

(Overview)

These statistics illustrate the depth of NIGGERtivity in New York City; however, this pattern exists in many cities with a substantial African-American population. In so-called "Chocolate cities," these harrowing statistics exponentially increase because they're prime real estate for NIGGERtivity. In fact, leading the "chocolate cities" in NIGGERtivity is Detroit, which coincidentally has the highest percentage of African-Americans *(84.3%)* among American cities with at least 100,000 residents. Even in places where there isn't a sizeable African-American community like Seattle (7.9% Af.Am) or Portland (6.3% Af.Am), NIGGERS (hiding amongst the small African-American communities) are still largely responsible for the mayhem. Regardless of region, Croakland (Oakland - 28% Af.Am) to Killadelphia (Philadelphia- 43.4% Af.Am), Gatlanta (Atlanta - 54% Af.Am) to Shotcago (Chicago - 32.9% Af.Am), NIGGERS always pose a threat to civility.

Enter At Your Own Risk: Police Union Says 'War-Like' Detroit Is Unsafe For Visitors

detroit.cbslocal.com

[Article's Quote: "The men and women of the Detroit Police Department believe the city is too dangerous to enter, and they want citizens to know it."]

Many young black men in Oakland are killing and dying for respect

sfgate.com

New Orleans Struggles to Stem Homicides

nytimes.com

[Author's Note: In 2010, New Orleans had a homicide rate that was 10 times the national average. According to an analysis of homicide cases by outside experts sponsored by the federal Bureau of Justice Assistance, "The killers and their victims are overwhelmingly young black men." Coincidentally, New Orleans has a 60.2% African-American populace.]

Kill-adelphia: Yet again, city tops list of homicide rates

philly.com

[Author's Note: According to the city of brotherly love's police commissioner, "arguments" were the common motive for murder. Yup, disagreements got people killed. The NIGGER subculture endorses killing over trivialities because murder is the ultimate form of "Keepin' it real."]

Violent crime in D.C. surges in 2012

washingtontimes.com

[Author's Note: With its 50.7 African-American percentage, D.C. routinely experiences NIGGERtivity.]

(Beneficial NIGGERtivity?)

Despite the detrimental effects of NIGGERtivity, it has strangely become advantageous for the military and inner-city trauma centers. How is NIGGERtivity useful to anyone, you ask?

Well, if manure can be used for fertilizer, then surely NIGGERtivity can be useful for something! The fact that African-Americans are more likely to die from a gunshot or other assault-related injury has enabled military doctors to use inner-city hospitals as training mechanisms to simulate the trauma likely to be encountered on the battle field. As reported by cnn.com, ***"Dr. John Renshaw is also Major John Renshaw, United States Air Force, and he's deploying to the front lines of Afghanistan to treat the wounded. But before he goes, he along with other military medical personnel will complete a tour of duty at the University of Maryland's Shock Trauma Center in Baltimore - sharpening their ability to deal with critical trauma patients. Colonel David Powers, a surgeon, ran the military training program here. He has since retired. 'The injuries that I have treated here, that I see here at this hospital, are the closest thing to the injuries I saw in Iraq, that I have experienced in the continental U.S.', Powers says."*** In other words, Bulletmore, oops, Baltimore (65.1% African-American population percentage) like other NIGfested cities exposes the military doctors to injuries comparable to a war zone. Wow, outside of the prison industry, the NIGGER subculture is actually beneficial. Other NIGfested cities that would be useful in preparing for battlefield trauma are Chicago, St. Louis, Detroit, and Philadelphia.

U.S. hospital work prepares military docs for battlefield injuries
cnn.com

(Wherever Af-Am's are Prevalent)

With the seemingly unshakable NIGGER cloud lingering over the African-American community, whenever or wherever African-Americans are present in a significant manner, NIGGERS eventually manifest, and a downward spiral ensues. Quality neighborhoods are transformed into third world dystopias. The police and realtors are especially familiar with this troublesome correlation between crime and African-Americans areas. An abundance of African-Americans (anywhere) provides cover for NIGGERS to infiltrate without being seen as invaders. A simple web search of *"Most dangerous zip codes"* or the *"Most dangerous U.S cities"* will consistently confirm this dark pattern. The NIGGER subculture characteristically aspires to appear on this infamous list because it's perceived as a praise-worthy, "keepin it real" achievement. On the other hand, a web search of *"The best places to live"* or *"Most peaceful cities or zips"* will reveal places void of a significant dark footprint. Is it coincidence that the dominant, dark footprint (that exists in the unfavorable places) is conspicuously absent from the highly favored places? The ultimate reality is that these *"peaceful"* environments have Anti-NIGGER interests, whereas the *"least peaceful"* environments are NIGGERfiliac based. Astoundingly, Chicago's 2012 gun-related homicide count outnumbered the gun-related homicide tally of these states combined: Wyoming, Vermont, Maine, New Hampshire, North Dakota, South Dakota, Montana, Minnesota, Idaho, Iowa, Hawaii, Alaska, Rhode Island, Delaware, and Utah. By the way, these states coincidentally have low African-American populations.

"Black communities face 'epidemic' of violent murders"
pittsburghlive.com

High Murder Rates in Cities with Large Black Populations
capitalismmagazine.com

[Author's Note: Honest articles such as this are non-existent; especially in the BLACK press.]

Crime 'It's a Black Problem': Fla. Black Panthers Call for End to Violence After 15 Shot in 2 Days
theblaze.com

We Live in Killadelphia
philadelphiaweekly.com

Chapter IV

The NIGGER-Tsunami's Destruction of Events & Public Commons

"Ah! Destructive ignorance, what shall be done to chase thee out of the World!" Cotton Mather

As a global community, we're familiar with the devastating "natural" oceanic phenomenon that the Japanese named "tsunami." Without prejudice, it brutally destroys whatever is in its path, and transforms thriving cities into ancient ruins. Although U.S cities have been spared from the oceanic tsunami's wrath, these cities, especially those with a substantial African-American population, should still worry. Why do I say this? Well, routinely witnessed by citizens, and captured on countless videos is an "unnatural" land based phenomenon that also devastates any environment it encounters. However, unlike the natural, oceanic tsunami, which is fueled by a combination of high energy and immense volumes of water, this unnatural, land-based tsunami, is fueled by the combination of high violence and immense episodes of mayhem. I dubbed it, "NIGGER-Tsunami." The reckless, feral behavior of the NIGGER subculture crashes onto events and public commons causing tsunami-like damage. Geologists may be unfamiliar with NIGGER-Tsunamis, but unquestionably, social engineers are cognizant of its existence. The NIGGER-Tsunami actually manifests in two forms, the adult NIGGER version, and the lesser (in age, not violence potential) JuviNIGGER Flashfloods. Similar to the natural tsunami, the unpredictability of this unnatural NIGGER-Tsunami requires attentiveness and warning systems to save lives and property. This chapter will examine the effects of the NIGGER-Tsunami and its offshoot (JuviNIGGER Flashfloods) on environments that aren't NIGGER-Tsunami ready.

Two different signs prepared for two different Tsunamis.

(Where Does It Occur?)

History has revealed that the NIGGER-Tsunami typically manifests at African-American events or hangouts. It has also appeared in places that weren't NIGGER-Tsunami ready, and places with the word "Public." Specifically, Public parks, Public pools, Public beaches, Public transportation hubs, etc. with the only notable exception being the Public library. The library is an Anti-NIGGER place that repels the NIGGER subculture (Refer to ***The Anti-NIGGER*** chapter). Even though the internet makes cataloging the different places impacted by NIGGER-Tsunami relatively easy, openly acknowledging this pattern is offensive to many in the African-American community. Fortunately, the veil is being lifted by books such as this, and *"White Girl Bleed A lot"* by Colin Flaherty, which documents the NIGGER-Tsunami's nationwide impact and the media blackout. Flaherty writes, ***"In hundreds of episodes in more than 50 cities since 2012, groups of black people are roaming the streets of America—assaulting, intimidating, stalking, threatening, vandalizing, stealing, shooting, stabbing, even raping and killing.*** Additionally, Flaherty's timely book addresses an obvious contradiction; ***"We learn that every day from black caucuses, black teachers, black unions, black ministers, black colleges, black high schools, black music, black moguls, black hair business owners, black public employees, black art, black names, black poets, black inventors, black soldiers. Everything except black violent crime. That is Taboo. Result: Few know about it. Fewer still are talking about it. The list of cities under attack is long and getting longer – with some cities suffering dozens of attacks in the last year alone: Chicago, Miami, Philadelphia, Las Vegas, New York, Atlantic City, Milwaukee, Charlotte, Mobile,***

Kansas City, Denver, Birmingham, Saratoga Springs, Seattle, Portland, Nashville, Washington D.C, Los Angeles, Rochester, Wilmington, Georgetown, Greensboro, Nashville, Peoria, Vallejo, Des Moines, Dallas, Rehoboth Beach, Baltimore, Montgomery County, Boston, St. Louis, Brighton Beach, And more, more, more." Although the NIGGER-Tsunami's infamous reputation is an open secret, political correctness has forced several police departments dismiss these felonious, destructive binges as teens *"blowing off steam."* Whom are these disingenuous police departments really *"protecting and serving"?*

Flash Mobs Have Police on Alert, City Fed Up
nbcphiladelphia.com

Woman's leg broken, others hurt in Spring Garden mob attack
philly.com

(Becoming Tsunami-Ready)

Due to its propensity to occur with little to no warning, many American cities that aren't NIGGER-Tsunami ready really suffer. In addition to the incurred physical/material damage, tourism suffers, potential business investments falter, citizens become frustrated, and overtime pay for law enforcement (which is disastrous to cash-strapped cities) increases. Adding to the dilemma is the public relations issue, which surfaces whenever environments decide to become NIGGER-Tsunami ready. Naturally, these preventative tactics cause many in the African-American community to yell "racism." Even so, the "separate but equal" mindset of the Jim Crow era is returning (without the attached legal reinforcement) as a remedy. The following headlines reflect the typical outcome of non-ready, NIGGER-Tsunami environments.

Random attacks cause concern in Chicago
chicagotribune.com

[Article's Quote: "Mob attacks create a sensitive issue for city officials eager to boost tourism and convention business."]

Call for crackdown on black-on-white terror
wnd.com

[Article's Quote: "A state lawmaker in Maryland concerned about "black youths" who are "terrorizing" Baltimore's upscale Inner Harbor, wants the governor to send in state troopers to make the area safe."]

'In hindsight, being in a public park at night is not the safest place'
katu.com

[Author's Note: Officers responded to reports of 150 JuviNIGGERS randomly attacking people in the park.]

(Iowa State Fair)

As a kid, I always enjoyed fairs and carnivals. Although the games were rigged, and food overpriced, its magnetism was undeniable. Now, as a parent, I still anticipate taking my children to carnivals and fairs, but under certain circumstances; my priority has shifted from fun to safety. Presently, fairs, carnivals, or other family-based festivities in the inner-cities, have unfortunately become the devil's playground. In fact, across the country, family-centered venues events are encountering an unbilled, dangerous sideshow that routinely interrupts the family experience... Flashfloods. In Des Moines, Iowa, a police report from a racially eventful evening at the 2010 Iowa State Fair, documented what Flashflooders deemed... ***"Beat Whitey Night."*** The police report stated (in part), "***there was a group of 30-40 individuals roaming the fairgrounds openly calling it 'Beat Whitey Night'. This incident may be connected to other assaults occuring*** *[sic]* ***on the Iowa state fairgrounds."*** Another police report was more racially specific, saying (in part), ***"A large group of black male and female juveniles was report*** *[sic]* ***to have started assaulting people again, like last Friday night. Officers were tripped to the Main Gate Bar reference to a large fight with black male and female juveniles assaulting white citizens."*** Amazingly, even with the police reports and eyewitness accounts, NIGGERfiliacs have argued that these targeted attacks weren't *"hate crimes."* If Flashfloods can occur in Des Moines, Iowa, which is 70.5% Euro-American and only 10.2% African-American, they'll manifest anywhere.

Westland officials could decide to ban carnivals
myfoxdetroit.com

[Article's Quote: "The carnivals have been attracting some unruly crowds, some gang activity, some fights, and not just our community, but

communities around us, and we're just kind of looking to see what we can do to keep everybody safe." - Westland Police Chief]

(Milwaukee)

I've never been to Milwaukee, Wisconsin. My only reference to the city stems from the 1980's sitcom *"Laverne & Shirley"* (My age is showing). Besides Milwaukee beer, and their professional basketball team (Bucks), I have no additional links. In fact, my lack of connection led to a presumption that Milwaukee was a lily WHITE city with no NIGGERtivity issues. That was, until I repeatedly heard about a "racially charged" open letter authored by two WHITE Milwaukee public officials. After reading the letter, and being surprised that the NIGGER subculture was being chastised in Lavern and Shirley's town, I was still stunned, until I discovered that Milwaukee had a 40% African-American population. Then, it suddenly made sense. With a 40% Af-Am populace, NIGGERtivity and NIGGER-Tsunamis will definitely occur. Council members Bob Donovan and Joe Dudzik simply released a joint statement voicing their frustration. Unsurprisingly, NIGGERfiliacs denounced the letter (which is actually a shorter, cleaner version of this book) as racist.

("Racism" or "Realism")

Let's analyze some of the "racist" joint statement. ***"As elected officials, we are shocked and concerned about the senseless violence displayed by the large mob outside State Fair Park last night. On behalf of our city, we apologize to the victims and good patrons who endured or witnessed such horrific behavior. Sadly, what transpired near State Fair Park last night is only the most recent mob riot spawned by a culture of violence that has been brewing in Milwaukee for some time. And let's face it, it also has much to do with a deteriorating African-American culture in our city. Are large groups of Hispanics or Hmong going out in large mobs and viciously attacking whites? No."*** Like most people, the well-intentioned Aldermen don't realize that the NIGGER subculture isn't interested in behaving agreeably for the community's sake. The letter later concluded, ***"The community was shocked when the violent mob of African-American youths attacked white people in Kilbourn***

Reservoir Park on July 3. Then, a few eyebrows were raised at the F-bombs and shocking disregard and disrespect for Milwaukee police officers shown by a large and unruly group of African-Americans at N. Richards St. and W. North Ave. last Saturday night. And now this horrific mob violence near State Fair Park. But for those who live in some city neighborhoods, this violence has been like a steady rain for far too many years now. And the reality is this summer it seems we have five or six shootings each and every weekend! Unfortunately, this behavior is now all too common in some parts of the Milwaukee community. Our hearts go out to the older generation of African-Americans in this city who remember when their community had one of the HIGHEST marriage rates in the city. Sadly, many of these same residents are now scared of their own children and grandchildren. Although we hope our law enforcement agencies are able to bring some of the thugs who were involved in these attacks to justice, no amount of millions of dollars in government spending or resources is going to truly address this problem. We can no longer wish this violence would just go away, and we cannot ignore it; we must see it for what it truly is. We cannot begin to address the underlying causes of the violence without change. We believe that change must come from within the African-American community, where new seeds must be sown." I emphatically agree with their assessment that change must first occur within the African-American community, ***"where new seeds must be sown."*** Essentially, this press release was an articulate way of expressing a sentiment that communities across America (impacted by the NIGGER subculture) are echoing. Due to fear of being labeled as racists, intolerable behavior from the NIGGER subculture has been regularly tolerated by Euro-Americans. Now, the public is increasingly venting their disgust with the NIGGER subculture, followed by expressed disappointment with the African-American community for being enablers. As NIGGERtivity worsens, and continues to spread, I expect more aggressive action and authentic denunciations from elected officials, regardless of race. In Philadelphia, Mayor Michael Nutter conveyed a similar "tough talk" message to this dysfunctional segment of the African-American community. He warned, ***"Please talk to your children because things are going to change ... There will be serious consequences for aggressive, violent, idiotic behavior. Everyone is gonna be held accountable. We're taking steps for the safety of citizens and of teenagers. This is about all of us—everybody. The bottom line is this nonsense must stop right now."*** Unlike Milwaukee Aldermen Bob Donovan and Joe Dudzik, Nutter is BLACK, and won't be charged with racism for speaking the obvious truth.

State Fair melees produce 11 injuries, 31 arrests
jsonline.com

Philadelphia mayor talks tough to black teenagers after 'flash mobs'
washingtontimes.com

(Another ~~Racist~~ Realist Observation)

In an article titled *"The Predicted Georgetown shooting and the Black Family"* posted (11/1/11) on the *dailycaller.com,* author Mark Judge detailed his observation of JuviNIGGERS on a Halloween night in Georgetown. He wrote, ***"We all know what the problem is. But we just don't have the guts to speak honestly about the issue of unsupervised black teenagers from broken homes and the havoc they can cause — to themselves and others."*** He later continued, ***"In all of that, no one would have the guts to tell the truth. It was not Asians or whites or Indians who were wilding in Georgetown. It was black teenagers. Illegitimacy and fatherlessness in black urban areas like Washington, D.C. has created an entire class of youth who have been weaned on gangster culture and have absolutely no impulse control. Being in the middle of the maelstrom in Georgetown, I was struck by a simple observation again and again: These kids have no impulse control. They scream to each other across the street at the top of their lungs, talk at the same time, say inappropriate things to adults and settle disputes with guns."*** Moving forward, I'm sure that affluent Georgetown will enact statutes to become NIGGER-Tsunami ready. Certain places have a very short tolerance for NIGGERtivity; perhaps, G-town is next.

(BLACKS Are Welcome... NIGGERS Stay Out)

In Akron, Ohio, a veteran teacher at a 52% Black high school, created a maelstrom after condemning the despicable behavior of JuviNIGGER 'trick or treaters' who annually migrated to his neighborhood. Using his Facebook page to vent about the (N)egro (I)ndividuals (G)enerating (G)rief (E)verywhere (R)outinely, he wrote: ***"I don't mind if you come from the ghetto to trick or treat. But when you whip out your teeny dicks and piss on the telephone pole in front of my front yard and a bunch of preschoolers and toddlers, you can take your nigger-ass back where it came from. I don't have anything against anyone of color, but niggers, stay out."*** So, what happened to the teacher after his rant was publicized? As expected, he was sacrificed on the altar of political correctness, and eventually fired, despite embarking on an apology tour. The PC gods were upset that he actually judged the miscreants by the content of their character. Meanwhile, the JuviNIGGERS that he admonished were treated as victims.

Firestone High School teacher placed on leave; district investigating alleged racist rant on Facebook
ohio.com

(African-American based Celebrations)

NIGGERtivity never takes a sabbatical, doesn't observe holidays; recognize sacred or holy environments, ceremonies etc., nor cares if the event has a positive, historic, theme. In fact, African-American themed events are especially susceptible to NIGGER-Tsunamis because of the high Af-Am attendance. Even on MLK day, the amount of NIGGERtivity that routinely occurs confirms their restless, sociopathic nature. In attempt to emphasize this point, I've documented a few incidences of NIGGERtivity and NIGGER-Tsunamis from African-American themed events. I find it amusing whenever NIGGERfiliacs triumphantly hold press conferences following any large African-American event that didn't experience a NIGGER–Tsunami. They're essentially proclaiming that applause should be given to NIGGERS for not behaving like NIGGERS. It's truly a damning indictment of a culture when praise is warranted for acting civilized in public.

NOPD arrests juvenile in Central City quintuple shooting near Martin Luther King Day parade

bayoubuzz.com

[Author's Note: JuviNIGGERS only recognize MLK as the dude who got them a day off from school.]

Dozen arrested after African-American Day Parade in Harlem

nydailynews.com

[Article's Quote: "Cops made more than a dozen arrests and recovered 14 illegal firearms after Sunday's African-American Day Parade in Harlem."]

Man opens fire at Brooklyn parade, toll rises to 46 shot since Saturday morning

nypost.com

[Author's Note: The parade also had fatal shootings in 2003 and 2005.]

[VIDEO] Fatal Shooting and WWE-Style Brawl Taint DC's Caribbean Festival

hypervocal.com

(Juneteenth)

Juneteenth, also known as Freedom Day or Emancipation Day, is a holiday in the U.S honoring African-American heritage by commemorating the announcement of the abolition of slavery in the State of Texas in 1865. Celebrated on June 19, the term is a portmanteau of *June* and *nineteenth*, and is recognized as a state holiday in 37 states of the United States. Juneteenth is the oldest known celebration commemorating the ending of slavery in the United States and has been an African-American tradition since the late 19th century. Traditions include an enunciated public reading of the Emancipation Proclamation as a reminder that the slaves have been proclaimed free. The events are celebratory and festive. Many African-American families use this opportunity to retrace their ancestry to the ancestors who were held in bondage for centuries, exchange artifacts, debunk family myths, and stress responsibility and striving to be the best you can be. Celebrants often sing traditional songs as well such as *Swing Low, Sweet Chariot*; *Lift Every Voice and Sing*; and poetry from Black authors like Maya Angelou. Juneteenth celebrations also include a wide range of festivities to celebrate American heritage, such as parades, rodeos, street fairs, cookouts, family reunions, or park parties that include such things as African-American music, dancing, or contests of physical strength and intellect. Some of the events may include black cowboys, historical reenactments, or Miss Juneteenth contests. Traditional American sports may also be played such as baseball, football, or basketball tournaments. Wikipedia provided this elaborate explanation of Juneteenth, but here's what it neglected to mention. NIGGERS (specifically JuviNIGGERS) aren't interested in Juneteenth or its tradition; this festival is simply another vehicle used to incite a NIGGER-Tsunami or Flashflood.

Man beaten to death by angry crowd at Austin's Juneteenth celebration
9news.com

Mayor Disgusted by Juneteenth Violence
todaystmj4.com

Juneteenth celebration turns ugly in Milwaukee
msnbc.com

(Black Expo)

The Indiana Black Expo Summer Celebration is the largest ethnic–cultural event in the U.S. It's held over ten days within the Indiana Convention Center as well as various places around Indianapolis. Participation at the 2006 Summer Celebration reached record highs, with over 350,000 in attendance. From the Black Expo's official website, their ***"Diversity Promise"*** states, ***"Indiana Black Expo, Inc. celebrates cultural diversity and inclusiveness across all races, ethnicities, nationalities, generations, socioeconomic levels and religious affiliations. We continue to strive for excellence by providing unique events and programs which reflect the changing landscape of Indiana and the world. Our commitment to excellence through personal enhancement and community development exemplify our dedication to improving the quality of life for all."*** Uh oh, this ***"Diversity Promise,"*** which ***"celebrates cultural diversity and inclusiveness,"*** is essentially an open invitation to the NIGGER subculture and associated NIGflation. Nevertheless, the city of Indianapolis was well aware of the costly NIGflation associated with the Black Expo, and took preventative measures to become NIGGER-Tsunami/Flashflood ready. The preparation even included utilizing an army of peacekeepers to assist the police. Detailing the measures taken to make the city NIGGER-Tsunami ready,

Indystar.com columnist Erika D. Smith wrote (7/19/11), ***"It looked like the government had declared martial law after the sun went down Friday. Police were dozens deep on Pennsylvania Street across from the American Legion Mall. They were on foot, on bikes and in cars. On Meridian Street, there were even more cops, plus civilians who had vowed to help keep the peace. Even people in the audience were peering through the dark, watching for trouble."*** Although the mobilization of a strong police presence is usually employed to maintain public order during massive protests or demonstrations, cities are learning that this show of force is necessary to exhibit their degree of NIGGER-Tsunami readiness. Question: Why aren't these drastic measures utilized at the other major, annual Indianapolis event called the Indianapolis 500 (Indy 500)? After all, it's also a popular annual event, and has comparable attendance. Is it because it's a predominately Euro-American affair? No, it's because rednecks attend the Indy 500 for pleasure, whereas NIGGERS attend the Black Expo for pain.

Smith: Finding the balance between safety, comfort at Summer Celebration

indystar.com

Black Expo shootings put cycle of violence back in spotlight

thegrio.com

10 people shot downtown after Indiana Black Expo event

Victims were between 10 & 18

wishtv.com

[Author's Note: African-Americans typically blame racism when permit requirements are suddenly toughened, exorbitant insurance retention is demanded, and a paramilitary police force is utilized as an overseer for American-American themed events. These precautionary measures are taken because cities have to factor the NIGflation when approving African-American events.]

Volunteers will help keep peace on streets for this year's Black Expo

indystar.com

[Author's Note: The HoG could really use these "volunteers."]

Indiana Black Expo working to overcome stigma of violence

The Indiana Black Expo's Summer Celebration is working hard to overcome the stigma of violence from year's past.

fox59.com

(Greek Picnic)

The Greek Picnic is an annual weeklong event during the month of July in Philadelphia, Pennsylvania. Originally designed as a reunion celebrating African-American college fraternities and sororities, it later gained popularity among the general (non-student) African-American population because of its various social activities. As it grew in popularity, it was eventually seized by the NIGGER-Tsunami, and regressed into an event spoiled by frequent cases of sexual harassment, physical/sexual assaults, gun-related violence, carjacking, and other NIGGERtivity. July after July, the NIGGER-Tsunami consistently unleashed its wrath. Eventually, the city was forced to become NIGGER-Tsunami ready. A super-heavy police presence, coupled with businesses closing their stores during the event, forced the Greek Picnic into obscurity. By implementing these extreme preventative measures, Philadelphia has joined the growing list of cities that've become NIGGER-Tsunami ready.

Black Greek Organizations Not Welcomed In Pennsylvania
newsone.com

NEWS ANALYSIS: U. police prevents fiasco at Greek picnic
thedp.com

(Freaknik)

Freaknik was an annual spring break meeting in Atlanta, Georgia, composed primarily of students from historically BLACK colleges and universities (HBCUs). Overall, Freaknik was the southern version of Philadelphia's Greek picnic. And like its northern sibling, the NIGGER subculture usurped the theme. After Atlanta (unable to afford the NIGflation) began using heavy-handed tactics to prevent the re-occurring NIGGER-Tsunamis, Freaknik lost its charm. In April 2010, Atlanta officials banned Freaknik-related events inside the city limits. As a result, the Freaknik organizers considered relocating to Miami Beach. However, the Miami Beach residents were well aware of the NIGflation associated with Freaknik and became oppositional to that idea.

Freaknik too lewd, crude for Atlanta?
chronicle.augusta.com

Atlanta Mayor Says He Won't Allow Freaknik Trouble
mysouthga.com

'Freaknik' Revelers Descend on an Apprehensive Atlanta
latimes.com

(Miami Beach)

Every Memorial Day weekend on South Beach (Miami), Urban Weekend seizes the town. Wikipedia explains, ***"Urban Beach Week has been likened to a de-facto continuation of Freaknik's cultural activities. The event has become known for its over-the-top parties and fashions, as well as incidents of bad behavior."*** Although Miami's tsunami warning system wasn't built to detect the land based NIGGER-Tsunami, the town is still well aware of its existence. Understanding the damage it causes, the town is now reacting similarly to the other impacted cities (Philly, Atlanta, and Myrtle Beach) by preventing its arrival, or becoming NIGGER-Tsunami ready. In fact, the president of Miami-Dade County's largest Hispanic gay-rights group wrote an open letter to the mayor, commissioners, and concerned citizens voicing his frustration with this event. He wrote, ***"When did perceived political or social correctness override the safety & well-being of a community? This is not a race, economic or ethnic issue, it is an issue of visitors who have a total lack of respect for our community, its property & citizens. I know hotel rooms are filled, but at what price and for how long? How many events, meetings, conventions & vacations have been CANCEELLED*** [sic] ***because of this nightmare we endure each Memorial Day? Almost everyone who lives here that I know, get out of Miami Beach for Memorial Day - including many of you - because of this unruly & dangerous mob that we seem to invite back every year and turn a blind eye to the irreparable damage they leave behind."*** Even though the event wasn't banned by the city, a Gestapo-inspired *"show me your papers"* tactic was utilized to minimize the NIGGER-Tsunami's impact. As reported on *miami.cbslocal.com (5/21/12),* ***"City Officials came up with an extensive traffic plan to discourage the general public from driving into residential neighborhoods. For the first time ever, residents are going to have to show "proof of residency" if they live in key sections west of Washington Avenue between 5th and 15th Streets and south of 5th street."*** Yes, this is a start, but only heavy-handed tactics, or complete bans will prevent NIGGER-Tsunamis.

Gunfire, Death and Crime Spur Calls For End to Miami Beach's Urban Beach Weekend
miaminewtimes.com

Fears Over Miami Beach Freaknik Event
nbcmiami.com

Miami Beach Police Get Strict For Memorial Day Weekend
miami.cbslocal.com

(Black Bike Week)

Myrtle Beach's Bike Fest, commonly referred to as Black Bike week, occurs on Myrtle Beach a week after the (majority Euro-American) Harley Davidson Spring Rally. Although these two bike-themed gatherings appear similar in theme, the news headlines, police reports, videos, and social networking sites reflect the differences. Recognizing these contrasts, Myrtle Beach has passed several ordinances that are seemingly NIGGER-Tsunami deterrents. According to *blackradionetwork.com*, ***"In recent years, the NAACP and African-Americans have filed and successfully settled federal discrimination lawsuits against the city of Myrtle Beach and area businesses for unequal treatment of Black Week visitors compared to those who attend Harley Week, traditionally held one week earlier and a predominately white event."*** Also, similar to the business communities' reaction during the Greek picnic, many businesses intentionally close for the entire week, instead of profiteering. It's truly a damning indictment of an event when businesses defy capitalistic logic by deciding against profiting from the influx of potential customers. Normally, cities and businesses eagerly anticipate hosting events of this magnitude because of the revenue potential, especially during these harsh economic times. Moreover, hotels and property owners overcharge for rentals, restaurants are maxed, and various vendors can expect walk-in traffic. So, is it racist for businesses to close doors? Au Contraire. Those businesses (along with City Council) understand that NIGflation outweighs any generated revenue; thus, reactionary, slow kill measures are logical. Even still, I'm unsurprised that Myrtle Beach's act of self-preservation via NIGGER-Tsunami prevention was considered racist. Especially since the NAACP has occupied the Myrtle Beach event for seven consecutive years monitoring for discrimination while ignoring the NIGGERtivity.

Myrtle Beach police inundated with crime during 8-hour window
myrtlebeachonline.com

Myrtle Beach asking Atlantic Beach to join them in canceling Bike Week
wwaytv3.com

(Movies Theatres)

The NIGGER subculture assumes that NIGGERtivity is justified wherever they've paid admission. Particularly, in movie theatres, where they habitually disregard the theatre imposed courtesy reminders by continuously texting, cell phone chatting, or collective blabbing. Moreover, they typically inject their personal soundtrack into the film by yelling advice and warnings to the actors like kindergarteners at an audience-participation play. Adding insult to injury, annoyed moviegoers risk being physically assaulted if they dare request that NIGGERS act considerately. This is why I only patronize Anti-NIGGER movies, and frequent theatres far from the HoG. Avoidance is relatively easy because their lack of horizon limits them to certain types of movies. Whenever fleeing isn't an option, it's time for Netflix.

Marine Home From Iraq War, Wife Allegedly Assaulted Outside Florida Theater by Teen Mob
foxnews.com

[Author's Note: The marine asked the JuviNIGGERS who were talking on cell phones to "be quiet."]

Suspects in Alleged Movie Theater Assault Caught On Camera
wnep.com

[Author's Note: A woman "shushed" JuviNIGGERS for talking loudly and cursing during the movie. They responded by breaking her eye socket.]

(Malls)

Why do most cities have so-called "Black and White malls?" Well, the answer is simple, WHITE people know that wherever many African-Americans consistently frequent, NIGGERtivity follows. Consequently, this mall abandonment for 'Whiter' pastures creates the "Black mall, White mall" phenomenon. As stated earlier, NIGGERS have triggered the resurrection of a *"separate but equal"* reality. The "Black" malls are familiar with NIGGERtivity and the associated NIGflation; therefore, may utilize NIGGER-Tsunami/Flashflood preventive strategies or remedies that probably aren't practiced in "White" malls. Some even have mini-police stations on site. Often, Black mall policies forbid the entry of teens during school hours. Even during non-school hours, teens may have to be accompanied by a parent or adult. It isn't uncommon for *"One Teen At A Time," or "Please Remove Your Hood,"* signs to be conspicuously displayed. Since federal law forbids merchants from outright saying *"No Af-Am teens allowed,"* these alternative forms of discrimination and profiling were developed to prevent NIGflation. Fortunately, internet shopping provides the ultimate protection against Flashfloods.

100 Teens Act A FOOL Inside MILWAUKEE Mall . . . Scaring Shoppers . . . A Gun POPS OFF Inside The Mall!!
indyhiphop.com

(Journalistic Advice)

Disappointed by a Flashflood that occurred at an area mall, a BLACK journalist penned an open letter (5/20/09) to the involved JuviNIGGERS. Here is an excerpt. ***"Look, as a working journalist I am supposed to stay neutral. But I really want to take a moment to offer you guys some big sister/motherly advice: Look... I know things may not be perfect in your house. I get that. Believe me, I get that. But through your actions last week you are making things worse on yourself, and the entire black community. You just reinforced that old standby stereotype that we are all nothing but uneducated troublemakers. And the next time you try and walk into a store and get some service, guess what? That sales clerk probably won't want to serve you. And guess what else? You've planted the seeds of your own destruction. Because they're talking about you. They're talking about what a lousy parent your mother is for letting you do such a thing at Mayfair. They're whispering that she's probably a single mother on welfare, and that you probably haven't seen your father in months, maybe years. And they're saying that you are just going to***

be a product of your environment, and will probably end up pregnant and poor... or in prison." I applaud any condemnation of this subculture; but BLACKS such as this well-intentioned reporter have to realize that NIGGERS aren't a representation of BLACKS just as White Trash aren't representative of WHITES. NIGGERS are simply representatives of their chosen subculture.

Shelley Walcott: Don't Tell The Boss
An Open Letter To The Kids Who Tore Up Mayfair
todaystmj4.com

(Transit Authorities)

In cities across America, the sporadic Flashfloods are wreaking havoc on transit authorities' ability to safely provide a necessary service to the public. The negative impact of JuviNIGGERtivity is forcing (already) cash short metro systems in a poor economy to somehow find money for high-tech surveillance systems and increased police patrols. Just as taxicabs utilize bulletproof partitions, the bus driver area may soon be next, especially in urban areas. The bus driver's chances of being assaulted are exponentially increased when confined with JuviNIGGERS. Simply asking a JuviNIGGER to pay the fare can result in a physical and/or verbal assault (including being spat upon). I'm sure that many incidents are unreported because it's always a public relations nightmare to call out this subculture. Even so, Detroit bus drivers were so frustrated with being assaulted that they refused to drive routes that heightened exposure to NIGGERtivity. As reported by CBS Detroit (*DDOT Drivers Refuse To Work: 'They're Scared For Their Lives', 11/4/11*), the spokesperson for the bus drivers' union stated, ***"Our drivers are scared, they're scared for their lives. This has been an ongoing situation about security. I think yesterday kind of just topped it off, when one of my drivers was beat up by some teenagers down in the middle of Rosa Parks and it took the police almost 30 minutes to get there, in downtown Detroit."*** Ironically, this particular bus depot is named in honor of Rosa Parks, yes, thee Rosa Parks whose historic action made it possible for the JuviNIGGERS to sit in the front (to cause trouble). Although job security is a crapshoot in bankrupt Detroit, rampant JuviNIGGERtivity caused bus drivers to abandon their precious jobs because they were ***"scared for their lives."***

The NIGGER subculture owes Rosa Parks an apology

(Chuck E. Cheese)

How pervasive is the NIGGER-Tsunami? It's so widespread that it has even tainted the image of the Chuck E. Cheese franchise. This historically reliable child-centered outlet, which bills itself as a place *"where a kid can be a kid,"* has instead, morphed into a place where *NIGGERS can be NIGGERS*. Is Sesame Place next? In order to reclaim their image, many Chuck E. Cheese locations (especially in urban areas) have implemented NIGGER-Tsunami preventing measures such as metal detectors, security guards (some armed), and even a contraband list. In fact, a Milwaukee, Wisconsin Chuck E. Cheese publically posted a contraband list that included chains, screwdrivers, gang colors, glasscutters, and knives. Coincidentally, these same items are also considered contraband and prohibited in HNCUs. The question that begs to be asked is... who would bring those items to Chuck E. Cheese in the first place??? Oh, wait... don't answer. Eventually, Chuck E. Cheese restaurants will require dress shoes and blazers for entry, while Chuck E. Cheese himself will probably be strapped; all because NIGGERS don't enjoy civilized atmospheres. They behave as if the games, toys, and merchandise belong to them, and the other children are trespassers. Their lack of etiquette and courtesy deters agreeable patrons from returning; consequently, the franchise loses quality money while our kids lose a place to be kids.

Calling All Cars: Trouble at Chuck E. Cheese's Again

online.wsj.com

[Article's Quote: "But in some cities, law enforcement officials say the number of disruptions at their local outlet is far higher than at nearby restaurants, and even many bars."]

(Flint, Michigan)

In Flint, Michigan (Flint is 56.6% African-American), Police Sargent Tim Jones's incident report (8/19/08, case# 2008-2354) documented the NIGGERtivity encountered once he responded to yet another Chuck E. Cheese disturbance call. The Officer wrote, ***"I exited my vehicle and entered into the Chuck E Cheese restaurant where I observed approximately 75-85 black males and females fighting in the rear of the restaurant. As I entered the restaurant, I noticed that pepper gas had been sprayed. There was a strong odor of the O.C. spray in the air. I noticed that Officers were trying to separate three black females that appeared to have been fighting. Two of the individuals appeared to have already been sprayed by OC. I also noticed a third female lying on the floor. Just as I got to the rear of the restaurant a second fight broke out near the front doors and the cash register area. Other Officers from the State Police, Sheriff's Department as well as Flint Township Officers were trying to control this incident. The fight continued for several minutes with several requests for more officers to respond to this location. This incident continued to escalate from the continued pushing, fighting and shoving."*** Although this report is from an urban location, don't think that this type NIGGERtivity is isolated to NIGfested locations. Like bedbugs, NIGGERS can manifest anywhere. Read on.

(Brookfield, Wisconsin)

In Brookfield, Wisconsin (1.2% African-American), Police Officer Mironischen's incident report (5/30/08, #K08-02585 DC) documented the NIGGERtivity encountered at a presumably NIGGER-free Chuck E. Cheese. The officer wrote, ***"Officer Knapp and I entered Chuck E Cheese and were directed to the eating area near the stage and observed approximately thirty to forty people gathered. There was a large amount of yelling and screaming and people engaged in physical fighting. Officer Kennedy was also enroute to our location at this time. Officer Knapp and I attempted to break up the altercation."*** After calling for assistance, the officer's report continued, ***"I made contact with the manager;*** (name was redacted in the incident report) ***and inquired which people were causing the problem. He directed me to two large groups of male and female African-American people. With the assistance of other officers they were escorted out of the business. While attempting to ascertain who the primary subjects involved were, we received little cooperation from patrons."*** Naturally, the NIGGERfiliacs will say that these two stories were isolated incidences, or the patrons were unfairly targeted. Undeniable stories (such as these) are routinely witnessed and reported by officers, parents, and employees around the country; they haven't conspired to tell the same lie. Although there is a Chuck E. Cheese location near my home, I drive to the exurbs where NIGGERS don't frequent. Yes, the commute can be a fiscal strain (i.e. gasoline), but paying for the extra gas is still cheaper than posting bail for fighting a NIGGER parent.

Chuck E. Cheese's again beset by fights

jsonline.com

[Article's Quote: "Five years after Chuck E. Cheese's restaurant hired private security because of excessive calls to police about disturbances, officers are making even more trips for fights and other problems at the children's party restaurant."]

***"Some nights we're afraid for our lives!"*-Anonymous house band member**

Chapter V

The Hood or Ghetto a.k.a the "HoG"

"I live in a neighborhood so bad that you can get shot while getting shot." Chris Rock

Albert Einstein said, ***"The world is a dangerous place to live: not because of the people who are evil, but because of the people who don't do anything about it."*** Mr. Einstein's profound observation is applicable to the state of affairs plaguing HoGs across America. This chapter explores the various factors and levels of dysfunction that inevitably transforms neighborhoods into HoGs. Nationwide, HoGs are essentially replicas of each other with varying degrees of dysfunction, violence, and apathy. Despite the slight differences, they undeniably share a common denominator... the NIGGER subculture.

(Defining Hood)

African-Americans always speak about the *"hood"* as if it's our sovereign and indigenous territory. But, what exactly is a *hood?* Moreover, what are the qualifying factors for a neighborhood to be deemed one? Is a *hood* any housing project, public housing location, or predominately African-American neighborhood? Is the single most relevant aspect that makes an area a *hood* determined by the amount of crime and poverty? I live in a mixed neighborhood; no, not racially mixed, but culturally mixed. In other words, it's comprised of three different segments of African-Americans: BLACKS, NIGGERS, and blacks (WNT). Is this a *hood*? I have WHITE friends that live amongst their three segments (WHITES, wiggers, White Trash) does this qualify as a *hood*? Or, is the term (*hood*) exclusive to African-American neighborhoods? If the term is indeed exclusive to African-American neighborhoods, then it makes sense that the words *"hood"* and *"ghetto"* are synonymous with African-Americans.

(Is My Neighborhood a Hood?)

On paper, my neighborhood is prime real estate. Within a two mile radius of my home exists: three banks, a credit union, two major supermarkets, hospital, public health center, several private practice dentist/medical offices, a historic college, two libraries, major mall, numerous shopping districts, two police precincts, a fire station, two recreation centers with baseball/football fields, tennis courts, two high schools/elementary schools, more than a few beauty/barbershops, daycare centers, numerous convenience/fast food stores, two public parks (including an arboretum), major bus routes/depot, local and regional rail train stations, churches, temples, masjids, Social Security building, unemployment office, and welfare office. Wow, even while writing, I'm realizing that this list isn't all-inclusive. Knowing that *"location, location, location"* is a general real estate mantra used to gauge a neighborhood's value, seemingly, my neighborhood's location should make realtors salivate, and property value soar. Unfortunately, neither has occurred, and that likely won't change until gentrification arrives. Indisputably, my neighborhood's potential is overshadowed by shootouts, homey-cides, police raids, hovering helicopters, drug dealing, armed robberies, assaults, twenty-four hour traffic, and high victimization rates. I've realized that the quality of life issues posed in real time by the NIGGER subculture trumps the paper version of my neighborhood, thus, making it a HoG.

(Dictionary "Hood")

In mainstream dictionaries, *"hood"* in slang context is simply defined as ***"A neighborhood, usually in the inner-city."*** Clearly, there should be more meat to this definition. I guess if NIGGERtivity continues at its current pace, an extended, descriptive definition of *"hood"* will be manufactured. Even the word *"bootylicious"* is descriptively defined in several mainstream dictionaries lol. Before NIGGERS redefined the term, I recognize that *"hood"* was once primarily used as a shortened form for neighborhood. After all, the word *"neighborhood"* is simply two words: *"neighbor"* and *"hood."* While a quality "neighborhood" encompasses the *"neighbor"* aspect, an inferior neighborhood encompasses the *"hood"* aspect. This *"hood"* aspect represents the interests of a *"hood"*-lum (hoodlum). What is a hoodlum? It's generally defined as a ***"gangster or thug."*** Both terms are NIGGER attributes. In other words, to be *"hood"* is to be *gangster-like, thug-like,* or ultimately *NIGGER-like,* and the *"hood"* is their lair. Did you know that *"hood"* could be a person, place, or thing? Well, NIGGERS know! This is why a *hood*, wearing a *hood*, representing the *hood* is highly revered in their subculture.

(JEWISH Ghetto -vs- NIGGER Ghetto)

Since the NIGGER subculture has made *"hood"* synonymous with African-Americans, how did the word *"ghetto"* also become associated with African-Americans? In today's society, it's understood that calling someone or something *"ghetto"* conjures images of Af-Am dysfunction, ignorance, and lack of class. Prior to this parallel, *"ghetto"* was an area where Jews were forced to live. In fact, the *Merriam-Webster* online dictionary specifically mentions "Jews" in its primary definition of *ghetto*: ***"a quarter of a city in which Jews were formerly required to live."*** Despite this definition, it bears repeating that any time *"ghetto"* is mentioned or referenced today, historical/archival film of JEWISH imagery typically doesn't come to mind *(unless the topic is specifically World War I or II).* Instead, an African-American neighborhood or person comes to mind. How and when did this change occur? I have diligently searched different dictionaries attempting to find the words Black, African-American, Negro, Afro-American, Colored et.al specifically mentioned (as Jews are) in any mainstream dictionary's *"ghetto"* definition. The closest term used was *"minority,"* which (NIGGERS will be surprised to learn) isn't exclusive to African-Americans. Again I ask, if Black, African-American, Negro, Afro-American, colored, et al. are not linked to the word *"ghetto"* in mainstream dictionaries (like the Jews), how did *"ghetto"* become synonymous with African-Americans? Did I miss the JEWISH press conference where they officially removed their affiliation with the word *"ghetto,"* and subsequently alley-ooped the term to African-Americans? This identity shift occurred as soon as NIGGERS affectionately claimed the word *"ghetto,"* just as they did with "NIGGER." Despite the undesirable inferences of both terms, they were rebranded in the image and after the likeness of the NIGGER subculture. Ironically, this subculture embraces the terms NIGGERS, hood, and ghetto, but despise being called out as such.

(Different Ghettos)

Again, the term *"ghetto"* is so culturally ingrained that African-Americans use it as if all African-Americans reside or have equity there. Laughably, NIGGERS believe that any African-American that doesn't or didn't reside in the ghetto lack street credentials, street smarts, or simply don't know "the struggle." While researching this topic, I've discovered that American ghettos were once termed ethnic enclaves, and were closely associated with different waves of immigration and internal urban migration. The success and development of these ethnic enclaves were rooted in hard work and self-sufficiency. Those fundamental attributes ultimately benefitted the enclave's economy. In fact, many of those ethnic enclaves evolved into thriving tourist attractions like Chinatowns, Koreatowns, Little Italys, etc. Nowadays, most ethnic enclaves have been seized by the NIGGER subculture, and the principles that served the Irish, German, Italian, Polish, Asian, and Jewish immigrants etc. are non-existent. The only time that the HoG could possibly be a tourist site is on Halloween.

(Conclusion)

Although history reveals that a variety of ethnic groups lived in ghettos, these groups didn't allow that word "ghetto" to define them. On the contrary, they communally persevered to build their legacy while leaving the ghetto and its connotations as historical footnotes. Unlike NIGGERS, other ethnicities understood that the ghetto was a place to escape, not personify. In the HoG, *hood* and *ghetto* are affectionately embraced as the way to be, and have manifested into a seemingly patented lifestyle. In summary, hoods and ghettos are the same entity with the same negative pathologies, which is why I simply refer to them as HoGs.

(Conditions)

As previously stated, most HoGs didn't start as such. Although poor, they were still principled, tight-knit neighborhoods. Furthermore, neighbors generally had permission to reprimand kids, and kids respected elders. In those times, disrespecting an adult was a brazen and cavalier act that oftentimes resulted in a public scolding or/and beating. Parents were generally appreciative whenever another adult attempted to correct their child's misbehavior because an unspoken united front existed between adults. But since the parasitic NIGGER subculture, has leached onto African-American neighborhoods, these principles have disappeared. Their preferred form of behavior (O.N.D) has transformed African-American neighborhoods into HoGs. Although the degree of dysfunction between HoGs may vary, the NIGGER subculture ensures that dysfunction and crime are constant. Presently, HoGs are third world out-posts in America's inner-cities, and the disregard for basic courtesy and curfews ensure that HoGs are open twenty-four hours a day, especially during the summer. Due to the lack of community upkeep and property maintenance, many HoGs have become urban wastelands, and the residents are desensitized to the stench. Moreover, NIGGERtivity is allowed to flourish, Ebonics is the official language, and low cultural standards are maintained through the "keepin' it real" mantra.

(24/7)

As evidenced by the FBI's annual list of most dangerous zip codes, HoGs are notorious for their crime rate. Certainly, NIGGERS enjoy the bloody reputation associated with their particular HoG making this shameful list, but in the real world, one can only sympathize for the good residents stuck in that quagmire. The gunshots, corner clustering, police sirens, sound of dirt bikes/four wheelers carelessly performing laps throughout the night, and music-thumping cars ensure that the few employed residents don't easily rest. I've gotten used to falling asleep to the sound of a metal bird (police helicopter) hovering my HoG in search of another usual suspect. Certainly, it's only a matter of time before drone attacks are authorized. Alarm clocks are obsolete because sleep is constantly interrupted by the unmistakable sound of gunfire, or other forms of NIGGERtivity. Due to the omnipresent "no snitch" policy (Refer to ***Abel Kills Cain*** chapter), the NIGGER subculture has established a monopoly in HoGs across America.

SW Philly Residents Wake Up to Find Cars Shot Up
nbbcphiladelphia.com

Trenton minister, activist: Hard spike in violence bringing hood to point of war

trentonian.com

Dalai Lama Brings Peace Message To Inner-City

huffingtonpost.com

[Author's Note: Peace??? He'd be better off bringing his "piece."]

(Fight, Flight, or Assimilate)

Co-existing with the NIGGER subculture is a living hell. Admittedly, socio-economics has stalled my ability to escape to a responsible, like-minded community. For most, taking cover has been the only alternative when fighting or fleeing is not. But, even when opportunities arrive for many to flee the HoG, the pervasive HoG mindset interprets leaving as an abandonment of Blackness. Yup, unbelievably, Af-Ams are expected to *"keep it real"* by raising families in these dangerous conditions. The HoG's gravitational pull is so strong that the crab in a barrel mentality is the accepted way of life. Whenever one tries to escape, others attempt to pull him/her back into the murky HoG conditions.

(The Cry for Help)

Many HoG natives claim that conditions are so dire that the only recourse is to seek government intervention. This collective cry usually occurs after continuous homey-cides, collateral damage, or other drastic manifestations of NIGGERtivity. A couple examples of the immediate, routine responses are, *"somebody needs to help us,"* or the *"police need to step up."* The natives always demand help from outside entities for internal conflicts; including usage of the National Guard. To them, these are viable and logical options since most already rely on the government for everything. Therefore, in their mind, there's nothing abnormal about requesting a government-provided security detail at taxpayers' expense. The fact that such proposals are even requested in HoGs is indicative of the circumstances created by the NIGGER subculture. Fundamentally, I don't believe that the government can police the HoG out of its NIGfestation; that's a temporary fix for a long-term problem. The policing should start from the community itself, with police assistance. In other words, a police presence should only supplement the community's Anti-NIGGER mindset. Even if the National Guard/police intensely patrolled the HoGs, I guarantee that racism, racial profiling, and police brutality will be alleged by the natives. Something as simple as cell phone video showing a cop tightly placing handcuffs on a suspect will be enough for the race-peddlers to arrange anti-brutality protests, while calling for law enforcement's departure. Helping the HoG is definitely a double-edged sword.

(Seniors in the HoG)

Due to my belief that we're all life's students, I possess a natural respect for seniors. Seniors are nearing graduation from this form of existence to another. So, for the seniors who are economically stuck in the HoG, I'm always concerned for their safety. It's depressing that they have to spend their remaining earthly time as vulnerable prey in neighborhoods they've inhabited before the local troublemakers were even born. I always hear the trapped residents reminisce about the once beautiful neighborhood of yesteryear. They'd frequently contrast the present HoG to the old neighborhood, and tell of a seemingly imaginary time when elders could fearlessly sit on their stoops and enjoy their golden years. The diehard seniors who refuse to forfeit their homes have watched their environment decay into a shadow of its former self; detonated by the NIGGER subculture. Again, I'm fearful for their safety because NIGGERtivity indiscriminately victimizes; even world-renowned BLACK trailblazers aren't shielded from it. The New York Times reported (9/1/94), ***"Her face bruised and her lip swollen, Rosa Parks, the mother of the civil rights movement, seemed more sad than angry today as she quietly described being robbed and beaten in her bedroom here on Tuesday night. 'I regret very much that some of our people are in such a mental state that they would hurt and rob an older person,' Mrs. Parks said as she sat in living room of her modest, rented home, five blocks from the boulevard named in her honor."*** The older generation always seems to forgive behaviors that I perceive as unforgivable. Perhaps, one day, I will evolve to that point, but for now, Urban Terrorists need to taste a swift and severe form of vigilante justice.

Sadness and Anger After a Legend Is Mugged
nytimes.com

Four teens charged in Detroit carjacking of 88-year-old Tuskegee airman

detroitnews.com

[Author's Note: While pointing his gun at the BLACK patriot, the JuviNIGGER had the audacity to call him a NIGGER. Wow, talk about role reversal.]

(Kids in the HoG)

Children are said to be living messages that we as parents send to the future. Additionally, it takes a village to raise a child, but if the village has NIGGERS then that village is doomed. In short, NIGGERtivity in the HoG exposes kids to things that children simply should not experience; shootings, stabbings, fights, murder etc. are all part of the landscape. Moreover, funeral preparations rival birthday celebrations. Although my kiddie eyes didn't recognize NIGGERS for who they were, I still realized that there were some abnormally bad people in the HoG, especially after my uncle was killed (shot) in a schoolyard. I believe that I was twelve years old when I saw my first homicide victim, which I now know was actually a homey-cide victim. I can still visualize the dude lying on the ground in a fetal position agonizing from a gunshot wound to the abdomen. His sister was crying uncontrollably as she clutched and begged him not to die. As the crowd grew, and the spectators tried to ascertain the facts, he died in her arms before an ambulance could arrive. Stunned, I didn't know how to process what I'd witnessed, except to think that this experience was a rite of passage in the HoG. In fact, I couldn't wait to get to school the following day to tell what I saw. This was one of many violence-related, childhood experiences from a housing project that was actually considered "good" when compared to other HoGs.

(Something from Nothing)

Although the HoG is typically a bleak bubble, somehow, children miraculously make fun where none exists. Poverty coupled with a hazardous environment still doesn't obstruct a kid's desire to be a kid; they remind me of grass that manage to grow through concrete. Childhood is a universal club where the members, regardless of race, naturally connect by virtue of simply being children. Their simplistic view of the world combined with the ability to be easily entertained is enviable. For most of his childhood, Frederick Douglass stated that he didn't know he was enslaved because he was preoccupied with being a kid. In the HoG, this same uncomplicated mindset is exhibited by its kids. They can be found enjoying themselves in many clever ways. To be clear, I'm not talking about JuviNIGGERS! JuviNIGGERS create alternative forms of recreation in attempt to "wreck-creation." I'm talking about the agreeable kids who get creative because the playground doesn't have functioning equipment, or doubles as a drug strip. I'm talking about those kids who no longer duck at the sound of gunshots because they've become desensitized, and still look forward to playing ghetto-games. As a kid, following a significant rainfall, we would stand on a hill and place Popsicle sticks or tree twigs into the curbside water stream to see whose stick would go downhill to the sewer fastest. There were plenty of Popsicle sticks, so the games lasted until the flowing water subsided. Although the sticks/twigs were often impeded by the curbside tires of parked cars, or trapped by curbside debris, those obstacles only increased our improvisation skills. After all, bragging rights would last until the next rainfall. Those days are long gone, but the NIGGER-inflicted realities facing children in the HoG remain.

St. Louis youth gunshot death rate second highest in U.S
stltoday.com

[Author's Note: St. Louis has a 49.2% Af-Am populace.]

Child shot on porch in north St. Louis
kmov.com

2-year-old critical after shooting at party
philly.com

Deputies: Robber puts gun to child's back for $5
wtsp.com

Police: 13-year-old stabs boy over bike
wsbtv.com

[Author's Note: "Chauntavious" was stabbed by his 13-year-old neighbor.]

Teen gunned down on Christmas Eve... just feet from where his cousin was killed at Thanksgiving
dailymail.co.uk

(Halloween in the HoG)

Unlike mischief night, which precedes Halloween, Halloween is primarily celebrated outside the HoG. Although Halloween decoratives plaster HoG landscapes, the actual candy-hunt traditionally occurs in Euro-American neighborhoods. As a kid, I wondered why we didn't trick or treat in my neighborhood, but as an adult, I now understand. The Halloween exodus isn't due to economic depravity, or Halloween falling on the 31st, narrowly missing the first of the month's food stamp allotment. First, dispensing Halloween candy in the HoG is a rarity because most residents are receivers (Quadruplers) instead of givers. Secondly, the fact that it's acceptable for NIGGERS to openly wear masks poses serious safety issues. The Quadruplers' mindset coupled with NIGGERS having free reign while disguised, makes the HoG non-ideal for trick or treating. But wait, this isn't entirely bad news for the NIGGER subculture; Halloween is the one time of the year when their subculture and entitlement mentality are actually tolerated in non-NIGGER neighborhoods. It's particularly easy to spot the JuviNIGGERS because they travel without adult supervision, trick or treat later than normal time, don't wear traditional costumes (street clothes and a dollar store mask), and their school backpack doubles as the candy bag. Smileless and unmannerly, they knock on doors, shove out bags, and then leave without expressing any gratitude. I remember when kids would at least say, ***"trick or treat, smell my feet, give me something good to eat***."

15 shot, 2 dead in N.O. Halloween shootings

wwltv.com

D.C. Halloween Violence: Georgetown Shooting Sparks Youth Confrontations; 6 Shot Across City

huffingtonpost.com

[Author's Note: D.C. has a gun ban.]

"Grandfather details Halloween shooting that left boy gravely injured"

latimes.com

[Author's Note: While showing off his Halloween costume in his backyard, 5-year-old Aaron Shannon Jr. was murdered.]

Another superhero killed by the neighborhood villain

(Security Measures)

Poverty itself is a struggle, but that poverty becomes a prison sentence when living amongst the NIGGER subculture. With the drugs, violence, and overall "watch your back" atmosphere, HoGs are essentially minimum-security penitentiaries without barbed wires. If escaping the HoG isn't financially viable, then the next best move is to toughen security measures (depending on the HoG, tripwires, and claymore mines may be ideal, lol). In all HoGs and nearby areas, the standard security trend is steel security doors and windows. Despite their cost, and impedance to escape a fire, heavy-duty security doors/windows are the HoG's mandatory investments. Drive through any HoG or places located near HoGs, and pay attention to the amount of security doors and/or windows. In fact, it's not an anomaly for entire porches to be enclosed with steel bars. Whenever I see a home that's completely barricaded with bars, I often wonder if they're meant to prevent the criminals from entering or prevent the occupants from exiting. The reality is that HoG residents are barricading themselves at the expense of keeping out NIGtruders. In non-NIGfested areas, the trend is cosmetically-based doors and windows, instead of security-based.

The HoG is intimately familiar with the various types of security bars

(The Plan)

In the HoG, the world is realized through a narrow lens. It's a place where their immediate, present day surroundings are the extent of the NIGGER subculture's concern. The HoG is their corrupted version of community, and it (HoG) exists wherever they exist. Society is slowly realizing that the NIGGER subculture creates HoG's wherever it dwells, and taking them from the HoG doesn't necessarily take the HoG from them. Futile attempts to reform or accommodate NIGGERS by relocating them from the HoG (via taxpayer-subsidized programs like Section 8) into NIGGER-free environments is like uprooting a fully developed tree from the forest and re-planting it in a desert. In other words, it simply doesn't work. I've witnessed the demolition then subsequent rebuilding of several housing projects, only to see the new, modernized, energy efficient, low-income housing developments morph into the HoG of old. How does the cycle return? Well, the dilapidation returns because the revamping of the homes didn't translate into the revamping of the NIGGER mindset. Presently, the priority of public housing administrations in several cities has shifted from 'assimilating NIGGERS into the mainstream' to 'targeted concentration.' This targeted concentration keeps NIGGERS confined to their renovated bubble. Cities intentionally remodel HoGs knowing that they'll eventually become dilapidated, but at least it'll help prevent the hyperghettoization of other areas.

Di Ionno: Snow plow drivers are robbed while cleaning Newark housing project

nj.com

[Author's Note: Society shouldn't help those that don't want to be helped!!]

(Out of Options)

Cash-strapped cities across America are scrambling to combat the NIGGER subculture, and if your city isn't prepared, it's next. The officers patrolling HoGs encounter so much NIGGERtivity that it's surprising they aren't issued a daily supply of *"no questions asked"* bullets. In fact, in certain sections of Washington D.C, the NIGGERtivity is so overwhelming that D.C's firefighters were required to assist police officers with crime fighting. According to the Washington Post (7/14/11), ***"Both D.C. firefighters and***

police officers are upset over a new program that forces the fire department to help fight crime. For the past three weeks, D.C. Fire and EMS personnel have been parking their trucks at high crime neighborhoods." Surely, desperate times call for desperate measures, but forcing firefighters to fight crime is as wise as sending cops to fight an inferno. Here's an alternative to sending firefighters to battle crime, send city council members instead.

D.C. Firefighters To Help Police Streets?
nbcwashington.com

(Streets Named After Leaders)

Like several inner-city schools named after honorable BLACKS, streets/avenues/boulevards (in the HoG) generally possess the same NIGGER-induced reputation. Presently, those streets/avenues/boulevards have been hijacked by the NIGGER subculture and converted into *"enter at own risk"* areas. It's accepted knowledge that some of the most violent streets/avenues/boulevards in this country ironically bear Dr. Martin Luther King's name. As a kid, I was inspired to see streets/avenues/boulevards named after BLACK people because they were permanent, positive salutations and not temporary fixtures that are only recognized during BLACK history month. Let's rename the streets if we can't reclaim their honor.

Victim of Muhammad Ali Blvd. shooting dies; police searching for shooter
wave3.com

(Does Bad Mean Bad?)

Whenever I hear people, (politicians, real estate agents, teachers, et.al) mention that an area, school, neighborhood, etc. is "bad," contextually, "bad" isn't slang for "good." Nope, it's actually a code word for NIGfested. The "bad" euphemism denotes a place where NIGGERtivity thrives or randomly manifests. If an African-American says, *"I avoid that neighborhood because it's bad,"* such information is heeded without issue. But, if a Euro-American says the same thing, it may be misinterpreted as racism. Regardless, if I were a Euro-American, and considered racist for saying that a certain Af-Am neighborhood was "bad," I wouldn't care! This form of alleged racism could really be lifesaving. Since following one's intuition and statistics are now considered racist, this latest piece of pending technology, which follows crime statistics to make a determination, will certainly make NIGGERfilacs irate. CBS-Seattle reported (1/6/12), "***Microsoft has been granted a patent for its 'avoid ghetto' feature for GPS devices.***" Part of Microsoft's controversial patent states that routes can be calculated to avoid unsafe neighborhoods. To protect the feelings of a criminally prone subculture, NIGGERfilacs will naturally denounce this statistically driven technology as racist. They'd rather innocent people be harmed or lose their lives by making a wrong turn. I strongly support this "*avoid ghetto*" feature because it's an idea whose time has come. Actually, its arrival makes an excellent, complimentary accessory to the "*avoid NIGGERS*" mobile application that I'm creating. LoL.

Microsoft Patents 'Avoid Ghetto' Feature For GPS Devices
seattle.cbslocal.com

Predictably, NIGGERfilacs will raise more hell about this sign while ignoring the HoG conditions that validates it

(Public Housing)

The HoG, specifically, public housing developments are incubators for the NIGGER subculture. I remember when a primary goal of public housing was to help people become independently solvent enough to transition out the system. Presently, the public housing game is currently fixed to where people can perpetually reside there as long as they follow the criteria and maintain the basic requirements. This is how the NIGGER subculture maintains their intergenerational lease-holding status. In Philadelphia, public housing tenants are only required to pay a third of their income in rent, which isn't asking much since the rent is already low. Once upon a time, a stigma was attached to living in the projects, but now Public housing is filled with entitled Quadruplers who (because of their heavily subsidized lifestyles) actually have disposable incomes. In the HoG, it's common to see expensive cars with pricey rims, residents wearing the latest fashion apparel (with matching footwear), and high-end accessories (smart phones, jewelry, handbags etc.). Furthermore, costly hair weaves, video games systems, big screen TVs, cable/satellite (with all the premium channels), and computers are plentiful. Often, their utilities are subsidized, so no conservation methods are employed. It's normal for air conditioners and heaters to carelessly run at maximum settings. Sure, there are residents like my mother who understood that public housing was simply a bridge to self-sufficiency, but most treat their temporary rental leases as if they are permanent property deeds. Outside of prisons, the government shouldn't provide lifetime housing.

(Section 8)

Due to the Housing Choice Voucher Program, also known as Section 8, the government (aka taxpayers) has become the biggest landlord in the country. Section 8 was designed to help low-income tenants rent property in the private market with taxpayer assistance. In other words, taxpayers pay a large percentage of the rent, and tenants pay the rest. As long as a unit is up to inspection code, the approved tenant is free to choose a private-sector unit anywhere in America, and is not limited to specific complexes. Often, the desirable properties are located in safe and stable NIGGER-free neighborhoods outside of the HoG. The Section 8 approval essentially allows NIGGERS to fly from their previous mess nest and restart the cycle elsewhere. They move into quaint neighborhoods and slowly transform them. Section 8 is another well-intentioned initiative, but this routinely abused program that forces integration, has actually proliferated the NIGGER subculture, and destabilized communities.

(Neighborhood's Decline)

I want to preface this paragraph by acknowledging that there are decent people in Section 8 housing, just as there are degenerates in mansions. Yet, the NIGGER subculture's pathologies have become linked to Section 8, which understandably makes any respectable neighborhood abhor prospective Section 8 properties. Those who may truly need this hand up (such as the handicapped and elderly) can blame the NIGGER subculture for the stigma that's attached to Section 8 renters. Homeowners know that the Section 8ers have no equity in the property and will most likely treat it like a throwaway. As a result, instead of watching the neighborhood slowly collapse into its own footprint, the natives that can afford to escape wisely do so. *JamesBovard.com* (*Raising Hell in Subsidized Housing*- 8/24/11) wrote, ***"In the 1990s, the feds were embarrassed by skyrocketing crime rates in public housing—up to 10 times the national average, according to HUD studies and many newspaper reports. The government's response was to hand out vouchers to residents of the projects (authorized under Section 8 of the Housing and Community Development Act of 1974), dispersing them to safer and more upscale locales."*** Further detailing the impact of this forced integration, he explained, ***"But the dispersal of public housing residents to quieter neighborhoods has failed to weed out the criminal element that made life miserable for most residents of the projects. 'Homicide was simply moved to a new location, not eliminated,' concluded University of Louisville criminologist Geetha Suresh in a 2009 article in Homicide Studies. In Louisville, Memphis, and other cities, violent crime skyrocketed in neighborhoods where Section 8 recipients resettled."*** Like pigs in slop, NIGGERS take solace in creating hyperghettoization conditions.

Section 8 Renters Facing Scrutiny In Los Angeles Suburbs
newsone.com

As Program Moves Poor to Suburbs, Tensions Follow
nytimes.com

Neighborhoods of CHA relocations experienced higher crime rates
suntimes.com

[Article's Quote: "Crime was worse in neighborhoods where former Chicago Housing Authority residents used vouchers to move into private apartments, a new study found."]

(Section 8 Shortages)

The NIGGER subculture has become accustomed with getting something for nothing. After the historic election of the nation's first BLACK president, Quadruplers characteristically assumed that (by virtue of his ethnicity) he'd automatically increase the goodies to their subculture; the handout expectations were astronomical. In record numbers, they eagerly stand in Section 8 lines anticipating a handout. From what I've seen, extensively waiting in these long lines for subsidies (such as Obama phones), is one of the few times that NIGGERS actually show incentive or upward mobility. Visit ***www.BLACKSvsNIGGERS.com*** for video of their entitlement mentality.

Craziness! Section 8 Housing Voucher Stampede Erupts In Dallas
newsone.com

Housing crisis reaches full boil in East Point; 62 injured
ajc.com

NIGGERgeddon ensued as officials handed out Section 8 applications

(Sexuality in the HoG)

As a pastime, NIGGERS leisurely possess multiple promiscuous relationships. Essentially, their polygamous affairs are nothing more than thoughtless breeding for simple pleasure. Although their hyper-sexuality, and irresponsible practice of 'procreation for recreation' guarantees astonishingly bloated illegitimacy rates (amongst other pathologies), careless mating remains standard practice in the HoG. Granted, reproduction is nature's method of advancing a species, and to that extent, NIGGERS excel; yet, this lone strength is an overtaxing liability to society. Ultimately, Baby Daddies and Baby Mamas share responsibly for this quagmire, and should be considered public nuisances. The time spent during the child's conception, typically represents the only significant time that these two are truly united in the child's life.

Man Calls 911 For Ride to Baby Mama's House
wreg.com

Deputies: Couple Fights Over Feeding Baby
Incident Report States Both Man, Woman Did Not Think It's Their Turn To Feed Infant
wyff4.com

[Author's Note: "Lavasha" and her "baby daddy" were still fighting when the police arrived.]

Mom accused of using infant to strike boyfriend
post-gazette.com

[Author's Note: "Chytoria" swung the baby at her boyfriend.]

Mom allegedly throws baby from moving vehicle seeking attention from baby's dad
katc.com

Mother's Day slaying blamed on cheap gift
mysanantonio.com

[Author's Note: The traditional flowers and card didn't suffice, so the Baby Mama stabbed her Baby Daddy to death.]

(NIGGERS and Health)

Given the sexual carelessness of the NIGGER subculture, and their avoidance of regular preventative check-ups and condom usage, it's highly probable that they're responsible for the widespread sexual health issues afflicting the African-American community. NIGGERS will claim that they don't get regular checkups or blood work because they don't like needles; yet, will get tattoos. Go figure.

(Baby Daddy)

In their subculture, Baby Daddies aren't really expected to play a significant role in the child's life. Yes, NIGGERS are "fathers" on paper (birth certificate), but taxpayers will ultimately be the provider. Baby Daddies are the reason that African-American dads have horrible reputations. In fact, Child Support Court seemingly makes a concentrated effort to financially "stick it" to the involved BLACK fathers as compensation for the deadbeat Baby Daddies.

On the flip side, Baby Mamas have it good because they typically receive society's compassion without being held accountable, whereas men are held accountable without society's compassion.

Man fathers 21 children by 11 different women... and he's only 29
dailymail.co.uk

Worst Deadbeat Dad Ever: Father Of 23 Children By 14 Different Mothers Jailed For Failure To Pay Over 500K In Child Support!!!
bossip.com

Tennessee's deadbeat dads: The three men who have fathered 78 children with 46 different women...and they're not paying child support to any of them
dailymail.com

Man Murders His Own Son To Avoid Paying Child Support
countercurrentnews.com

(Government to the Rescue...Again)

On Father's Day 2008, while campaigning for President, candidate Obama gave a speech in which he cleverly rebuked a primary NIGGER subculture tenet. He quipped, ***"Chris Rock had a routine. He said some—too many of our men, they're proud, they brag about doing things they're supposed to do. They say 'Well, I- I'm not in jail.' Well you're not supposed to be in jail!"*** After hearing this comment, which nationally exposed the NIGGER mentality, I wished that he'd said more. After all, his truthfulness wasn't going to jeopardize losing votes because most African-Americans are unshakably allied to the Democrat Party. Even though Senator Obama clowned the NIGGER subculture while on the campaign trail, he still threw them another taxpayer-subsidized lifeline after becoming president. A *root.com* article (6/14/11) titled, *"Can the Government Create Better Dads?"* by Cynthia Gordy reported, ***"the Obama administration in 2009, created the Task Force for Responsible Fatherhood and Healthy Families, to advise the administration on ways that the government can help strengthen fatherhood."*** The Obama administration was, ***"rolling out new initiatives to help dads maneuver around some of the obstacles to fatherhood, from economic hardship to uncertainty after leaving the criminal justice system."*** The help didn't stop there, ***"The Department of Health and Human Services will announce additional funding for local fatherhood programs. Originally created***

under the George W. Bush administration, HHS already provides "Promoting Responsible Fatherhood" grants for community-based organizations that focus on workforce development, healthy relationship skills, parenting classes, financial/child support management and other family-affirming services to low-income and ex-offender fathers. The agency is increasing its support for the next round of grants, from $50 million a year over five years, to $75 million." Yet again, the government is coddling the NIGGER subculture. For responsible and involved fathers, waiting for superman isn't a viable option; yet, Baby Daddies get another government bailout for simply being NIGGERS. Instead of the government trying to create better baby daddies, perhaps it should first focus on creating a better government.

Obama's Father's Day Speech Urges Black Fathers To Be More Engaged In Raising Their Children
huffingtonpost.com

Black Dads Complain They Get A Bad Rap In New Poll
newsone.com

[Author's Note: Yeah, stop confusing us with NIGGERS!]

(Reality Check)

This administration's effort to jumpstart fatherhood in the NIGGER subculture by infusing millions of dollars into this initiative is futile. NIGGER fathers will ultimately raise JuviNIGGERS; the apple usually doesn't fall far from the tree. In their subculture, active parenting is an afterthought (more often, never a thought), and the responsibility of the child is always forwarded to the government. Although Philadelphia Mayor Michael Nutter is a supporter of President Obama, I'm assuming that he's not on board with the President's ambitious initiatives. Regarding absentee fathers, Nutter stated, ***"Part of the problem in the black community—in many communities, but in particular, the black community—is there are too many men making too many babies and we don't wanna take care of your children. We're not a babysitting service; we're a government."*** I wonder if there's a way to upload Nutter's message onto President Obama's teleprompter.

Father, Son Suspected in Father's Day Armed Robbery
ferndale.patch.com

[Author's Note: He was only spending quality time with his son. Now, they can bond even longer at an HNCU.]

Police: Man brings 5-year-old son along when he robs store

fox8live.com

[Author's Note: He was just showing lil man the ropes.]

Black fathers and sons behind bars together: How common is it?

thegrio.com

[Author's Note: Actually, it's quite common in the NIGGER subculture because it's tradition.]

(Baby Mama)

Just as a fish doesn't know it's in water, the typical Baby Mama doesn't know that she's a liability. Baby Mamas are shortsighted, low educated, self-entitled incubators who are complicit in perpetuating this HoG epidemic. Despite burdening the conceived children with a dim future and taxpayers with another mouth to feed, their multi-partner birthing marathon thrives. I use the word "partner" loosely because as previously stated, the partnership doesn't extend pass the procreation phase. Consequently, these babies, who are the byproduct of people that shouldn't have had children in the first place, are likely to become JuviNIGGERS. Although Baby Mamas usually possess meager earning capacities, their reliance on the Sugar Daddy Government allows them to be worry-free from costly baby-associated expenditures such as medical care, clothing, food, education, day care, etc. In other words, their ability to casually conceive is fueled by their entitlement mentality and taxpayer-provided safety net.

Judge frees jailed mom of 15; kids stay in foster care

tbo.com

Children Left in Car with Loaded Gun during Manicure

abc24.com

[Author's Note: Their ages were 4, 2, and 9 months, which is old enough by Baby Mama standards.]

(The Baby Endorsement)

In the HoG, it's culturally acceptable to give birth before the legal age of obtaining a learner's permit, thus perpetuating the cycle of "babies having babies." There's no shame about teenage pregnancy because it's an income-generating, taxpayer-sponsored venture. Due to the financial incentives offered to Baby Mamas, this venture usually marks the beginning of an everlasting marriage to her Sugar Daddy Government. Contractually, more kids equal more benefits. If a raise is needed, simply have more kids. This quid pro quo exchange is a slap in the face to parents like me. In the real world, working parents understand that children are a financial liability, but to Baby Mamas, their children are financial assets. On the welfare plantation, babies are the "must have" accessories. Whenever I see a pregnant, teenaged Baby Mama, I can't help but to feel sorrow for the unborn child. Undoubtedly, the child will face uphill battles, starting with the burden of a HoG name that ultimately won't be in their best interest outside the HoG. Even so, their arrangement with Sugar Daddy allows them to confidently proclaim, ***"I don't need no man... my baby will be alright".*** Rearing children is a serious endeavor, yet, Baby Mamas brazenly hold taxpayers liable for a job that we didn't apply.

Judge orders dad of nine children with six women to stop procreating until he can afford to support his existing offspring

dailymail.co.uk

[Author's Note: Why aren't more judges doing this to Baby Mamas and Daddies???]

(The Odds)

According to *marchofdimes.com*, ***"Teen mothers are more likely to drop out of high school than girls who delay childbearing. Only 40 percent of teenagers who have children before age 18 go on to graduate from high school, compared to 75 percent of teens from similar social and economic backgrounds who do not give birth until ages 20 or 21. With her education cut short, a teenage mother may lack job skills, making it hard for her to find and keep a job. A teenage mother may become financially dependent on her family or on public assistance. Teen mothers are more likely to live in poverty than women who delay childbearing, and more than 75 percent of all unmarried teen mothers go on welfare within 5 years of the birth of their first child. About 64 percent of children born to an unmarried teenage high-school dropout live in poverty,***

compared to 7 percent of children born to women over age 20 who are married and high school graduates. A child born to a teenage mother is 50 percent more likely to repeat a grade in school and is more likely to perform poorly on standardized tests and drop out before finishing high school." Detailing the financial costs, *thenationalcampaign.org* stated, ***"Teen childbearing in the United States cost taxpayers (federal, state, and local) at least $10.9 billion in 2008, according to an updated analysis by The National Campaign to Prevent Teen and Unplanned Pregnancy. Most of the costs of teen childbearing are associated with negative consequences for the children of teen mothers, including increased costs for health care, foster care, incarceration, and lost tax revenue."*** Although these statistics paint a bleak reality of teenage parenthood, the NIGGER subculture remains comfortably undeterred because of their Sugar Daddy.

(Did M.J Warn Baby Mamas?)

Although several reality TV shows have attempted to make single parenthood enviable, this manufactured reality is not actuality. Even the late king of pop Michael Jackson knew the strife of such a disadvantageous lifestyle. From the biggest selling album of all time *(Thriller)*, is a song titled *"Wanna Be Startin' Somethin,"* in which one particular verse holds an eternal truth. ***"If You Can't Feed Your Baby (Yeah, Yeah)---- Then Don't Have A Baby (Yeah, Yeah)---And Don't Think Maybe (Yeah, Yeah)---- If You Can't Feed Your Baby (Yeah, Yeah),---- You'll Be Always Tryin'----To Stop That Child From Cryin'----Hustlin', Stealin', Lyin',----Now Baby's Slowly Dyin'."*** In the HoG, the *Thriller* album is to music what the *Bible* is to books, yet, even while blasting this song, Baby Mamas conveniently ignore these particular lyrics. I've seen MJ do the impossible during his concerts (like make grown men cry like little girls), but even MJ couldn't prevent the increase of Baby Mamas.

(Baby Mama & Son Relationship)

The typical Baby Mama and son relationship resembles that of a girlfriend-boyfriend relationship. In fact, parenting is second to friendship. The son views the Baby Mama as his equal, whereas she perceives him as a little version of her ideal man. His overall persona reflects the style to which the Baby Mama is attracted. Often, Baby Mamas are barely twice their son's age, and as a result, both grow up together. The household lacks rules, authority figures, oversight, and consequences. Add the never-ending compromises and the result is a structure-less home running on autopilot. The molding of her lil' man starts at birth with the HoG name. Although breast milk is the best nourishment and most economically logical, it's too much of a chore for Baby Mamas to breastfeed. So, the baby is usually left crib-bound with a bottle of (WIC provided) milk propped against a pillow, while she *"does her."* As the infant grows, toddler pictures are taken of him dressed in attire exclusive to the NIGGER subculture (bandana, Fitted New ERA hat, Timberlands, or the latest HoG fashion). Additionally, his mannerisms, slang, and "swag" are taught and encouraged. Educational programs such as "Hooked on Phonics," which assist with development of reading skills, are shunned for name brand apparel or video games.

Georgia Mom Checked Son, Friends Out of School to Rob Bank, Say Police
cbsnews.com

[Author's Note: She was simply taking the boys on a field trip to learn the financial aspects of "keepin' it real."]

NYPD Puts Collar On Alleged Mother-Child Shoplifting Team
newyork.cbslocal.com

Woman Accused Of Taking 5 Children Shoplifting
tbo.com

Mother Takes Child To Drug Deal; Dealer Puts Gun To Child's Head
wreg.com

[Author's Note: I'm sure that mom's friend "Cordarel" the drug dealer, would never engage in such recklessness! This type of unprofessionalism is uncharacteristic of drug dealers.]

Cops: Mom gave her children beer and cocaine
ctpost.com

[Author's Note: Is this the new milk and cookies?]

Police Say Louisville man stomps mom over Kool-Aid
wdrb.com

[Author's Note: Luckily, it was only Kool-Aid and not "Lequan's" 40 ounce of Malt Liquor.]

(Free So & So tee shirts / Baby Mama's Delusion)

Another tradition in the HoG is the wearing of hats or tee shirts that read "*Free* (fill in HoG name)" after he is incarcerated. Only in the HoG, is it actually fashionable to wear paraphernalia that endorses the release of self-serving criminals who care nothing about the community. Basically, they're saying, "*Free Ray-Ray*" so that he can return to the HoG and continue the NIGGERtivity that sent him to the HNCU in the first place. Although Ray-Ray's crimes aren't an outcry or expression against systemic oppression, somehow, he's honored like a political prisoner. Meanwhile, the actual victim(s) of his crimes receive no support. On the flip side of the "*Free so & so*" spectacle are the "*In memory of*" tee shirts. These shirts usually have an angelic-like picture of the deceased who probably died from NIGGER on NIGGER ***(N/N)*** violence. Laughably, the eulogy typically reads as if this person was a Gandhi or Mother Theresa-like humanitarian, even though the lengthy rap sheet proves the opposite.

(He was a Good Kid)

Trivia Question: What's the predictable response from a Baby Mama after finding out that "Ray-Ray" was charged with a violent crime, or became a homey-cide victim? Of course, it's ***"Ray-Ray a good kid, he would never hurt nobody...He my angel."*** Yeah, he was good...good at being a NIGGER. Actually, I have no issue with Baby Mamas calling their children angels. However, she needs to be specific because there are two types of angels (good/bad). The Ray-Ray type of "angels" personifies the reality that "*one person's angel may be another person's demon.*" Adding insult to injury is that following every arrest or homey-cide, the public is always made to believe that Ray-Ray was in the process of turning around his life, and was a proud father who provided for his many kids by several Baby Mamas. The bar is set so low in the NIGGER subculture that doing the minimum of what society considers normal behavior deserves accolades. In spite of Ray-Ray's extensive rap sheet and notorious reputation, delusional Baby Mamas will unwaveringly promote that her son was really a good person, if only we had gotten to personally know him. Grandmomma Starkes always said, ***"A mother's milk nourishes heroes as well as villains."*** Apparently, Baby Mamas are in denial about their propensity to nourish the latter.

Family: Hadiya Pendleton slaying suspect 'good kid'
chicagotribune.com

[Author's Note: So, if this gang member is a "good kid," then what was the Honor student that he killed? Clearly, the NIGGER subculture has its own, warped definition of "good."]

Fayetteville man shot in the face; suspect is sought
wral.com

[Author's Note: A warrant was issued for "Boo-Boo" with charges ranging from attempted 1st degree murder, to assault and attempted robbery with a deadly weapon. Despite the pending charges, I'm sure that "Boo-Boo" was a sweetheart when he wasn't robbing and shooting people.]

(The True Perpetrators)

Baby Mamas perpetuate a notion that the violence occurring in the HoG is actually the result of a racist system. Allegedly, this so-called "racist system" villainizes HoG children while ignoring the true perpetrators. Ok, I'm going to give Baby Mamas the benefit of doubt; what if these ***N/N*** homey-cides are indeed caused by outside entities, but conveniently blamed on the guiltless, do-gooders in the NIGGER subculture? Perhaps the police should re-investigate the homey-cide case that Ray-Ray was charged with because here's what I heard really happened. According to an unnamed Baby Mama, there's an ongoing turf war between Amish and Buddhists teenagers. Both groups covertly canvas the HoG for potential converts. Whenever these two groups cross paths in the HoG, tensions intensify; the Amish teens feel that the Buddhists teens aren't *"keepin' it real."* The spiritually disciplined Buddhists usually ignore the malicious stares and threatening gang signs from the conservative Amish Mennonite teens. But one day, (the day that Ray-Ray was coincidentally arrested) tensions peaked. An Amish teen deliberately steered his horse and buggy towards the direction of a Buddhist who was meditating on a prayer rug. Sensing that this was an Amish drive by, the Buddhist quickly dove behind some unkempt brush (typical in the HoG) and soon after, a shootout ensued. Until this day, no one is certain which group fired shots first, but when the commotion settled, Jayquantavious (who, according to his Baby Mama, was on his way to feed the homeless after returning from Bible study) was shot multiple times. Of course, the gun found on Jayquantavious must've been planted by the "po-po" (police). Although Ray-Ray was quickly charged with Jayquantavious' homey-cide, the true culprits (Amish and

Buddhists) were never indicted. Thanks to the Baby Mama's version of events, I now see why the *"Free Ray-Ray"* shirts are worn... he was framed.

Mother, aunt of Georgia baby slaying suspect De'Marquise Elkins arrested for lying to police
nydailynews.com

[Article's Quote: "He was with us the whole time. There is no doubt in my mind that he is innocent," said Baby Mama about her son De'Marquise.]

(Businesses in the HoG)

When businesses abandon the HoG, racism is the default reason. HoG residents complain about the lack of thriving businesses or jobs within the HoG, but with so much endemic violence, normal business productivity simply cannot function or flourish. In any city, people know that they can patronize Chinatown or Little Italy without the fear of being robbed or assaulted by the natives. In the HoG, the opposite is true. Most legitimate businesses (particularly small businesses) can't afford the NIGflation (robberies, graffiti, loitering etc.), so when they flee, many HoGs become "food deserts." They are areas with high poverty rates and low access to healthy food. These food deserts are often forced to depend on small stores with limited food selections at substantially inflated prices. The remaining merchants inflate the prices knowing that they are the HoG's principle food source.

City Council Votes for Armed Guards to Patrol Newark Fast-Food Joints at Night
Restaurant owners balk at security costs; initiative would take effect next month unless Booker intervenes.
nbcnewyork.com

Gas Station Looted Amid Owner's Family Crisis
Owner Returned To India For Mother's Funeral
myfoxphilly.com

(The Mainstays)

Miraculously, certain businesses have managed to endure the NIGflation, and are now staples in the HoG's landscape. Businesses such as check cashing/payday loans, bodegas, barber shops/beauty salons, laundromats, liquor stores, fast food joints, Asian/Arab stores and gas stations (which double as convenience stores), continue to persevere. In any other neighborhood, these "convenience stores" would be considered "inconvenience stores." Yet, despite their bloated HoG prices, they remain "convenient" for flash flooding, loitering, and other NIGGERtivity. Sometimes, if a corner store wants to be favored, it may offer higher exchange rates for food stamps on the underground market. It's a fact that the HoG would almost be void of legitimate businesses if other minorities (Asians, Arabs, and Latinos) didn't brave the NIGGER element, especially the Asians. The Asian's admirable ability to survive long-term in the HoG isn't based on any ancient Chinese secret; instead, their longevity is centered around bulletproof Plexiglas (literally). NIGGERfiliacs argue, ***"The over-saturation of these types of establishments within the economically disadvantaged communities is simply a continuation of the exploitation of the poor."*** Really? The NIGGER subculture created the conditions for these types of bottom-feeding establishments to develop. Ironically, they will also cause many of them to fold.

Only in the HoG can these types of stores exist

(Merchant's Constant Threat)

As previously stated, Asians, Arabs, and Latino entrepreneurs are the few merchants courageous (or arguably desperate) enough to open and maintain businesses in the HoG; perhaps they interpret high risk as high reward. However, due to the persistent NIGGER threat, the merchant's "entrepreneurial spirit" puts them at risk of becoming literal "spirits." In other words, these merchants are endangering their lives (and family member's lives) in exchange for providing a service to the HoG. I recall reading about one such scenario of a HoG storeowner and his family being murdered during a robbery, even after complying with the Urban Terrorist's demands. Describing the incident, the police captain stated, ***"Right now it is believed that they did not resist at all, it's just an all-out assassination."*** Remember, NIGGERS have no honor, so armed robbery isn't limited to simply robbing the storefront business; they will also follow the business owner home to execute a home NIGvasion. This subculture will definitely bite the hand that feeds it.

Owner, family killed inside W. Phila grocery store
abclocal.go.com

Phenix City crime: Store owner followed home, robbed at gunpoint
ledger-enquirer.com

(Delivering in the HoG)

Any job that entails delivering to the HoG requires the delivery people to be mentally and physically prepared in a soldier-like manner. In the HoG, where conditions are hostile, and residents are stereotypically bad tippers, many businesses still offer delivery service as a convenience. For those who deliver for a living, danger is always one delivery away. Despite the fact that delivery people usually don't carry large sums of cash, NIGGERS are too stupid to know that whatever little money taken, won't even be nearly enough to post bail. Whether it's pizza delivery, Chinese delivery, newspaper delivery, USPS mail carrier, or even Santa, all are potential prey in the HoG. As a result, several municipalities are drafting legislation that allows delivery drivers to exercise their constitutional right ***"to bear arms"*** while on the job. Last year, on my block, a ***C/N*** scenario occurred; a pizza deliveryman fatally shot a NIGGER who called in a bogus order in attempt to rob him. Suffice it to say, more stories of delivery people defending themselves will become normal as people fight back.

Boston police say 'vicious thugs' killed pizza delivery man
cnn.com

Mailman Murdered Over Mail Box Key: Feds
nbcmiami.com

Chinese Food Delivery Man Killed in Brooklyn by Two Teenagers
yellowworld.org

Cops Warn Restaurants About Orders Called In From Cell Phones
chicago.cbslocal.com

(The Ice Cream Man)

Even the beloved ice cream man, who we fondly remember as children, isn't exempt from the effects of NIGGERtivity. While the ice cream truck's unique and familiar sound causes hysteria amongst the children (as they hustle parents for loose change), NIGGERS plot. Therefore, the ice cream man has to be extremely selective about the routes, and time of day it travels into the HoG. The killing and robbing of ice cream men personally resonates because I was briefly employed as a server on an ice cream truck as a teen. I was even promised my own truck after obtaining my driver's license. I enjoyed watching the children rush and huddle at our route stops. At each route, I'd often have kids spell words for a free treat. "Ogre" was my favorite word for kids to spell because it was misleadingly easy (This was pre-Shrek). I would say, ***"Anyone that can spell this four lettered word will get a freebie."*** Of course, all the kids would get excited because it was only a four-lettered word, and they figured that it was probably spelled the way it sounds. *"O-g-e-r"* was always the most obvious spelling followed by *"O-g-a-r,"* then *"O-g-u-r."* After repeated attempts, and sometimes outright yelling of random spellings (some spellings were all consonants lol), the kids would become upset, when no one won. After all, they had shouted every conceivable letter combination and still no prize. At that point, I'd always be accused of lying. They assumed that one of those numerous spellings had to be correct. When faced with that accusation, I would submit and give the correct spelling. Afterwards, they'd be dumbfounded by the simplicity of the word, but, without fail, a kid would usually say. ***"I said that, I said that! O-G-R-E right? I said that, I swear!"*** I really enjoyed those experiences, but not enough to risk my life to obtain them. I resigned after just one summer.

Ice cream truck driver shot and killed
daytondailynews.com

Ice cream truck driver robbed, shot in Blue Springs

examiner.net

[Author's Note: Fortunately, it was a BB gun. Unfortunately, these NIGGERS will upgrade weaponry for their next robbery.]

(Does Poverty Create HoGs?)

NIGGERfiliacs argue that outside of racism, poverty is the culprit for HoG conditions. I vehemently disagree. Poverty isn't an anomaly or new phenomenon; it's simply a lack of money or resources, and doesn't justify NIGGERtivity. Poverty isn't indicative of a person's worth, so being poor is no excuse to behave poorly. Poverty is used to justify NIGGERtivity because there's an absence of logical explanations for the mayhem caused by this minority within a minority. In this age of technology and information, any phrases used to justify NIGGERtivity or HoG conditions such as *"born in poverty, raised in poverty,"* etc. should be scoffed. Yes, I know that poverty disproportionally affects African-Americans, and intergenerational poverty can create social unrest, but poverty in America (intergenerational or not) isn't exclusive to African-Americans. Quite simply, African-Americans don't have a patent on poverty. In fact, a 2011 Congressional Research Service report stated, ***"In 2011, 27.6% of blacks (10.9 million) and 25.3% of Hispanics (13.2 million) had incomes below poverty, compared to 9.8% of non-Hispanic whites (19.2 million) and 12.3% of Asians (2.0 million). Although blacks represent only 12.8% of the total population, they make up 23.6% of the poor population; Hispanics, who represent 16.5% of the population, account for 28.6% of the poor."*** Further scrutiny of this study reveals that numerically there are more Euro-Americans *(19.2 million)* and Latino-Americans *(13.2 million)* with incomes below the poverty line than African-Americans *(10.9).* Surely, these numbers are racist.

(What's West Virginia's Secret?)

The state of West Virginia, which has a super majority 93% Euro-American population (3.5% African-American), is consistently one of the poorest states in the country, and is tops amongst states with the largest food stamp payouts. Yet, it somehow maintains a crime rate that's lower than the national average. In fact, West Virginia ranked first on *247wallst.com*'s

2012 list of *America's Most Miserable States*. It possessed the eighth lowest adult population with a high school diploma or higher, second lowest median household income in the country, and sixth-highest rate of poverty. Moreover, its health statistics were just as grim.

- The highest rate of people who have had heart attacks or suffered from coronary artery disease
- The third highest rates of cancer and diabetes
- The highest rate of smokers
- The second highest rate of obesity
- The lowest life expectancy

With the common perception that high poverty equals a high crime rate, West Virginia must be underreporting the homicides, rapes, and other mayhem that are surely occurring because of its dire poverty (and equally worst health). Overall, the entire redneck-infested Appalachian region is high in poverty and food stamp payouts. Nationally, there are nearly twice as many Euro-Americans living in poverty than African-Americans. So if poverty is the reason for the astronomical crime rates in HoGs, then those poverty-stricken rednecks should be committing violent crimes at almost twice the rate of their NIGGER counterparts. Again, I ask, why aren't these communities suffering from poverty-related violence stemming from disenfranchisement? Whenever I pose that question, the NIGGERfiliacs utilize their *"break glass in case of an emergency"* term when the other excuses fail, *"WHITE Privilege."*

(The Great Depression)

The Great Depression was the longest, most widespread, and deepest depression of the 20th century. It's commonly used as an example of how far the world's economy can decline. I often ask NIGGERfiliacs, *"Why didn't the Great Depression result in thousands of 'Black on Black' homicides?"* After all, this form of poverty was so extreme and wide spread that history actually labeled it as, *"The Great Depression."* Somehow, my great-grandparents' generation lived through the Great Depression and didn't commit violent crimes as a coping mechanism. Alternatively, neighbors became family, and the community persevered by supporting each other. The common-unity (community) was each other, which is a foreign concept in the self-centered NIGGER subculture.

(Re-Evaluating Poverty)

The NIGGER subculture's Sugar Daddy has been so dependable that their definition of poverty is warped. Their Sugar Daddy has shielded them from experiencing the unadulterated, global version of poverty (where a basic human necessity such as clean water isn't government provided) and instead, provided the Americanized variety (which they still complain). In other words, the American version of poor doesn't qualify as poor in a global conversation. Ever notice the amount of overweight people in the HoG? Any anorexic looking people (in the HoG) are typically that way because of other factors besides poverty. Historically, obesity or fatness was a sign of wealth (plentiful food), but funny how times have changed; fat people are now "poor" lol. Citizens in countries such as Haiti, Somalia, Iraq, and Afghanistan would laugh at the NIGGER subculture's shallow definition of poverty. In fact, the NIGGER subculture would lack the ability to cope as poor people in a third world country. The HoG isn't a dystopia because of poverty; the NIGGER subculture created those conditions.

(Lessons from Cairo & India)

Traveling to Cairo prior to the Arab Spring uprising, I got an up close and personal view of "real" poverty, void of substantial government assistance. It took little time to deduce that the oft complained about HoG poverty isn't equivalent. In Cairo, a widespread accepted means of generating income was begging. Families literally sent their children to beg tourists for money. At the time of my trip, the average Egyptian employee made approximately $55 a month, and since 1984, the basic monthly minimum wage was $6.35. Yet, the Egyptian's frustration at the socio-economic conditions didn't result in continued massive homicides of each other. Instead, unlike NIGGERS, they collectively channeled their grievances into a massive political uprising for change. India is another country where the poverty is pervasive. A Huffington Post article by Muneeza Naqvi titled,

"India's Stingy Poverty Definition Irks Critics" (5/27/11) stated, ***"India's Planning Commission, which helps sets economic policy, told the Supreme Court that the poverty line for the nation's cities was 578 rupees ($12.75) per person a month – or 2,312 rupees ($51.38)."*** The article continued, ***"The World Bank global poverty line, at $1.25 a day or about $38 per month, is three times higher than India's urban level. Local activists say a better name for India's standard would be "the starvation line."*** Under these conditions, the so-called *"keepin' it real," and "street smart"* NIGGER subculture would collapse within weeks. NIGGERfiliacs need to understand that societal circumstances don't create NIGGERS; NIGGERS choose to be such. America has the richest poor, including those in the HoG.

Poverty does not breed extremism in Pakistan, study finds
telegraph.co.uk

(The Formula)

After the Civil Rights Act was passed, many Euro-Americans began opting out of the new diversification plan, and White flight ensued. Racism is always blamed for WHITE flight, even though, Euro-Americans (specifically WHITES) escape from each other as well. WHITES isolate themselves from so-called White Trash, but oddly, BLACKS don't run as quickly from NIGGERS. Seemingly, African-Americans have a higher tolerance for NIGGERtivity than WHITES have for wiggertivity. Unlike BLACKS, WHITES will not allow their community to be held captive by a degenerate underclass. I used to think that racism was the primary force for WHITE flight, but I've come to the realization that they (WHITES) may be on to something. Due to the NIGGERS causing the African-American community to descend into a bottomless pit of dysfunction at seemingly free fall speed, I too, have become a separatist. I, like many others, want to live in a quality neighborhood around a specific type of people; so yes, I'm prejudiced. Euro-Americans who intentionally avoid NIGGERS are unfairly labeled as racist while BLACKS are called "sell-outs." Either way, I still have no issue with anyone bidding NIGGERS a fare-well. Actually, I endorse such measures.

(Trailer Park -vs- Projects)

Although Euro-Americans are 36.9% and African-Americans are 43.4% of my city's population, there is no predominately Euro-American public housing in my city. Apparently, Euro-Ams have abandoned public housing and settled in areas free of the NIGGER subculture. Decades ago, most of housing projects were predominately Euro-American, even the housing project where I was raised until African-Americans arrived. Somehow, even then, the poor Euro-Americans that lived amongst us managed to leave. Although officially poor, those Euro-Americans still found the resources to escape this change of landscape. Presently, it seems that even the economically lowest of Euro-Americans would rather live in trailer parks on the outskirts than cohabitate in public housing with the NIGGER subculture. BLACKS need to adopt that mindset.

(Religion)

Regardless of whichever religious cloak NIGGERS claim to subscribe, NIGGERS are frauds! Don't be fooled by their necklaces with a Jesus charm, or any other religion-related item; it's for attention, not religious piety. In other words, they only use religion to forward their agenda. Besides, NIGGERS don't pray, they prey. That's why the light at the end of the tunnel that most NIGGERS will likely see, won't be GOD, it will be a muzzle flash. They take religious traditions and pervert them. For instance, Passover a.k.a Easter is the remembrance of Jesus Christ's resurrection after his crucifixion. Understandably, most people celebrate in humility. However, in the pseudo-religious NIGGER subculture, Easter is another excuse to self-indulge. Easter means purchasing new name brand apparel, sneakers/shoes, etc. just to style and profile in the HoG. Moreover, it's a day where the entire HoG tries to out dress each other in the latest fashion apparel. Thanks to them, several urban clothing stores pop up solely to accommodate the Easter clothing sales. Simply put, the pseudo-religious NIGGER subculture isn't concerned about the purpose or details of Passover, or any other religious tradition, just the benefits. At the end of the day, retailers, not religion reap the benefits from them.

Police: robber uses Christian shirt as disguise

myfoxatlanta.com

Teen Stabbed At National Zoo During Black Easter Celebration
newsone.com

Macon Easter egg hunt canceled after past violence
ajc.com

Only on 12: Woman robbed in church lobby speaks out
wrdw.com

Robbers Loot House of God
nbcwashington.com

[Author's Note: It wasn't their church or God so they didn't care. Wait, either way, it still wouldn't have mattered.]

Chapter VI

NIGGERnomics

"Anyone who has ever struggled with poverty knows how extremely expensive it is to be poor." – James Baldwin

In life's natural order, each generation should advance further than the previous one. But in the NIGGER subculture, the practice of NIGGERnomics ensures generational stagnation. As long as their Sugar Daddy continues to provide the basics, NIGGERnomics will remain unconcerned with generational progress, national affairs, or state of the economy. In other words, their focus is never on the future, just the present, their present; not America's present. In the HoG, NIGGERnomics is practiced more than capitalism. NIGGERnomics is embraced because it remains undisturbed during major economic downturns, recessions, double-digit unemployment, hyperinflation, austerity measures, budget sequesters, record gas prices, outsourcing, etc. Also, 401k plans, mutual funds, IRAs, money market accounts, stocks, bonds, and hedge funds, are shunned in favor of NIGGERnomics. Knowledge of the three major credit bureaus is as foreign as knowledge of the three government branches (except Judicial). Moreover, NIGGERS are more likely to know ESPN scores than their credit scores. Actually, the only credit that truly concerns them is "street credit." If their Sugar Daddy ever reroutes the sugar, NIGGERnomics will suffer, and then, NIGGERgeddon will commence.

(NIGGERnomics Root)

The basis of NIGGERnomics is welfare, crime, child support, and menial jobs. NIGGERfiliacs routinely argue that gainful employment will offset NIGGERtivity. Admittedly, this theory sounds plausible, but NIGGERS deduce, ***"Why work forty hours a week when I can rob in a few minutes?"*** They simply want the fruit, not labor; income has to be quick and non-laborious, which is why welfare and other government handouts are so appealing. Welfare, Section 8, and other taxpayer-subsidized goodies provide shortcuts that aren't extended to actual taxpayers. Baby Mamas are even provided a plastic card that doesn't have a minimum payment date or interest rate like other plastic cards (Visa, AMEX, MasterCard, etc.). In fact, it doesn't require repayment at all. Yup, I'm talking about a HoG pillar... the infamous E.B.T card, which is another D.E.B.T for taxpayers.

Convicted Drug Dealer Tries To Use EBT Card To Post Bail
newsone.com

Woman is arrested after trying to buy Ipads using food stamp card
dailymail.co.uk

[Article's Quote: "When the transaction was denied, she allegedly assaulted a store clerk and fled from the store with the merchandise."]

Welfare cards used for cash withdrawals at strip clubs, porn shops and liquor stores
dailymail.co.uk

[Article's Quote: "The New York Post combed through more than 200 million Electronic Benefit Transfer records from January 2011 to July 2012 and concluded that untold amounts of taxpayer funding meant for food and diapers was likely paying for strippers, booze and adult videos."]

(The Welfare Plantation)

President Franklin D. Roosevelt issued an ominous warning regarding the impact of a welfare state: ***"The lessons of history, confirmed by evidence immediately before me show conclusively that continued dependence on relief induces a spiritual and moral disintegration fundamentally destructive to the national fiber. To dole out relief in this way is to administer a narcotic, a subtle destroyer of the human spirit. It is inimical to the dictates of sound policy. It is a violation of the traditions of America."*** This historic quote concisely describes the NIGGER-subculture, whose lifestyles are taxpayer-subsidized from cradle to grave. Over decades, their Sugar Daddy has been so reliable that they categorically reject self-sufficiency. Once the "wel-fare" benefits arrive, they happily say "fare-well" to any attempt of upward mobility. This is how Baby Mamas became the poster child for welfare dependency and abuse, despite being numerically outnumbered on the welfare dole by Euro-American women. Even the toughened measures of the Personal Responsibility and Work Opportunity Act (PRWORA) couldn't shake their desire to circumvent the system. In fact, their resolved was strengthened. Consequently, many states are suffering from dwindling tax revenues while this welfare lifer's club grows. It doesn't take a complicated mathematical equation to calculate that a financial collapse is eminent, if recipients continue to outnumber the producers, and revenue is removed faster than it's deposited.

(Fair is Fair)

I'm open-minded when it comes to the numerous systems of "social safety nets" for citizens; granted that these safety nets don't become hammocks. I don't mind helping the helpless, but I refuse to shift the shiftless. Frankly, I'm not going to pay for the rope that'll eventually be used to hang me. The misallocation of taxpayers' monies is a direct result of the government's unwillingness to separate those who can't support themselves from those who won't support themselves. I know, it's a damned if you do, damned if you don't scenario; but helping those who refuse to help themselves will never yield positive results. My ideology of *"all for one and one for all"* only extends to contributing citizens who've helped fund the system. Again, I don't downright object to programs that help those who have experienced trouble through no fault of their own; my objection is towards the swindlers who are essentially stealing the temporary assistance allocated for the needy. In the HoG, the majority of able bodied, healthy individuals facing dismal financial circumstances are in that position because of self-inflicted wounds (school dropout, multiple children, criminal record etc.). In these instances, taxpayers shouldn't fund their lifestyles or early retirements. Time after time, the numerous deductions on my paystubs make me cringe, but even still, I accept that taxes help maintain civilization. I pay child support because it *"makes sense to me,"* but paying to support lazy adults *"makes cents for them."* Sure, make use of government services when needed, but remember that the system is a temporary "hand up" not a permanent "hand out." Despite the fact that public assistance should be paid forward once stability is established, the NIGGER subculture generationally lives from womb-to-tomb on the taxpayer's dime without contribution.

(My Suggestions)

Society should re-create the stigma that used to be attached to receiving welfare. Perhaps this would eliminate the *"something for nothing"* entitlement mindset embodied by the NIGGER subculture. With them in mind, I've developed a short list of suggestions to be applied when public assistance is requested. My plan would have all able-bodied applicants sign a contract emphasizing self–sufficiency in a pre-determined amount of time. Additionally, the contract would be an agreement that applicants would not indulge in any self-defeating behavior that would further cost taxpayers. Furthermore, EBT cards would be replaced with the original, old school, tangible food stamps that recipients would have to physically tear from the food stamp booklets. Lastly, the booklet's serial numbers had better match the individual food stamps! Listed below are additional contractually binding requirements that would be reinforced by surprise inspections. The elderly and mentally/physically disabled citizens would be exempt from this application process, but still have first preference on available housing units.

1. For starters, a high school diploma, G.E.D, or trade should be obtained if the applicant doesn't have one.

2. Like most employees in the private sector, drug tests would be required for applicants and recipients. This keeps the recipients job ready, and ensures that benefits aren't used for illegal substances. Additionally, it's unfair for drug-tested taxpayers to pay for the welfare of "un-tested" beneficiaries.

3. As a precondition for receiving benefits, utilization of birth control (IUD, implant, tubes tied etc.) would be mandated. If a pregnancy occurs while receiving benefits, an automatic suspension of all welfare will result.

4. Comparable to military barracks, random home inspections will occur to ensure the upkeep of the taxpayer-subsidized property. Furniture, appliances, electronics, entertainment apparatuses, etc. should reflect one's income level. If the recipient can afford to purchase

high-end items, then taxpayer assistance is no longer needed. Moreover, if such pricey items are found on premises, they should be confiscated, inventoried, and returned once the recipient becomes self-sufficient.

5. If the applicant is unemployed, he/she will be required to perform community service as deemed necessary in his/her environment. The community service may include but isn't limited to, trash removal, volunteering at local schools, blood donation, curfew/truancy enforcement, painting/removing blight etc.

6. All applicants must be finger printed. Again, if taxpayers have to be fingerprinted for employment, so should those seeking taxpayers' assistance.

7. Food stamps are not accepted for any food outside of what is considered nutritionally necessary. Items such as, fast food, soda, candy, junk food, and other treats would have to be purchased with the applicant's earned money. This rule isn't telling people what to eat, but only limiting what can be eaten with other peoples' (taxpayers) money. Besides, having a "sweet tooth" is different from having hunger pains. In short, food stamps are for sustenance.

Replace the EBT card with the "original" food stamps

(The Rebuttal)

Of course, NIGGERfiliacs and the NIGGER subculture will insinuate that these proposals are a violation of rights or civil liberties, yet disregard the fact that all the mentioned requirements only apply to those who request taxpayers' assistance. These requirements would deter Quadruplerism since beggars can't be choosers. Presently, the current system is exploited by the NIGGER subculture because it rewards them for being NIGGERS. Welfare is not "free" money!

Black People Strongly Support Drug Tests For Welfare Recipients
newsone.com

(NIGGERfiliacs Rebuttal)

There are two talking points where the NIGGERfiliacs and I actually agree: (One) Not all poor people are uneducated or on welfare. (Two) There are financially secure people who are also cheats. Even though a poor person is (statistically) likely to be undereducated or uneducated, not all poor exploit the system; just as all corporations aren't corporate welfare cheats. The NIGGERfiliacs asked, ***"How can the so-called NIGGER subculture be singled out when the government spends BILLIONS on unnecessary wars, and overlook government fiscal waste?"*** Hey, I don't excuse wasteful government spending in any capacity; the welfare state is perpetuated on both Main and Wall Street. However, my ire is with the NIGGER subculture because I'm intimately familiar with their deliberate dependent mind state, and no one is holding them accountable. Besides, there are plenty of books, documentaries, websites, organizations, etc. that speak truth to power. But, on this controversial mission, I'm a lone shooter (for now).

Michigan Lottery winner Leroy Fick wins $2M and is still collecting food stamps?
examiner.com

[Author's Note: Leroy is Euro-American.]

Feds: Seattle welfare recipient lives in million dollar home
king5.com

[Author's Note: The couple allegedly lived in the home for 8 years while receiving more than $1,200 a month in public housing vouchers, federal and state disability, and food stamps.]

(Quadruplers)

Baby Mamas are called *"Quadruplers" because* their lifestyles are usually taxpayer-subsidized in at least four different ways. It's standard operating procedure for them to receive subsidized housing, daycare, food stamps, cash, medical etc. Quadruplers think that public assistance is their *40 acres and mule.* They view welfare and other social programs as reparations, or rights established with the Civil Rights Act. This disconnect from reality exists because their Sugar Daddy rewards them with a steady stream of benefits while the taxpayers do the heavy lifting. In essence, Sugar Daddy feeds them without teaching them how to feed themselves. As the saying goes, ***"If you give a man a fish, you will feed him for a day; if you teach him how to fish, you will feed him for a lifetime."*** On the other hand, that proverb reads differently when applied to NIGGERS. ***"If you give a NIGGER a fish, he'll ask for salt, pepper, and ketchup; if you teach a NIGGER to fish, he'll leisurely spend his days fishing instead of looking for a job."*** The taxpaying class is funding a dependent class of permanent harvesters on the welfare plantation who don't care about a negative perception... as long as the subsidized crops continue to grow.

Alabama nightclub raises eyebrows with 'Food Stamp Friday' party

dailycaller.com

(Independent Women???)

Generally, Quadrupler Baby Mamas lack work ethic and possess little interest in becoming self-sufficient. They firmly believe that child rearing is equivalent to gainful employment. In other words, they believe that they should be compensated for taking care of their own children. In the HoG, these delusional females are always claiming to be *"independent women or divas,"* and will publically strike the pose of self-sufficiency while disregarding the obvious truth. They'll loudly profess their independence (to any listening or non-listening ear), and their social network postings further corroborate the fallacy. Contrary to the Quadrupler's facade of independence, there's actually a small number of mother's stuck in the HoG (my mother used to be one) who are actually striving to be "independent women." However, these women aren't yelling and advertising their independence because it's hypocritical to claim independence while still receiving taxpayer provided benefits. Instead of yelling independence, these uncommon women are too busy working to become independent. Just because Baby Mamas claim independence, doesn't replace the statistical truth that they're extremely dependent. In fact, they're the First Ladies of the hand out society.

(Converting Quadruplers)

The Quadrupler's familiarity with living on the taxpayer's dime makes it almost impossible to convince them that welfare is temporary assistance. The length of time receiving government support usually trumps their actual work history (if such a history ever existed). For generations, they've successfully exploited the various "public" assistance programs without changing course, which is why their taxpayer-subsidized course is easy to chart. It starts with a "public" hospital birth. Next, is the "public" housing upbringing while attending a "public" school. At some point, they commit a crime, and then a "public" defender is appointed. Geesh, with so little return on the taxpaying public's money, the very least that NIGGERS can do is behave in "public." Adding insult to injury, they complain about benefits or services without acknowledging the pain of the taxpayers who are forced fund this Ponzi scheme. Dr. Adrian Rogers accurately observed, ***"What one person receives without working for, another person must work for without receiving. The government cannot give to anybody anything that the government does not first take from somebody else."*** Quadruplers should be forced to swim like the rest of us. Even though, changing the mindset of Quadruplers is like trying to empty an ocean with a spoon.

(Spending Habits)

Despite having food stamp budgets, NIGGERS inherently maintain caviar taste. Logically, their subculture should have an economic advantage because of the disposable income gained during its taxpayer-subsidized existence, yet, there will never be any wealthy NIGGERS! Why is this? Well, the simple answer is based on an eternal truth; a fool and his money eventually part. On the other hand, there are and will always be wealthy, self-made BLACK people such as *Madam C. J. Walker.* Wealth is tied to financial literacy, astuteness, perseverance, sacrifice, and delayed gratification; all of which, are Anti-NIGGER attributes. Their lack of fiscal discipline and responsibility will keep them dependent on Sugar Daddy and shackled in perpetual, inter-generational poverty (which they seem quite content). Yes, there are "hood rich" NIGGERS and they're always easily noticed because of their characteristically flossy ways. But, being "hood rich" only makes them the big fish in a little HoG pond, which is the only legacy that matters to them, not intergenerational wealth.

Madam C.J. Walker (December 23, 1867 – May 25, 1919), born Sarah Breedlove, was an African-American businesswoman, hair care entrepreneur, and philanthropist. She made her fortune by developing and marketing a hugely successful line of beauty and hair products for black women under the company she founded, Madam C.J. Walker Manufacturing Company. The Guinness Book of Records cites Walker as the first woman to become a millionaire by her own achievements.
*Source: Wikipedia

(Perpetrating a Fraud)

NIGGERS are infatuated with looking like they have money. To them, the appearance of having money is just as important as physical possession of it. In the HoG, everyone tries not to look poverty-stricken or poor to each other, but it's all a ploy. Moreover, it's indicative of their childish "look at me" syndrome. NIGGERS will perpetuate the "look at me" syndrome by doing extreme things such as: "Making it rain" (the act of throwing money in the air then watch it fall like rain) in clubs, purchasing over-priced rims (which further depreciates the car), buying flashy jewelry, and clothes with the designer's logo in plain view etc. Laughably, they believe that these trivial material possessions are actually assets that accumulate equity. I guess this is their method of portfolio diversification. The *"get rich or die tryin,"* mindset remains in effect, even though most *"die trying"* or incarcerated. Their impulsiveness combined with the desire for immediate gratification and HoG recognition, keeps them financially stagnant. The truth is that their inflated sense of self is a defense mechanism used to escape the ultimate reality of their dismal state.

Car rims so coveted, some people will kill for them
chron.com

(Athletes)

Outside of drug dealing and other criminal enterprises, rich Niggers or blacks (WNT) are primarily found in the entertainment field (Actors, Athletes, Rappers, Musicians, Boxers, etc.). As evidenced by the fact that African-American athletes (and their entourages) tend to get into more worldly trouble than their Euro-American counterparts, financial status doesn't mean immunity from Obsessive NIGGER Disorder (O.N.D). National Football League (NFL) All-Pro Jared Allen, (who is Euro-American) had wise advice for bling-hungry African-American draft picks entering the league during a lockout season. Speaking to *thevikingage.com* (5/6/11), Allen stated, ***"I think the bigger disappointment was to see the jewelry on these kids' arms and ears. Are you kidding me? You haven't played a down in the league yet and [there are] thousands and thousands of dollars on these kids arms and I'm like, "You guys understand you're getting drafted into a lockout where you don't know what rules you're playing under or how much money you possibly might get?"*** Predictably, NIGGERfiliacs interpreted his sage advice as racism, just as they did when the National Basketball Association (NBA) instituted a professional dress code. Despite the fact that approximately 8 out of 10 NBA players are African-American, the dress policy was denounced as racist because most of the banned items were predominately worn by African-American athletes, whose fashion was inspired by the HoG. Yup, billionaire owners telling their millionaire employees what to wear to the workplace is racist. Unsurprisingly, this "racism" hasn't deterred African-American youth from eagerly aspiring to make the NBA their preferred place of future employment.

Jared Allen Wishes Rookies Would Tone Down the Bling
thevikingage.com

NBA's New Dress Code Policy Sparks Furor
npr.org

(Knowledge of Money)

Would it be a contradiction if I acknowledged that NIGGERS are actually very expressive and conversant? Well, it's true... sort of. If asked about drugs, they'll effectively explain the different terminologies, detail the ways to cook, package, and flip them. If asked about guns, they'll give a thorough tutorial. If asked about gangsters/drug dealers, they'll give a detailed history lesson. If asked about women, they'll quickly tell you about "hoes and tricks." If asked about rap music or NBA basketball, they'll talk for hours. See, they are knowledgeable, as long as the topic is limited to entertainment and criminality. There's no need to even question them about the dollar bill they worship because they're content with believing that the government has a printing press that never runs out of ink. Additionally, asking about the institutions (Federal Reserve, World Bank, International Monetary Fund etc.) that print, control, regulate, and set interest rates, is equivalent to asking how many rocks are on the moon. Their willful and blissful ignorance of money (itself) is another reason why there will never be wealthy NIGGERS. All of America's wealth could be distributed equally amongst American citizens, and within months, NIGGERS would be insolvent. Soon after, another hand-out would be demanded, even though they couldn't account for their initial fiscal mismanagement. The book, Atlas Shrugged explains money in a way that's foreign to the NIGGER subculture. It reads, ***"Money will not purchase happiness for the man who has no concept of what he wants; money will not give him a code of values, if he's evaded the knowledge of what to value, and it will not provide him with a purpose, if he's evaded the choice of what to seek. Money will not buy intelligence for the fool, or admiration for the coward, or respect for the incompetent. The man who attempts to purchase the brains of his superiors to serve him, with his money replacing his judgment, ends up by becoming the victim of his inferiors. The men of intelligence desert him, but the cheats and the frauds come flocking to him, drawn by a law which he has not discovered: that no man may be smaller than his money."***

(Brand Loyalty)

NIGGERS are a consumer group that doesn't differentiate between wants and needs; they produce nothing yet consume everything, which is why companies exploit them. Every item worn in the NIGGER subculture has to have a designer's name or logo in plain sight to offset any impression of poverty. Even simple items like headscarves and socks are typically emblazed with fashionable logos as status symbols. They willingly indulge in corporate worship, and has pledged allegiance to certain name brands with no reciprocity. Think of many episodes of NIGGERgeddon that occurred at stores across America in attempt to get the latest Air Jordans. Think of the many senseless murders that occur for clothing, footwear, sunglasses, cell phones, etc. In fact, NIGGERS killed my cousin for his leather jacket during my youth. NIGGERgeddon and violent NIGGERtivity will transpire over trivial material trappings, especially items from long-term, HoG fashion fixtures. Companies such as Timberland, Ralph Lauren Polo, Gucci, New Era, etc. maintain their HOG residency because "Brand loyalty" is the only loyalty that NIGGERS truly know, unless the company is BLACK owned (remember FUBU).

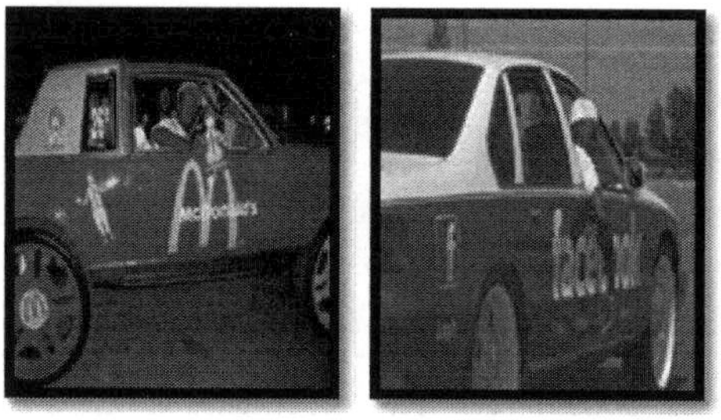

This foolishness is not endorsed by McDonald's "365 Black" campaign or Facebook

(Paying Retail)

Again, NIGGERS love to pay retail for name brand items because it validates them. Budget conscious people know to avoid paying retail, whereas the NIGGER subculture doesn't differentiate between the 'price versus worth' of an item. They don't know how foolish they sound when bragging about the hefty price paid for a recently purchased item, meanwhile living in the projects. The obvious truth is that they enjoy being non-compensated, human billboards advertising a financial falsehood. I wholeheartedly support any exploitation of people that exuberantly participate in their own exploitation. Should I be upset with Ralph Lauren for the following story?

(Polo Party)

A Quadrupler Baby Mama (living in the projects) hosted a "Polo Party" to celebrate her son's third birthday. The invitation mandated that attendees wear Ralph Lauren Polo clothing or entry would be denied. Additionally, it emphasized that children couldn't wear polo shirts made by any other comparable (cheaper) designers such as the U.S Polo Association (U.S.P.A). Apparently, the party was more about Ralph Lauren, and less about kids wanting to genuinely celebrate her son's birthday. Due to their misplaced priorities, Baby Mamas will spend thousands of dollars to ensure that their children have the latest name brand designer clothes and accessories, but won't invest that same money into academic endeavors. By making their name brand dress a principle part of themselves, they essentially are of no more value than their dress.

(Earning Money)

NIGGERS will complain about working for minimum wage, yet, won't hesitate to work for cents per hour at an HNCU. I guess that their preference for the cents per hour HNCU jobs over regular minimum waged jobs is because HNCU jobs come with street cred. After all, "Keepin' it real" is the only true currency in the HoG, and it's peddled like stock. This sentiment is especially true for JuviNIGGERS. The Center for Labor Market Studies at Northeastern University released its executive summary (10/09), which documented, ***"A disturbing number of the young men and women crowding America's jails are high school dropouts, suggesting that the destructive path to prison begins when these young adults leave school often before they officially drop out. This pipeline to prison is disproportionately filled by young Black men ages 16 to 24. On any given day, nearly 23 percent of all young Black men who have dropped out of high school are in jail, prison, or a juvenile institute. In other words, approximately 23 of every 100 young Black male dropouts are in jail compared to only 6 to 7 of every 100 Asian, Hispanic or White male dropouts."*** The odds of obtaining gainful employment are further diminished when the blatant tattoos, Ebonics, saggin' pants, entitlement attitude etc. are factored.

Study: Young Black & Hispanic men likely to end up jobless, imprisoned or dead
wwaytv3.com

(Alternative Income)

In 2008, while running for congress, Republican candidate Jack Davis proposed (to help offset high teenage African-American unemployment) that African-American teens be bused to rural farms where many farmers rely on migrant workers. Davis said, ***"We have a huge unemployment problem with black youth in our cities. Put them on buses, take them out there [to the farms] and pay them a decent wage; they will work."*** Naturally, this practical idea was shunned by the NIGGER subculture, and condemned as racism by NIGGERfiliacs. The NIGGERfiliacs suggested that this proposal invoked memories of a painful past and considered it insensitive. Yeah, it was insensitive to NIGGERnomics. This opportunity should've been embraced because it's honest work and builds character. At twelve, I had my first job as a dishwasher at a high-paced and demanding Japanese restaurant. I can still hear the manager telling me in broken English, *"We need more soup bowl, we need more soup bowl!"* (He always said it twice lol) Although I was paid "under the table" (not knowing exactly what that meant at the time), I developed work ethic and was elated about earning my own money. NIGGERfiliacs are disingenuous; they know that statistically, African-Americans teens are more probable (than any other group) to end up on a rural farm anyway (prison). Therefore, why not utilize this idea as a means of earning an income. I'm very familiar with the historic connection between African-Americans and plantations, but with menial graduation rates, limited social skills, and no marketable trade, these teens' job prospects are almost non-existent. The fact is that JuviNIGGERS aren't equipped for today's global economy; gone are the twentieth century factory jobs that supported non-skilled, lowly educated individuals whose only commodity was general labor. In this competitive, post-industrial age where diplomas no longer suffice, the JuviNIGGERtivity will increase.

Republican Says Blacks Should Be Bused To Farms To Pick Crops
newsone.com

(Limited NIGGER Reach)

One positive aspect of NIGGERnomics is that it limits their prospective employment fields. One is more likely to encounter a black (WNT) on the work front than a NIGGER. Outside of professional entertainment (including sports), NIGGERS will never attain any legal salaried profession where specialized education is a prerequisite; everything about their subculture is physical not cerebral. Consequently, one doesn't have to worry about NIGGER doctors, dentists, lawyers (except jailhouse lawyers), or scientists of any kind, etc. Their herdish, "monkey see-monkey do" mentality typically concentrates them into the same occupations (Drug Dealer, Rapper, Welfare Lifer, Exotic dancer, Athlete, etc.). They're not proprietors of constructive, positive ideas, which is why they don't run things... they "ruin" things.

(NIGGERS Own/Contribute Nothing)

Aside from the businesses and industries that exploit them, NIGGERS will never be of any value to society. Although some NIGGERS excel at athletics or entertainment, it doesn't compensate for the overall cost of NIGGERtivity. In the HoG, they characteristically don't own any businesses or homes; yet willingly die "representing" a terrain where they own nothing. Even the drug strip isn't legally theirs. Heck, I probably own more of their "turf" than they do lol. Unbelievably, their subculture excuses this extreme territorial tribalism as if it's some kind of Palestine/Israel scenario. As another testament to their sociopathic existence, these self-proclaimed soldiers are actually toy soldiers fighting a senseless material war (against each other) for street credibility. I just wish that their battles would occur in some remote desert far away from civilization.

<u>*Chapter VII*</u>

Historically NIGGER Correctional Universities (HNCUs)

"He, who opens a school door, closes a prison" – Victor Hugo

HNCUs are *"Historically NIGGER Correctional Universities that specialize in providing an alternate, specialized form of education to the NIGGER segment of African-Americans";* better known as prisons. Even though NIGGERS are generally economic liabilities, and as valuable as a penny with a hole in it, HNCUs have effectively converted them into major economic assets. The HNCU's unique method of recycling society's waste (NIGGERS) should make them the envy of environmentalists. Despite being a tiny fraction of the total national population, NIGGERS typically are the majority student body at many HNCU campuses across the country. NIGGERfiliacs routinely question how their (NIGGERS) overrepresentation at HNCUs is even possible since they're a minority. They rationalize that this disproportionate HNCU makeup must be the result of socio-economics, disenfranchisement, and racism. Of course, their conspiracy soup wouldn't be complete without that reliable ingredient of "racism." The true answer as to why NIGGERS are the HNCU poster-child isn't due to socioeconomics, disenfranchisement, racism, or even P.T.S.D (Post Traumatic Slavery Disorder); it's simply a result of O.N.D. (Obsessive NIGGER Disorder)

(blacks With NIGGER Tendencies Enrollees)

There are also many blacks (WNT) enrolled at HNCUS, and I have witnessed several of them return to society as changed men with no intent of re-enrolling, myself as an example. After being incarcerated, I went through a self-realization process. In full disclosure, my HNCU enrollment was brief, and short stints don't garner any "street cred." Even so, I ultimately used that negative experience to mentor others. In the NIGGER subculture, the length of any HNCU enrollment has to be substantial or it isn't considered "real time." The only consolation for not doing "real time" is if one repeatedly does short enrollments a.k.a "jailbird." Aside from that, NIGGERS will say, ***"you dint do no real time!"*** Even though the NIGGER subculture embraces HNCUs as a rite of passage, it literally took one minute (after the bars slammed behind me) to realize that HNCUs weren't for me. Subsequently, I enrolled into a traditional HBCU. And for the record, it wasn't socio-economics, disenfranchisement, racism, or P.T.S.D that landed me inside an HNCU; nope, it was a consequence of having NIGGER tendencies.

(X)

I often reference another black (WNT) named Malcolm Little, who also went through a transformative process while enrolled at an HNCU. History has documented his metamorphosis and eventual rejection of NIGGER tendencies. Following his HNCU graduation, the world was introduced to Malcolm X. Although Malcolm's celebrity was linked to his commitment to Black upliftment, he eventually abandoned his Black Nationalist viewpoint in favor of universal brotherhood. The well-travelled X eventually realized that no one wins the race of racism, and declared, ***"In the past, yes, I have made sweeping indictments of all white people. I will never be guilty of that again — as I know now that some white people are truly sincere, that some truly are capable of being brotherly toward a black man."*** Arguably, this spiritual evolution led to his murder (by NIGGERS). Today, the race-peddlers ensure that the gun-toting, radicalized, *"By any means necessary"* Malcolm X, is emphasized over the wiser, diversity-preaching Malcolm X.

(My Friend on Death Row)

One of my childhood friends is currently on death row for an armed-robbery turned homicide. Like many of us growing up in the HoG, he was a black (WNT). At one point, he ill-advisedly started hanging with NIGGERS, and that's when things from bad to worst. After being inducted into their guild, he learned how to generate income via armed-robbery. Prior to indulging in that form of NIGGERtivity, he was a gifted singer who won talent shows. Sadly, my friend's life, and that of many others, was permanently changed by his fateful decision to hang with shady individuals who made evil appear fair-seeming. During his final act of NIGGERtivity, which landed him on death row, one of the NIGGERS fatally shot the robbery victim after she resisted his demand for her items (gold earrings). Even though my friend didn't pull the trigger, he was charged as the shooter after his NIGGER cohorts strategically blamed him. I always tell blacks (WNT) to watch the company the keep. One can't lay with dogs and then complain about the fleas.

(HNCU -vs- College)

Today, there's an ongoing debate as to whether more African-American men are in HNCUs than college. This debate is usually based on flawed math because the number of HNCUs enrollees includes "all" adult African-American men seventeen years or older, whereas the college numbers reflects a narrower student-age (late teens – early twenties). Therefore, this discrepancy will always give the numerical advantage to HNCUs. However, even if the factors were equal, NIGGERS would still attend HNCUs at a higher rate than BLACKS attend traditional colleges because NIGGERS prefer "State pen" to "Penn State." Prison is a hallmark of street credibility, and "doing time" is stupidly worn as a badge of honor. Their delusional subculture believes that going to prison is equivalent to attending college, which is why I characterized prisons as HNCUs. To them, being willfully ignorant is parallel to being educated. In other words, ignorance is their preferred method of learning. Noteworthy is the fact that blacks (WNT) will attend traditional and non-traditional colleges (HNCUs).

(Prison Industrial Complex)

The cost of the NIGGER subculture to taxpayers and society is (in my estimation) incalculable; the cost-benefit analysis is extremely lopsided. From the birth of a NIGGER, to the death of a NIGGER, and the drama in between, taxpayers have paid on all levels. Including the pain and suffering inflicted on civilian families, and the massive amount of civilian lives lost or altered by NIGGERtivity. Yet, despite their cost to society with little noticeable return, they've been an invaluable and profitable resource to a few niche business and industries. Gun and bullet manufacturers, stuffed animals makers (which are placed at homicide and homey-cide scenes), tee-shirt makers, urban funeral parlors, etc. should all send NIGGERS a "Thank You" card. However, the biggest "Thank You" card should come from the leading profiteer of NIGGERtivity, the Prison Industry.

(The New Jim Crow?)

According to the Bureau of Justice, at the end 2010, there was an estimated 561,400 *"sentenced"* African-American men in federal and state HNCUs. Within the last decade (2000 to 2010), no other race crossed the half million "sentenced" enrollee benchmark; meanwhile, African-American men averaged 564,454 enrollees during that time. In her book titled, *"The New Jim Crow,"* Michelle Alexander, an Ohio State Law professor, placed the aforementioned statistics into perspective. She observed, ***"There are more African-Americans under correctional control today—in prison or jail, on probation or parole—than were enslaved in 1850, a decade before the Civil War began."*** Surely, her comparative analysis is stunning, but the reality is that those HNCU numbers overwhelmingly reflect the NIGGER subculture, and not BLACKS. Besides, the best method to substantially decrease those staggering numbers isn't by playing the "blame game," but by not committing crime in the first place. Evidently, such logic is easier said than done.

More Black Men in Prison Today Than Enslaved in 1850, Author and Professor Says
rollingout.com

(Bet on Black Skin)

From 1980 to the present, the U.S. prison population has ballooned from half a million to almost two and a half million. The U.S. is only five percent of the world's population, yet leads the world in prison population (25%). Unquestionably, the prison industry has tapped into a niche market of reNIGable (renewable) material that can be eternally exploited. According to the Justice Policy Institute, ***"From FY2005 to FY2009, state spending on corrections increased 25 percent nationally, more than any other expenditure. During these tough fiscal times, many states are starting to look toward alternatives to***

incarceration for improving public safety and reducing prison populations, but states still spend more than $53 billion per year on corrections." In other words, states are "looking" for alternatives but still actively investing in HNCUs. They're betting on NIGGERtivity. HNCUs will continue to thrive because they possess a fulltime, expendable, non-union workforce who are never late, and paid cents on the dollar. Moreover, sick/comp/vacation time and unemployment compensation are never a factor. Despite this exploitation, NIGGERS still enroll at record numbers, ensuring that HNCUs remain American staples.

Prospect.org (Education vs. Incarceration, Steven Hawkins, 12/6/10) documented, ***"As the prison population skyrocketed in the past three decades, researchers began to notice that high concentrations of inmates were coming from a few select neighborhoods- primarily poor communities of color- in major cities. These were dubbed "million-dollar blocks" to reflect that spending on incarceration was the predominant public-sector investment in these neighborhoods."*** Even though these "million-dollar blocks" are located within HoGs across America, they become worthless to the prison industry whenever gentrification occurs. The absence of NIGGERtivity means the absence of profit.

(HNCU Campus Life)

For many reasons, HNCU recidivism rates remain high. The most prominent reason is the benefits package included with their taxpayer-funded scholarship: free medical, vision, dental, housing, uniforms, attorneys, and (fill in the blank). Actually, HNCUs had Obamacare before Obamacare. Along with the meal plan (three squares a day), access to television, radio, and the chance to earn a degree/diploma, HNCUs are their natural preserve, sanctuary, and social club. Also, sex or sexual activity is easily obtained. Additionally, lifting weights, playing sports, or exercising in the yard allows them to form new alliances by joining one of the many HNCU fraternities (gangs). Often, blacks (WNT) enrollees will be promoted to minimum-security status, which allows them to perform supervised jobs (work-study) in the community such as highway cleaning. With all these scholarship-provided benefits, a study suggests that HNCUs actually extends the NIGGER life span. The same claim is also made about captive animals versus their wild counterparts. Regardless of reason for HNCU enrollment (even murder), the taxpayer-funded (full) scholarship provides them with basic needs that free citizens in third world countries (heck, in this country) would envy, especially the healthcare benefits.

Black men survive longer in prison than out: study
Black men are half as likely to die at any given time if they're in prison than if they aren't, suggests a new study of North Carolina inmates.
reuters.com

Shocking prison video results in indictment of 14

[Article's Quote: "The shocking video of Orleans Parish Prison inmates shooting drugs, drinking beer, and handling a loaded gun inside a jail cell has led to the indictment of 14 current and former inmates on contraband charges."]

(Jailhouse Lawyers)

Allow me to introduce an HNCU mainstay known as the Jailhouse Lawyer. The Jailhouse lawyer specializes in giving advice on all HNCU-related matters. Sometimes, a Jailhouse lawyer appears to be so knowledgeable that many (inmates, family, court-appointed lawyer etc.) become deluded into thinking that this person just needs another chance, or perhaps their criminal charge is indeed bogus. This pseudo-oracle purportedly knows the rights, laws, statutes, and everything else applicable to criminal cases or HNCU campus life. They'll also frivolously file grievances or lawsuits for any perceived violations of their entitlements. Oddly, with all their supposed experience, inside information, and knowledge, they somehow can't manage freedom. Once, I overheard a Jailhouse lawyer ebonically explain how the mandatory minimum sentencing guidelines (established with the federalized "War on Drugs" declaration) were racially biased. Ironically, this Jailhouse lawyer was incarcerated (again) for indulging in the same drug-dealing NIGGERtivity that he preached was sending disproportionate amounts of African-Americans to prison. Although, he was well versed regarding the mandatory minimum sentencing guidelines, crack versus cocaine sentencing disparity, three-strike rule, and the other techniques used to deter NIGGERtivity, he characteristically faulted the system for his incarceration and not himself. Admittedly, I felt no pity for his decision to play with fire (committing crimes) knowing the high probability of being burned (incarcerated). The so-called war on drugs, mandatory minimums, forcing inmates to pay for their stay, and other diversionary tactics won't reduce HNCU enrollment. NIGGERS simply don't fear HNCUs.

(General Math)

NIGGERS are prone to crime because it defines their culture. A *Bureau of Justice Statistics* bulletin (2/9/12) stated, ***"At year end 2010, black non-Hispanic males had an imprisonment rate (3,074 per 100,000 U.S. black male residents) that was nearly 7 times higher than white non-Hispanic males (459 per 100,000).*** Moreover, a *Bureau of Justice Statistics* press release (6/23/10) stated, ***"Black males, with an incarceration rate of 4,749 inmates per 100,000 U.S. residents, were incarcerated at a rate more than six times higher than white males (708 inmates per 100,000 U.S. residents) and 2.6 times higher than Hispanic males (1,822 inmates per 100,000 U.S. residents)."*** For clarity, the Bureau of Justice Statistics' definition of *"Imprisonment rate"* is the number of prisoners under state and federal jurisdiction sentenced to more than one (1) year per 100,000 U.S residents, while the *"Incarceration rate"* is the number of inmates held in custody of state or federal prisons or in local jails, per 100,000 U.S residents. As the saying goes, *"people lie, numbers don't."*

(JuviNIGGERS' Profitability)

Despite the fact that today, African-Americans (including NIGGERS) have attained unprecedented positions of power and influence, the NIGGER subculture still preaches that 'skin color' obstructs African-American success. In turn, JuviNIGGERS are encouraged to explore criminality as a method to attain success. These law-breaking endeavors lead directly to HNCUs. Following any HNCU enrollment, they again blame 'skin color,' and not their criminality. As the NIGGER subculture continues to eat our young, HNCUs continue to devour theirs. JuviNIGGERS are a godsend to the private prison industry because of their early entry, late release, age benefit. In other words, their early induction into the prison system usually extends into adulthood, guaranteeing the industry a handsome profit for years. A capitalist's dream investment is one that requires low investment with the potential of high return. Therefore, based on the likelihood that JuviNIGGERS will eventually graduate from probation officers to parole officers, investors prefer HNCUs to HBCUs. Frequently, JuviNIGGERS are from families that have at least one HNCU alumni, so having a probation/parole officer, or wearing a court ordered ankle monitor only furthers the family's legacy in the HoG.

Two of Saginaw triplets convicted of July 2010 robbery, could join third brother in prison

mlive.com

Teen parolee from Crosby charged with killing Atascocita father

khou.com

[Author's Note: Similar to sex offenders, violent HNCU parolees should be labeled upon release.]

(JuviNIGGERS Know the Laws)

Laws don't deter JuviNIGGERS because they know that the sentence structure for juvenile crimes is different from adult sentencing guidelines. Unless charged as adults, the most stringent sentence that teenagers typically receive is juvenile life (max out at age 21). Moreover, they know that it's unconstitutional to impose the death penalty on minors. While I understand the sentiment that it's barbaric to punish juvenile offenders like adults, JuviNIGGERS aren't normal teenagers! Regardless of age, the sentences for murder and other violent acts should pack as much power as possible! Ignore the NIGGERfiliacs' narrative of poverty and disenfranchisement as justifications for JuviNIGGERtivity. NIGGERfiliacs always prefer the sentencing for any JuviNIGGER crime (regardless of viciousness) to be limited to counseling, treatment, or community service. In today's apologetic society, it seems that the adage ***"If you can't do the time then don't do the crime"*** has lost its validity. The following headlines reflect the savagery of JuviNIGGERS. Quick question: Are these headlines reflective of 'good teens' simply doing 'bad things,' or are these actually 'bad kids'? I already know the NIGGERfiliacs' answer.

4 Teens Arrested in "Unprovoked" Murder of 18-year-old Bobby Tillman at GA House Party

wltx.com

[Author's Note: I wouldn't trade a strand of hair on Bobby Tillman's head for the lives of "Quantez" and the three other charged JuviNIGGERS.]

Teen charged in fatal Chester shooting spree
philly.com

[Author's Note: "Kanei" decided that the birthday party would be more entertaining if he shot it up. His version of fun left two dead and eight wounded.]

Teens killed man over 99-cent lighter, prosecutors say
chicagotribune.com

[Author's Note: Of course, a little bit of counseling will fix these boys.]

Bronx teen arrested in death of college student shot over 50 cents
nydailynews.com

[Author's Note: "Dasheem" and his JuviNIGGER crew were charged after a college student was killed while trying to protect his little brother from being robbed.]

Teens Charged in Madisonville Church Robbery
kbtx.com

[Author's Note: "Dakeldric" and two other JuviNIGGERS (including "DeBrandon") robbed the pastor and worshippers following a Thanksgiving service. Thanksgiving to these JuviNIGGERS meant "thanks" for "giving" up the valuables.]

Detroit teen could face life in prison for robbing nun at gunpoint
mlive.com

[Author's Note: "Raylon's" Mama said that he did it because he was hungry. Hey Baby Mama, instead of being a NIGGERfiliac, tell "Raylon," that he simply could've asked the nun for food. After all, what's the likelihood that a nun (who has dedicated her life to helping the needy) would shun a hungry kid?]

Police: Teen Picked Dying PNC Park Usher's Pockets, Stole His Car
clipsyndicate.com

[Author's Note: Victim was found face down in the street.]

Teen Charged with Murdering Blind Man
belair.patch.com

[Author's Note: JuviNIGGERtivity has no bounds.]

Police: Forestville teen confesses to stabbing 92-year-old neighbor to death
gazette.net

[Author's Note: Another urban terrorism case that likely won't result with the death penalty.]

Two teenagers accused of robbing paralyzed woman
oaklandpress.com

[Author's Note: "Dazmon" and "Keywania," pretended to be Good Samaritans.]

(Lesson Learned)

One day before entering my home, I approached a group of corner-clustering JuviNIGGERS and spontaneously asked, ***"Which day of the week is best for going to jail?"*** Amused by the awkwardness of the question, they chuckled aloud and simultaneously yelled different days. I could barely contain my laughter as each explained their answer like Jailhouse lawyers. According to the group's consensus, Friday is the worst day because it usually entails sitting in a cell over the entire weekend, while Monday was a coin toss, heavily dependent upon the local National Football League (NFL) team's weekly performance. In other words, if the presiding judge's favorite team lost on Sunday, trouble was in the forecast for Monday's defendants. It was surprising to learn that football scores, and not evidence, decided the case outcomes. Perhaps that's how O.J Simpson miraculously won his 1995 case lol. After briefly entertaining their Jailhouse lawyer-like answers, and seeing that they didn't realize it was a trick question, I candidly informed them that the best day to go to jail is... ***"No-day!"*** The reality of my answer hit them like a sniper's bullet. Satisfied with the outcome, I proceeded to walk away thinking that my message was successfully conveyed. Then suddenly, after a brief moment of silence, one yelled a rebuttal. ***"Yeah, Mr. Starkes, if a crime is done right, you don't have to worry about which day is best, or going to prison at all... for that matter!"*** This rebuttal generated hi-fives and choir-type verbal confirmations amongst them. I immediately made a 180 degree turn and began to re-engage. After verbally sparring for approximately thirty additional minutes, I realized that their unanimous endorsement of *"Do the crime correctly"* ideology, versus my *"No-day is the best day"* approach was a testament to the NIGGER subculture's power. Following this exchange, I entered my home, hugged my kids, and prayed that they'd never subscribe to the subculture's ideologies.

<u>*Chapter VIII*</u>

Mistaken Identity & NIGGER Tax

"Our names are labels, plainly printed on the bottled essence of our past behavior." - Logan Pearsall Smith

Dr. Martin Luther King eloquently emphasized the importance of judging a person by the content of their character, and not skin color. However, application of that wisdom is increasingly difficult when a consistent and statistical correlation exists between crime, dysfunction, and black skin color. To BLACKS, this parallel, which is actually fueled by the unrelenting wrongdoings of the NIGGER subculture, has become unshakable and essentially leads to continuous cases of mistaken identity and so-called *"BLACK tax."* BLACK tax, as defined by *urbandictionary.com*, is ***"the notion that Black people have to work and perform regular task twice as well as White people."*** I agree with the context of this definition, but I'd add that BLACKS have to work twice as hard because of NIGGERS. Furthermore, BLACKS are unfairly obligated to be spokespeople for the entire African-American community (including NIGGERS), and account for all pathologies. *"Black tax"* should rightfully be renamed *"NIGGER tax,"* since it's the result of NIGGERS' dysfunctional and criminal behavior affecting BLACKS. Due to our shared pigmentation, *"NIGGER tax"* also accurately describes the humiliating costs that BLACKS are forced to pay. Quite simply, this subculture has essentially made BLACK skin synonymous with dysfunction and crime. The superficial correlation between skin color and behavior has NIGatively affected BLACKS, and reinforces an overall sense of paranoia against African-Americans. Guardian Newspaper journalist Joseph Harker wrote, ***"To be a black professional means every day having to assume you may be judged according to some negative stereotype; how can you prove to the next person you meet that you're not some street thug; or that your background is so broken and scarred that you'll never conform to the workplace culture?"*** In other words, the

NIGGER subculture's persistent strengthening of undesirable stereotypes imbeds a NIGative image that detrimentally affects BLACKS. Even Anti-NIGGERS have to remain conscious about the NIGGER tax, but as James Baldwin said, ***"No people come into a possession of a culture without having paid a heavy price for it."*** I hate being the bearer of bad news, but this tax is a price that we'll continue to pay until a clear distinction is created and maintained between the two cultures.

Being black and middle class doesn't mean you face less prejudice

Social status and wealth don't protect people from prejudice, new research reveals. Race is not a subset of class

guardian.co.uk

Professor's Arrest Tests Beliefs on Racial Progress

nytimes.com

[Author's Note: A prominent BLACK Harvard University professor was arrested at his home for disorderly conduct after someone called 911 and stated that a "breaking and entering" was occurring at the professor's home.]

(The Talk)

There comes a time in every BLACK household when BLACK parents should have "the talk" with their children, especially the males. This "talk" isn't about sex (that's the other conversation lol) instead, it's a race-realist, survivalist conversation addressing the NIGGER-created quagmire facing BLACKS. "The talk" teaches life skills that prepare the BLACK child for the reality of paying the NIGGER-tax, which includes (but not limited to) profiling, proper reaction to any police encounter, and double diligence in all endeavors (academia, career, etc.). Double diligence is required because NIGGERS are doubly lazy. Moreover, "the talk" emphasizes that the only commonality between BLACKS and NIGGERS is melanin content, but society (via cultural conditioning) may still lump BLACKS with the worst elements of the African-American community. For what it's worth, NIGGERfiliac parents use "the talk" as a platform to blame racism, and not NIGGERS for the NIGGER tax.

Lawyers Seek Reprieve for Inmate Based on Race Testimony

texastribune.org

[Article's Quote: "When Duane Edward Buck was on trial for capital murder in Houston in 1997, Dr. Walter Quijano told jurors that Buck was more likely

to be violent in the future because he was black." No, Doc... Buck is more likely to be violent in the future because he's a NIGGER.]

(NIGGERS & NAZIS)

The complacency of BLACKS is another reason why NIGGERS have become the defacto face African-Americans. This hands-off approach has allowed NIGGERS to create a distorted and abstract image of African-Americans. Here's the truth: NIGGERS are to BLACKS, what NAZIS were to GERMANS. The NAZIS, like NIGGERS, were a small, parasitic group that committed mass atrocities after hijacking the image of their people. Eventually, the NAZIS brought GERMANY to the brink of destruction, just as NIGGERS are doing to the African-American community. Both subgroups (NIGGERS and NAZIS) were not and are not representatives of BLACKS or GERMANS. Although NAZISM was a gloomy chapter in the GERMAN peoples' history, GERMANS rebuilt their image after NAZISM imploded. In America, NIGGERS are a disgraceful chapter in BLACK history, and once NIGGERS are marginalized, BLACKS can rebuild.

(Acting BLACK)

Since NIGGERS consider self-improvement, expanding horizons and intelligence as *"acting White,"* this question begs to be asked... what is *"acting BLACK?"* Is committing crimes acting BLACK? Is having multiple Baby Mamas or Daddies acting BLACK? Is being permanent government dependents acting BLACK? Is behaving impulsively, irrationally and having a penchant for violence acting BLACK? Is contributing nothing to society, yet expecting everything acting BLACK? Is speaking an unintelligible, off shoot version of English acting BLACK? No, none of this is acting BLACK! On the contrary, it's acting like a NIGGER! These traditional NIGGER subculture's tenets are routinely misinterpreted as *"acting BLACK,"* when actually, *"acting BLACK'* is the opposite. Henceforth, just call it what it rightfully is...*"acting NIGGER-ish."*

Rock Hill teen says she was bullied on school bus, beat for 'acting too much like a white person'
thestate.com

(Wigger Days)

An African-American student filed a Class Action lawsuit against a Minnesota High School for allowing its Euro-American students to hold *"Wednesday Wigger Days"* during Homecoming Week. During these *"Wigger Days,"* Euro-American students would parody the NIGGER subculture (mislabeled as BLACK culture) by dressing, acting, and displaying NIGGER attributes. The lawsuit stated, ***"The students who participated in Wigger or Wangsta day wore clothes that, from their perspective, mimicked Black culture. These costumes included oversized sports jerseys, low-slung pants, baseball hats cocked to the side and 'doo rags' on their heads. Some of the students displayed gang signs."*** In my opinion, events such as these provide teachable moments for any BLACK that's offended whenever the NIGGER subculture is exposed. Firstly, this *"Wigger Day"* tradition is an accurate, satirical portrayal of the NIGGER subculture, so unless you're a NIGGERfiliac, stop defending NIGGERS. Secondly, an exacting judgment of the NIGGER subculture by another race isn't an indictment of all African-Americans; NIGGER culture is different from BLACK culture. Finally, witnessing Euro-Americans have fun by wearing oversized jerseys, saggin jeans, Timberland boots, with fitted baseball caps (pulled over doo-rags) isn't a traumatic, racist event. Since the delusional NIGGER subculture thinks that their talk, attitudes, behavior, and overall style are well regarded, why is it racism when they are parodied? Oh yeah, that's right, just like homicides, and the use of the word NIGGER, it's only acceptable when African-Americans are the source. Newsflash... any parody of NIGGERS isn't the exclusive right of African-Americans. Actually, I applaud the event, and ultimately hope that BLACK students across America join hands with their counterparts to spoof the NIGGER subculture. The Reverend Dr. Martin Luther King Jr. captured the essence of the NIGGER subculture when he stated, ***"Nothing in all the world is more dangerous than sincere ignorance and conscientious stupidity."*** Wigger Day is simply mimicking a subculture that embraces ***"sincere ignorance and conscientious stupidity."***

Black Student Sues White School Over Racist "Wigger Day"
newsone.com

(Fake it 'til They Make It)

As sociopaths, NIGGERS will manipulate others to achieve desired goals or outcomes. Although they typically lack etiquette in all public and private places, there is one particular place where they inherently know that being a NIGGER is disadvantageous ...criminal court. The courtroom is one of the few places where they try to conceal their NIGGER identity and portray themselves as misunderstood, victimized BLACKS to garner sympathy. It's hilarious to observe a NIGGER defendant who rebuked education on every level suddenly scrap together his/her best Ebonics to mislead the judge or jury. From my vantage point, their attempt to misrepresent themselves as misconstrued BLACKS is as obvious as an analog television being advertised as high definition. Whenever NIGGERS utilize this ploy, BLACKS should press charges for attempted identity theft lol. Grandmomma Starkes advised, ***"A fool will expose himself when trying to emulate a wise person, but a wise person can easily play the fool."*** With that said, it's difficult for NIGGERS to pretend to be upstanding BLACKS, but BLACKS can effortlessly portray NIGGERS. After all, it takes nothing to be nothing. Despite their (NIGGERS) fraudulent misrepresentations, as long as *"I'm a victimized African-American"* is the defense, NIGGERfiliacs always excuse the NIGGERtivity.

(NIGGERS Misidentify BLACKS)

Human beings naturally have allegiances and loyalties. But ultimately, paths are decided individually. My path is incontestably a non-NIGGER path, yet, in spite of this affirmation, the NIGGER subculture still presumes FIVE myths about all African-Americans:

1. Our shared skin color naturally makes us allies or "brothers."

2. All African-Americans are NIGGERfiliacs.

3. All African-Americans are inherently NIGGERS, and our inner-NIGGER can be accessed with some "keepin' it real" dialogue. *[Author's Note: If a BLACK person isn't responsive or doesn't speak, dress, or subscribe to the NIGGER subculture, then they're labeled a sell-out, non-street, WHITE wannabe, etc.]*

4. All African-Americans speak Ebonics as if it's our native tongue.

5. Every African-American person that successfully escaped the HoG is supposed to return and help those who don't want to help themselves.

(Mistaken Identity Cases)

Due to the extremely lopsided levels of violent crime committed by the NIGGER subculture, xeNIGphobia is prevalent. They've fashioned themselves into the perfect "boogey man" in which all malevolence can be scapegoated. Furthermore, their criminal propensities have created an environment where a simple insinuation or allegation that it was a *"black"* person establishes instant credibility without reservation. During those "All points bulletins" (APB) or "Be on the Lookout" (BOLO) scenarios, vigilance is heightened, and the Department of Homeland Security may even increase the national threat level to catch the "black person." In fact, these Euro-American women, *Ashley Todd, Bonnie Sweeten*, and *Susan Smith* have all summoned the NIGGER boogeyman to serve as distractions. Even though their stories were fraudulent, unrelenting NIGGERtivity ensures that all *"black man"* allegations maintain equity.

Kidnap hoax case stereotypes fictional black male villain
thegrio.com

The white robber who carried out six raids disguised as a black man (and very nearly got away with it)
dailymail.co.uk

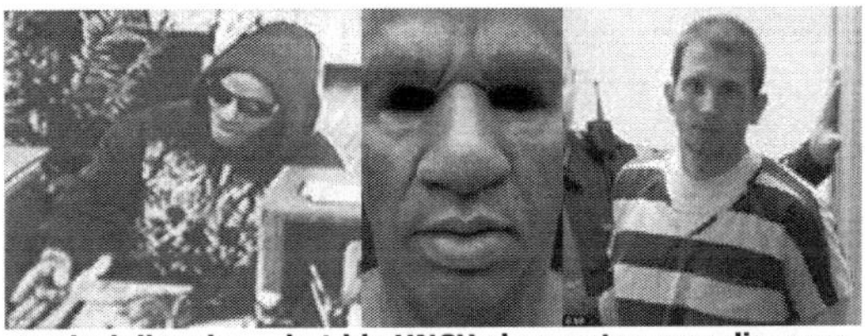

Logical disguise... but his HNCU classmates may disagree

(Profiling)

Profiling, in its many forms, is another extension of the NIGGER-tax that BLACKS disproportionately pay. But, instead of blaming the NIGGER subculture for creating the need for profiling, racism is instinctively charged. Racial profiling is actually criminal profiling; and since NIGGERS commit disproportionate amounts of crime, BLACKS will likely be impacted by profiling. We all profile, it would be asinine not to do so. Here's a hypothetical question: If a minority-owned airline company, which only made up thirteen percent of the industry, but accounted for more than half of the industry's total plane crashes, was scrutinized by the Federal Aviation Administration (FAA), and the minority-owned airline screamed racism, would the racism claim be legitimate? Of course not! In fact, this warranted scrutiny would be supported by the public because of the company's statistically hazardous history, just as scrutiny is warranted for the NIGGERS' statistically hazardous history. Whether it's driving, shopping, renting, dining, or hailing a cab, the NIGGER subculture has generated an existence for all African-Americans (especially men) where virtual "potential criminal" signs hover over our heads, and profiling is a consequence.

(DWB)

Driving While Black (D.W.B) is a scenario where BLACKS probably pay the highest NIGGER tax. The criminalization of BLACK drivers is the result of the police habitually casting wide nets (in the form of pretext stops) to catch a few fish. A *root.com* article titled, *"Minorities More Likely to Get Tickets, Have Vehicles Searched" (Jenée Desmond-Harris 7/15/11)* analyzed minority traffic stops utilizing data from a 2010 Illinois Department of Transportation study. It stated, ***"After a traffic stop, minority drivers are more likely to receive traffic tickets and have their vehicles searched by police."*** It added, ***"While less than 1 percent of all stops involved consent searches, the study showed that minority drivers were nearly twice as likely to undergo such searches. Despite the fact that minority motorists' vehicles were searched more frequently, police turned up contraband more frequently while searching white motorists' vehicles, according to the data."*** Although this study concluded that Euro-Americans more often possessed contraband, noticeably, WHITES rarely pay a White Trash-tax.

Driving While Black: Racial Profiling On Our Nation's Highways
aclu.org

(Number 28)

Warrick Dunn, a humanitarian and former National Football League (NFL) All-Pro running back, was a victim of mistaken identity. He paid the NIGGER-tax via a DWB encounter. During a traffic stop, Dunn said that four Euro-American officers targeted him with several personal questions, and stated that he had the ***"characteristics of people transporting drugs and guns."*** In other words, the police implied that he had the ***"characteristics"*** of a NIGGER. Despite Dunn's philanthropic efforts such as the establishment of the Warrick Dunn Foundation, and Homes for the Holidays program, which helps struggling single parents purchase homes, he didn't escape the NIGGER tax. Despite receipt of the Giant Steps Award in civic leadership from former President Bill Clinton for the aforementioned program, he didn't escape the NIGGER tax. In spite of petitioning all NFL players to donate at least five thousand dollars towards the Hurricane Katrina effort (which ultimately received over $5 million in contributions), he didn't escape the NIGGER-tax. Even though he received the Walter Payton Man of the Year Award in 2005 (which is the only NFL award that recognizes a player for his community service as well as for his excellence on the field), he didn't escape the NIGGER-tax. Although he received the Athletes in Action/Bart Starr Award, which is annually given to an NFL player who best exemplifies outstanding character and leadership in the home, on the field, and in the community, he didn't escape the NIGGER-tax. Ironically, Dunn's mother was a police officer who was killed in action by NIGGERS; yet, her peers assumed her son might be one. Unfortunately, possessing a charitable, philanthropic resume, and losing his crime-fighting mother to NIGGERtivity, still didn't shield him from the NIGGER-tax or mistaken identity.

NFL Legend Told He Looks Like A Drug-Dealer During Traffic Stop

newsone.com

Dunn receiving the Walter Payton award

(Stop and Frisk)

One spring day, my co-worker decided to walk to the corner store (bodega) for lunch. As he crossed the street, police officers unexpectedly jumped from their cruiser and frisked him. Before releasing him, they explained why it occurred. As the scenario unfolded, I watched with full understanding that this was another form of the NIGGER-tax, which is especially prevalent in any high crime, NIGfested area. However, my co-worker, a recent college graduate, interpreted this scenario differently; to him, it was blatant racism. At that moment, I immediately realized the public relations dilemma that "Stop and Frisk" posed, even though the cops were patrolling a "hot spot." Wikipedia explains Stop and Frisk as, ***"a law enforcement officer may briefly detain a person upon reasonable suspicion of involvement in a crime but short of probable cause to arrest."*** Despite being demonized, the Stop and Frisk policy has been credited with turning around New York City's crime-ridden reputation, making it one of the safest big cities in America. In fact, Mayor Bloomberg confidently defended New York City's Stop and Frisk program to a predominately African-American church congregation in Brooklyn. He explained, ***"Police officers make stops in Brownsville and East New York not because of race- it is because of crime."*** The disproportionate usage of Stop and Frisk in African-American neighborhoods is simply the police fishing wherever the fish swim, and NIGGER fish primarily swim in African-American ponds. If Robocop patrolled NYC, and the violent crime statistics were uploaded to his hard drive, he'd automatically spend his time profiling in HoGs because of their high crime probability. I can picture the HoG natives yelling, ***"Robocop is racist!"***

New Orleans police commander reassigned after alleged instructions to target young black men
nola.com

[Author's Note: The Af-Am community wants to stop the violence but doesn't want the police to stop the perpetrators.]

(Curfews)

In attempt to prevent or quell JuviNIGGERtivity, cities across America have implemented or strictly enforced curfews, which some contend are authoritarian, unconstitutional, knee-jerk reactions. Even more alarming is that pervasive NIGGERtivity has forced several cities to declare State of Emergencies. Essentially, State of Emergencies are desperate measures utilized when curfews and other strategies fail; it gives police expanded powers, and enacts a quasi-police state. These curfews and State of Emergencies are nothing less than the NIGGER-tax being forced upon law-abiding citizens.

Despite curfew, Chester records 5th killing this month
philly.com

[Author's Note: Chester has a 74.7% African-American population.]

Chester placed under a state of emergency
delcotimes.com

[Author's Note: Violent NIGGERtivity caused Chester to implement plan "B."]

Week of shootings led to Darby state of emergency
philly.com

[Author's Note: Darby has a 78.9% African-American population.]

(The Cost of Safety)

Following another Flashflood in Cleveland Heights, Ohio, columnist Michael O' Malley painted an accurate description of the quandary faced by many cities. He wrote, ***"This city, known for its liberalism, tolerance and racial diversity, finds itself in the thick of a social dilemma: How do you crack down on trouble-making groups of teenagers—mostly black—without violating civil rights or appearing to be racist?"*** As far as safety, cities should do what's best for their citizens; if a few eggs have to be cracked to make omelets, then so be it. Of course, if Euro-Americans are the ones cracking down on the NIGGER subculture, it'll automatically be interpreted as racism. But honestly, African-Americans aren't doing an efficient job of cracking, and most politicians would rather do what's popular instead of what's right. During a curfew announcement conference, Philadelphia Mayor Nutter voiced his discontentment with the Flashflooders, and acknowledged the reality of the NIGGER tax. He stated, ***"I apologize to the law-abiding citizens and teens. I am forced by the stupid, dumb, ignorant actions of a few to take actions tomorrow that will affect many. I don't want people to think we have thousands and thousands of bad young people running around ... But a few, less than 1 percent, are really bad ones. Unfortunately, they engage in violent behavior."*** Perhaps this ***"1 percent"*** that was referenced by Mayor Nutter should be the focus of the next Occupy movement. If that were to happen, I'd enthusiastically join.

Cleveland Heights' teen curfew brings questions in regard to legality, and whether it targets minorities
cleveland.com

Philadelphia mayor talks tough to black teenagers after 'flash mobs'
washingtontimes.com

Baltimore Opens City Curfew Center
www.baltimore.cbslocal.com

(Profiling NIGGERS)

Many businesses, such as nightclubs, bars, after-hour spots, etc. have discovered that the best way to avoid NIGflation is by preventing African-American patronage. Nevertheless, that endeavor can be tricky since federal law prohibits discrimination based on race. Therefore, businesses circumvent the law by "deterring" instead of "preventing" African-American patronage. I've witnessed clubs/restaurants/sports bars that were once *"come as you are"* relaxed environments, suddenly transform into *"don't come as you are."* Whenever this type of change occurs, African-Americans are quick to cite "racism," but I know differently, NIGGERtivity is usually the reason. Places that are untouched by NIGGERtivity have zero NIGflation, so their *"come as you are"* atmosphere remains intact. On the other hand, places touched by NIGGERtivity use multiple methods to reduce future NIGflation, including *"don't come as you are"* NIGGER-deterring dress codes, and non-catering music. These unsophisticated measures are only two of many used to discourage NIGfestation while avoiding lawsuits. Ironically, BLACK establishments utilize similar, preventive measures against NIGGER patronage, yet, appear puzzled when Euro-Americans establishments do the same.

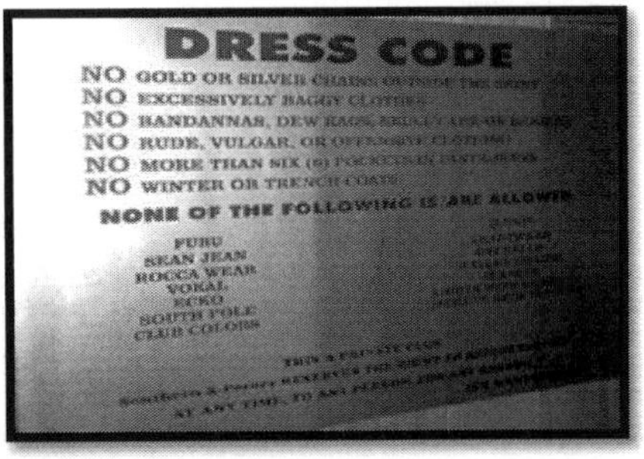

Deterring NIGGER clothing, NIGGER accessories, and NIGGER behavior ultimately means "No NIGGERS"!

(Catching Cabs)

We all know the history between African-American men and cabs, especially at night; again, this NIGGER-tax is due to the NIGGER subculture. Although cabbie homicides are senseless murders with little financial gain, robbing cabbies remains a favorite NIGGER pastime. Cabbies know that NIGGER money equals blood money. NIGGERS' reputation is so vicious that even in these tough economic times, some cabbies would rather err on the side of caution than pick up African-Americans. Even with increased safety measures such as installing bullet-resistant partitions, NIGGERtivity hasn't been deterred. So, to counter the unending NIGGERtivity, funerals, and hospital visits, the leader of the New York City cabbies union proposed a radical remedy. He openly urged his constituents to racially profile when deciding on a fare. He stated, ***"I don't care about racial profiling. You know, sometimes it is good we are racially profiled, because the God's honest truth is that 99 percent of the people that are robbing, stealing, killing these drivers are blacks and Hispanics."*** Of course, most cabbies were already profiling before he publicized his feelings, but holding a press conference symbolized the growing angst towards the NIGGER subculture. Sadly, even non-threatening BLACKS such as "Miles" from Sesame Street will suffer from mistaken identity by cabbies.

Well, maybe not... if he's accompanied by his diverse Muppet co-workers.

Having braids may get him profiled, so he should carry this pic showing he's no JuviNIGGER

Taxi big: "fair to profile
***Select riders by race:*" union boss**
nypost.com

United Cab driver slain after accepting fare that another shunned, police testify
nola.com

[Author's Note: "Quintina" and two JuviNIGGERS murdered the cabbie who didn't profile.]

4 teens charged with murder after cab driver found shot, killed
wistv.com

[Author's Note: "Demondros" and "Demandre" were two of the four implicated.]

3 charged with murder after another taxi driver found dead in Orlando
baynews9.com

(African Immigrants)

Why do (Black) African immigrants often maintain a distinction between themselves and native African-Americans? Surely, there are many answers; but the one that jumps at me is that they (unlike the native African-Americans) seem to recognize the (NiGative) stigma attached to African-Americans. Therefore, many distance themselves from the native African-Americans and strive to raise Anti-NIGGER children. Educator Edward Hayes articulated the educational prowess of many African immigrants, ***"According to U.S. Census Bureau data, in an analysis performed by the Journal of Blacks in Higher Education, African immigrants here were more likely to be college educated***

than any other immigrant group. Not only that, but African immigrants are also more highly educated than any other native-born ethnic group including white Americans. (Gasp) The 48.9% of all African immigrants that have earned a college degree is slightly higher than the percentage of degreed Asian immigrants, twice the rate of native-born whites, and four times the rate of native-born African-Americans." While the NIGGER subculture cites institutional racism for lack of progress, somehow these African immigrants have taken advantage of the plethora of opportunities unique to America. Understandably, in order to lessen their chances of paying the NIGGER-tax or mistaken identity, immigrants frequently remain detached and self-segregated from the native African-American community. In fact, many Nigerians use the word *"akata,"* to describe African-Americans. *"Akata"* translates as *"wild animal"* or *"ghetto*." I applaud the African immigrants for not succumbing to tenets of the NIGGER subculture. Even still, NIGGERS have so deeply criminalized black skin that no Black immigrant will ever be fully exempt from the NIGGER-tax or mistaken identity.

African immigrants out-graduate American Caucasians and Asians
examiner.com

(NIGGER Names)

Although I was a young father with no assets, a limited worldview, and lived in the HoG, I still wanted to give my firstborn something of value; a purposeful name that emphasized positivity and futuristic hope. Of course, having a positive name doesn't automatically guarantee success. Clearly, parents will ultimately name their children whatever they desire; but I believe that a good name is a good start. Of course, a "good name" is relative, as evidenced by a couple that named their children *"Adolf Hitler,"* *"Aryan Nation,"* and *"Hinler"* respectively. Perhaps, in their environment, these are "good names" just as *"Darealyst"* (pronounced "Da-realist") or *"Quantavious"* are "good names" in the HoG. Just sayin'.

Parents who named children 'Adolf Hitler' and 'Aryan Nation' will not receive custody of newborn son Hons
dailymail.co.uk

(Name Association)

Despite our best parental efforts, it's impossible to fully shield our children from life's many challenges. Yet, in the HoG, Baby Mamas actually create the obstacles, and one of which is giving children HoG names. Laughably, many of the names sound like chemical compounds found on pharmaceutical labels. Perhaps some of those HoG names are actually misspellings of the original intent since spelling isn't the NIGGER subculture's strongpoint. Or, maybe these names are simply the result of children naming children. Regardless, society is well aware of the name pattern associated with this dysfunctional and criminally prone subculture. These distinctive names advertise that the mother is probably a young, poor, uneducated, and single Baby Mama from the HoG who also may have a HoG name. Although these scribble-scrabbled, HoG rooted names are unique to the NIGGER subculture, they (NIGGERS) still don't understand why they're stereotyped, and will characteristically blame racism. Summarizing a study, *nationalpost.com* published an article (1/4/12) by Misty Harris titled, *"Bad baby name could leave your child sadder, dumber: study."* The study advised, ***"A poorly chosen baby name can lead to a lifetime of neglect, reduced relationship opportunities, lower self-esteem, a higher likelihood of smoking and diminished education prospects."*** Furthermore, ***"[U]nfortunate first names evoke negative reactions from strangers, which in turn influence life outcomes for the worst."*** Arguably, the only time this logic isn't applicable is when it's professional athletes, entertainers or their kids. Apparently, their exploitable talent makes them exempt from the societal standards that govern the rest of us.

Woman Named Fellony Arrested On Felony Battery Charge Following Bloody Indiana Bar Attack

thesmokinggun.com

[Author's Note: What were the odds that this would happen to poor Fellony?]

(Listen!!!)

The ultimate reality is that name association is a fact of life, and HoG names are definitely an indictment. Perhaps if HoG names were overrepresented amongst professional occupations instead of HNCU databases, they wouldn't be such a curse. Whenever a potential employer sees a HoG name on a resume or application, HoG pathologies are associated with the applicant. Moreover, whenever the media release the name of a perpetrator/suspect without identifying race, a HoG name tells the rest. To be fair, maybe there's a "Quantavious" studiously preparing for his bar exam at a prestigious Ivy-league university. Realistically, Quantavious is probably preparing for rec time at an HNCU, or "keepin it real" in the HoG. Like it or not, people are superficially judged and evaluated by their name/appearance; this is especially true for NIGGERS.

Escort ad bought by suspected thief who used funds from mall heist, police say
wptv.com

[Pop Quiz: "Shantwanice" and "Arshantayvia" were arrested for this crime. What is their ethnicity?]

(What about "Barack?")

I've heard the argument that President Barack Hussein Obama is an example of a name having no bearing on achievement. NIGGERfiliacs are quick to reference the name *"Barack"* as an example of a non-traditional name achieving mainstream success, however, Barack isn't a HoG name. In fact, ***Barack*** is the Anglicized version of Baraka, which means *'blessing'* in Kiswahili (aka Swahili), a language spoken by his Kenyan father. Some may even assume that I'm being hypocritical because my name is *Taleeb*. However, **Taleeb** is derived from the Arabic word *"Talib,"* which means *"student or knowledge seeker."* With that said, I challenge NIGGERfiliacs to explain the name *"Shitavious"* (from this first headline), and any other HoG name that's emphasized in quotations throughout this book.

15-year-old charged with three counts of first degree murder in Rutherford death
herald-review.com

[Author's Note: I "shit" you not..."Shitavious" was fifteen at the time of this horrendous crime, so the media shielded his identity. Even still, with that name, his cultural identity is obvious.]

Teen charged in robbery at Rock Hill barber shop
onlyinrockhill.com

[Author's Note: "Johnquavious" and his homey robbed the barbershop after receiving haircuts.]

Arrest made in murder

natchezdemocrat.com

[Author's Note: "Davarious" was arrested for the homicide that occurred on MLK street.]

Cops: Teens Beat Man Over $2 Beer

wcti12.com

[Author's Note: "Trekwan," "Xaviera" and 4 others were charged.]

Man Arrested After Blind Singer Robbed At T Stop

thebostonchannel.com

[Author's Note: "Ledonte" literally robbed the man blind."]

Teens Charged in Mob Attacks

nbcchicago.com

[Author's Note: Shockingly, "Dvonte, Trovolus, and Derodte" were charged.]

(Dress Code)

In yet another attempt to extinguish the NIGGER lifestyle and all that is associated with it, mounting frustration has forced municipalities across America to draft or impose legislation that bans a form of NIGGER dress called "saggin." Naturally, NIGGERfiliacs challenge the legality of such legislation because it profiles. Sure, it's profiling, but NIGGERfilacs shouldn't worry because this ban isn't designed to deter NIGGERtivity. Instead, it only mandates that NIGGERS cover their asses (literally). Since their dress intentionally illustrates that they're HoG stock, these bills force them to at least dress civilized, even though they don't act civilized. I say, the problem isn't the pants; it's the person wearing the pants.

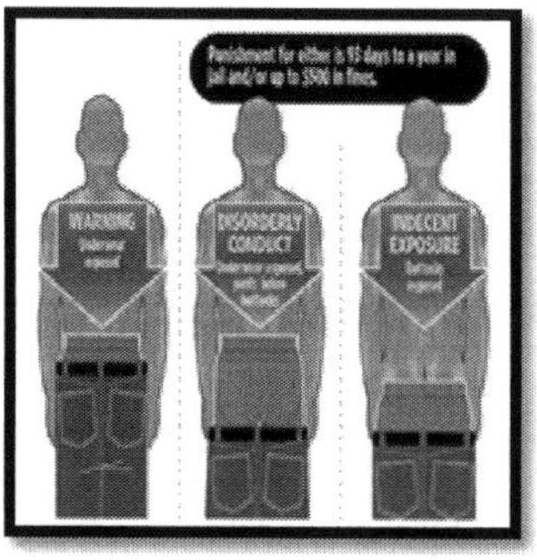

Many cities are desperately trying to punish NIGGERS for dressing like...umm... NIGGERS

(Saggin')

The saggin' pants style (or lack of) is the wearing of pants in a way that deliberately exposes one's buttocks. In the HoG, this is considered a form of "swag," which exemplifies style or confidence. This so-called "swag" that's proudly flaunted by NIGGERS is as artificial as a three-dollar bill. Outside the HoG, saggin' is generally perceived as moronic and classless, yet, even when they're outside the HoG, NIGGERS sag for attention. Saggin' is so normal in the HoG that a fashion company has actually created jeans to enhance the saggin experience. Its website states, ***"Consumers can 'sag' their jeans at different levels without having to constantly pull up their pants, resulting in more time to be active, express themselves and show their SWAG."*** In essence, this company is selling pants to the NIGGER subculture that deliberately exposes butt cheeks at different angles. Sometimes, truth is indeed stranger than fiction.

(Saggin' in School)

Although several school districts across America have implemented a dress code, and adopted a "dress for success" mentality, JuviNIGGERS still sag their school pants. As a result, the state of Florida enacted a "*Pull up Your Pants*" bill, requiring school districts in the Sunshine State to discipline students who wear clothing that expose undies. In Philadelphia, Mayor Michael Nutter countered the NIGGER subculture's version of "keepin' it real" with society's version of "keepin' it real." Speaking to JuviNIGGERS and teen blacks (WNT) he advised, ***"Pull your pants up and buy a belt—no one wants to see your underwear. Comb your hair. Learn some manners."*** Unfortunately, legislation, stern lectures, or sage advice won't yield positive change in their subculture. In fact, it's no coincidence that *"saggin"* spelled backwards is *"niggas."*

No more saggy pants for Ark. school children
Governor signs a bill banning attire that exposes 'underwear, buttocks or the breast of a female'
msnbc.com

(The Source)

The genesis of saggin' is a subject of much speculation, ranging from a dress to hide drugs/weapons or prison style. The prison theory suggests that this loose fit style is an invitation or summons for homosexual activity. Even so, regardless of origin or intent, this uncivilized dress that exposes one's buttocks correlates to those who stereotypically cost society more than they contribute (with the exception of plumbers lol).

Saggy Pants Robber Gets Depantsed in Court
nbcmiami.com

Indiana Man In Saggy Pants Bust
thesmokinggun.com

[Author's Note: Dude told police that he "was just swagging."]

Sagging pants hamper rape suspect fleeing Memphis police
commercialappeal.com

(Let em' Dress that Way)

In order to reverse the NIGative effects of mistaken identity between BLACKS and NIGGERS, a clear distinction has to be maintained. Saggin' pants are a simple indication of NIGGER affiliation, and is actually helpful because it visibly differentiates our two cultures. My advice to those wanting to limit their chances of mistaken identity is to not dress like them. I often tell kids about the dangers and associated consequences of adopting a NIGGER look. Dressing like a NIGGER authorizes one to be treated as such, so, do it at your own risk. If a woman dresses in a manner that's consistent with prostitutes, how can she be offended if someone inquires about her services? As comedian Dave Chappelle joked, ***"Fine, you're not a whore, but you're wearing a hooker's uniform."*** Likewise, NIGGER dress suggests antisocial predispositions, yet, they expect opposite treatment. I remember scouting potential neighborhoods to live and raise a family. After finding a listing that satisfied my search criteria, I eagerly drove to the neighborhood (located in a bordering state) without contacting the listing agent. I simply wanted to get a feel for the environment. It was a cool autumn afternoon, and as I approached the property, I immediately became enchanted with the neighborhood's quietness and solitude. After slowly scanning the home's exterior and mentally notating the necessary improvements, I pictured my children happily playing in the spacious yard. I enthusiastically rushed back to my car to call the listing agent for a full viewing. Then, while dialing, a discouraging sighting prevented the call's completion. An adult, African-American male, wearing a wife beater, bandana, saggin pants, and Timberland boots strutted from a neighboring home with a pit bull dog (off the leash). Even now, I'm still unsure as to whether he was walking the dog or the dog was walking him, but nevertheless, that NIGGER sighting gave an intangible glimpse of the neighborhood that the appraisal or real estate agent couldn't accurately convey. Seemingly, at the blink of an eye, the house that I envisioned as my future home had suddenly become a safety hazard. Ok, I didn't confirm if the dude was actually a NIGGER, but since he dressed like a NIGGER, and exhibited NIGGER attributes, I assumed as much. In other words, if it walks like a duck and talk like a duck... you know the rest.

Chapter IX

Who's to Blame for NIGGERtivity?

"Take your life in your own hands and what happens? A terrible thing: no one is to blame." – Erica Jong

In this information age, it's difficult to fathom that a people would actually prefer ignorance to intellect. Yet, that's how the NIGGER subculture pompously rolls. Many wonder how it's even possible that these extremely irresponsible beings manage to be responsible for disproportionate amounts of societal damage. Yes, these and other self-defeating aspects of the NIGGER subculture continue to baffle everyone... except NIGGERfiliacs. While society struggles to ascertain the catalyst(s) for NIGGER behavior, or more aptly, misbehavior, NIGGERfiliacs simply blame external entities. But, by charging outside entities, NIGGERtivity is essentially excused just as fast as it's occurring across the country. Moreover, this scapegoating of everyone/everything only empowers the NIGGER subculture while doing incalculable harm to the rest of us. Listen, I grew up under the same cultural conditions that NIGGERfilacs use to excuse the NIGGER subculture. In fact, I was an illegitimate (*excuse #1*), public housing project child (*excuse #2*), who was raised during the crack era *(excuse #3),* by a poor *(excuse #4),* single parent *(excuse #5).* Also, I was a Hip-Hop enthusiast *(excuse #6),* watched B.E.T *(excuse #7),* incessantly played video *games (excuse #8),* and had access to illegal guns *(excuse #9).* Even still, none of these circumstances and pastimes mandated that I did anything that ultimately wasn't my choice. Undeniably, background and circumstances influences development, but, individuals are eventually responsible for who they become. With that, NIGGERfiliacs should acquit any external entity indicted for NIGGERtivity, and acknowledge the true reason... O.N.D. This chapter was written to scrutinize and refute some of the NIGGERfiliac excuses for NIGGERtivity. HNCUs are notably absent from this short list because they aren't a cause; they're an effect.

*<u>Usual Suspect</u>: *Guns**

Although the Second Amendment of the United States Constitution partly states, ***"the right of the people to keep and bear Arms, shall not be infringed,"*** nonstop NIGGERtivity has forced several cities to enact legislation intended to turn this Second Amendment ***"right"*** into a privilege. Even with gun restrictions/bans, gun show closures, judicial deterrents, NRA demonization, or the outright elimination of the Second Amendment, gun-related NIGGERtivity would still flourish because stricter gun laws don't halt NIGGERtivity. NIGGERS simply don't follow laws, so wherever guns are outlawed, only outlaws will have guns! On the other hand, these gun laws/bans increase the number of potential victims because NIGGERS habitually target law-abiding, unarmed citizens. Seemingly, cities with the strictest gun laws suffer the most from gun-related NIGGERtivity. It's interesting to compare the extent of gun violence in cities/states that have stringent gun laws (Chicago) versus states/cities (Utah) that don't. How do places like Wyoming (0.8% Af-Am), Idaho (0.6% Af-Am), and Vermont (1% Af-Am) have a high rate of gun ownership, yet negligible gun violence rates? Well, places with a low percentage of Af-Ams have an even lower percentage of NIGGERS, thus yielding trivial amounts of gun-related NIGGERtivity. Furthermore, in the HoG, high gun possession annually results with more gun-related violence, whereas the opposite is generally true for places outside the HoG. Therefore, instead of instituting stricter "gun control" measures to combat NIGGER-sponsored violence, the focus should be on stricter "birth control" measures to combat the NIGGER-sponsored violence. Gun control will never affect those lacking self-control.

Chicago Mayor Attempting To Reinforce Handgun Ban After 60 Shootings This Weekend

hiphopwired.com

[Author's Note: Due to an increase in NIGGERtivity, in June 2011, the Illinois State Rifle Association issued a "travel advisory" for any members headed to Chicago.]

Southern U.S. town proud of its mandatory gun law

reuters.com

[Author's Note: In this town, north of Atlanta, gun ownership is mandatory. I'm sure that this NIGGER-Tsunami ready environment doesn't experience Flashfloods or "Knock-out King."]

(Buyback Program)

A handgun to NIGGERS is what water is to fish; statistically, handguns are their weapon of choice. Realizing this correlation, NIGfested cities and municipalities' have taken preventative measures such as bribing citizens (especially HoG residents) to surrender firearms via gun buyback programs. These gun buyback programs are knee-jerk reactions to gun-related NIGGERtivity, and are primarily inner-city occurrences; rural America is normally resistant and suspicious of any gun-stripping endeavor. Usually, with no questions asked, an official body institutes the gun buyback programs in exchange for money, gift cards, or food. Politicians know that these ploys won't stop gun-related NIGGERtivity. Such measures are merely bandages on a wound that requires nothing short of amputative surgery. As NIGGERtivity continues its national trend, these programs will likely evolve into more aggressive and desperate campaigns that encourage citizens to physically apprehend urban terrorists. Advisedly, leave this dangerous undertaking to constitutionally protected militias. Lol.

No takers on hoagies for guns swap in Pt. Breeze
whyy.org

[Author's Note: In Killadelphia (Philadelphia), where NIGGERtivity is rampant, a unique and perhaps desperate bartering system exists; a restaurant offered hoagies for guns.]

(An Unorthodox Strategy)

Following the trend of cities with a sizeable African-American population, Newark, New Jersey (52.4% Af-Am.) is also riddled with NIGGERtivity. So, in attempt to send a message of intolerance, Newark officials did something unprecedented; they hosted the city's (and probably the nation's) first toy gun exchange. Yes, "toy" gun exchange. Although there is no known correlation between water pistols, super soakers, and actual gun violence, Newark's mayor (Cory Booker) stated that the ***"children's toy gun exchange illustrated just how important such initiatives had become to curbing the cycle of violence."*** Actually, this kindergarten version of a gun exchange was utilized to culturally condition the youth into believing that guns are bad, and only bad people possess them.

The late comedian George Carlin captured the absurdity of such public relations stunts when stating, ***"And now, they're thinking about banning toy guns – and they're gonna keep the fucking real ones!"*** In attempt to make sense of this initiative, I conducted an exhaustive, statistical search of Newark's toy gun related violence, and surprisingly discovered that no cases were reported. Despite the fact that toy guns have existed as long as the real ones, and most children have had them, somehow, toy guns haven't influenced generations of children to grow up and commit armed violence. Yet, Newark's government has audaciously demonized toy guns for NIGGERtivity instead of NIGGERS themselves. Unfortunately, for Newark's kiddies, the classic, childhood game of cops and robbers will never be the same. Well, at least for the pretend cops. I guarantee that the pretend robbers (like their real life counterparts) will still manage to have guns.

Mayor Cory Booker of Newark Holds First Toy Gun Exchange
examiner.com

(My Experiment)

Periodically, I conduct an unscientific study to test the theory that 'guns' not 'people' are responsible for violent crimes. The incessant *'guns cause violence'* belief made me wonder if my gun is guilty of causing violence. Perhaps, it sneaks from the house, victimizes someone, and then returns unnoticed. Hmmm... one can never be too sure. With that, I normally initiate the experiment by placing my gun on the nightstand before going to sleep, and then noting its placement position. After waking, I'd document any noticeable changes such as missing bullets, damage, temperature, and position change. Strangely, nothing ever appears to be unchanged. Even so, being a diligent pseudo-scientist, I don't allow factual observations to conclude my study. For that reason, I intensified the research by installing a surveillance system to monitor the gun's activity while I slept. To this day, no evidence of foul play has materialized. So, since my numerous studies yielded the same exonerating result, I was forced into accepting the reality that my gun doesn't cause violence; but still, random studies are ongoing. *Disclaimer:* My unscientific gun results are unique to my anecdotal situation and may conflict with the experiences of the *"gun causes violence"* theorists. Surely, their guns behave differently.

(Guns Kill)

So, if guns not NIGGERS, are the reason for gun-related NIGGERtivity, let's scapegoat other inanimate objects as well. Automobiles should be blamed for drunk driving accidents right??? Mothers Against Drunk Driving (M.A.D.D) should wage a campaign against the automobile industry for creating vehicles of mass destruction right??? Silverware makes people fat right??? Pencils and pens are responsible for misspelled words right??? Wrong!!! None of these items (including guns) operates by themselves. It's time to blame violence on violent people, not guns!

1 hurt with bowling ball, 2 others injured during fight downtown
baltimoresun.com

[Author's Note: Ok NIGGERfiliacs, let me guess... it was the bowling ball's fault for being at a bowling alley. Perhaps bowling balls should be banned within city limits.]

(Castle Doctrine / Stand Your Ground)

I often chuckle at the way NIGGERS increase their knowledge of any law after it detrimentally affects their subculture. For example, the *Stand Your Ground Law* and comparable *Castle Doctrine* serve as two examples of laws that NIGGERS never cared to know until it affected them. Now, their subculture is intimately familiar with these two laws because they've become preventative measures against NIGGERtivity. The Castle Doctrine and comparable Stand-Your-Ground Law, which are enacted in many states, essentially declares that a person may use deadly force in self-defense when there is reasonable belief of a threat, without an obligation to retreat first. Again, NIGGERS were oblivious to such laws until they were exercised on them across the country in real time. Laws such as the Castle Doctrine and Stand Your Ground legally level the playing field against NIGGERtivity.

Corbett signs the 'Common-Sense' Castle Doctrine Bill
http://blogs.philadelphiaweekly.com

(Gangsta' Style)

The primary reason why civilians are injured, and collateral damage consistently occurs during gun-related NIGGERtivity, is because NIGGERS aren't interested in their level of shooting proficiency. In fact, while holding their weapons sideways to look gangsta, they shoot first, aim later. Reacting to news of two violent Atlanta carjackings (where Stand Your Ground is law), Atlanta based radio host Neal Boortz said, ***"This town is starting to look like a garbage heap. And we got too damn many urban thugs, yo, ruining the quality of life for everybody. And I'll tell you what it's gonna take. You people, you are - you need to have a gun. You need to have training. You need to know how to use that gun. You need to get a permit to carry that gun. And you do in fact need to carry that gun, and we need to see some dead thugs littering the landscape in Atlanta. We need to see the next guy that tries to carjack you shot dead right where he stands. We need more dead thugs in this city."*** Even though Boortz didn't mention race, and his rant applies to any ***"thug,"*** NIGGERfiliacs interpreted this as a threat to NIGGERS. He was instantly accused of racism. Yup, Mr. Boortz, even self-preservation is racist.

Critics condemn Boortz rant on violent crime
11alive.com

Usual Suspect**: ***Hip Hop Music

The Oscar Wilde saying, ***"Life imitates Art far more than Art imitates life"*** is especially true for Hip Hop. The subculture's inability to separate entertainment from reality has arguably made Hip Hop most culpable for inciting NIGGERtivity. While I don't cite Hip-Hop as the catalyst for NIGGERtivity, its complicity is undeniable. With more than 70% of African-American children being raised in single parent households, Hip-Hop oftentimes serves as a surrogate parent, and consequently, this outsourcing of parenthood has naturally yielded dysfunctional results. In the HoG, Hip-Hop is omnipresent and is by far the most influential form of entertainment. In fact, it's more than entertainment; it's a chosen lifestyle. Understandably, it's easily demonized because of its suggestive lyrics and close alignment with the impressionable

NIGGER subculture, but ultimately, NIGGERtivity is a choice; certain Hip-Hop genres simply provide theme music. If Hip-Hop is responsible for NIGGERtivity, as the NIGGERfiliacs claim, explain why Euro and Asian-American teens (Hip Hop's biggest costumers) aren't wreaking collective havoc in their communities like their African-American peers. Do Euro and Asian-American teens possess impenetrable defenses against Hip Hop's seductive spell? Or, is it that they simply choose not to behavior like NIGGERS? I think the latter.

ATF and D.C Police Impersonate Rap Label; Arrest 70 in Year Long Guns and Drug Sting

allhiphop.com

[Author's Note: Over 7.2 million in drugs and 161 weapons were confiscated including a rocket launcher. For some strange reason, I doubt that if the ATF impersonated a Country Music label similar results would've been generated.]

(Hip Hop's Past -vs- Present)

There's a noticeable difference between Hip Hop from my teenage years to today's version. I'm not going to waste ink debating which era is better or authentic because it's relative. However, I can confidently claim that my era maintained more Hip Hop variety. Similar to today, NIGGERtivity existed during my adolescence, yet, unlike today's top Hip Hop artists, the old school artists collaborated to make anti-violence songs. For example, symbolic songs such as *"Self Destruction"* (artists from the East coast) and *"We're all in the Same Gang"* (artists from the West coast) confronted NIGGERtivity and its destructive impact. In fact, on *Self Destruction's* first verse, Hip-Hop legend *KRS-One*, called out the NIGGER subculture. He rapped, ***"Well, today's topic self-destruction; It really ain't the rap audience that's buggin'. It's one or two suckas, ignorant brothers, tryin' to rob and steal from one another. You get caught in the mid, so to crush that stereotype here's what we did. We got ourselves together, so that you could unite and fight for what's right; not negative, cause-- the way we live is positive, we don't kill our relatives."*** Later in the song, rapper *D-Nice* advised, ***"It's time to stand together in a unity, cause if not, then we're soon to be; self-destroyed, unemployed, the rap race will be lost without a trace--Or a clue, but what to do, is stop the violence and kick the science. Down***

the road that we call eternity, where knowledge is formed and you'll learn to be, self-sufficient, independent, to teach to each is what rap intended." Overall, my favorite verse belonged to Kool Moe Dee, ***"I never ever ran from the Ku Klux Klan so I shouldn't have to run from a black man."*** Additionally, *Self-Destruction's* video (released in 1989) even streamed important statistics at the bottom of the screen such as, ***"One out of every 22 Black American males will be killed by a violent crime"*** and ***"84% of violent crimes against Blacks were committed by Black offenders."*** Presently, even though those daunting statistics have actually worsened, this issue receives little mention from today's top Hip Hop artists. As a teen, I enjoyed the variety that Hip Hop provided, but today, it's imbalanced and tilted towards the NIGGER subculture.

*Usual Suspect: *Black Entertainment Television (B.E.T)*

Despite the overabundance of cable and satellite channels today, the NIGGER subculture remains solely obsessed with B.E.T (Black Entertainment Television). B.E.T is blamed for NIGGERtivity because it promotes HoG values and themes to the highly gullible NIGGER subculture. Again, being a NIGGER is a choice, so don't blame B.E.T for NIGGERS choosing to be NIGGERS. If NIGGERS watched the National Geographic Channel with the same intensity, would they become geologists? Of course not!!! It must be clarified that regardless of its name, B.E.T is not the voice or face of BLACK people! It's frustrating to constantly hear African-Americans proclaim that B.E.T is "our" channel when realistically; B.E.T is no more our channel than MTV (Music Television) is the Euro-Americans' channel. B.E.T is simply an entertainment channel that primarily caters to a certain segment of African-Americans. Actually, both channels are owned by the media behemoth Viacom, whose core principles centers on one color... green; any content that obstructs their bottom line is disregarded. Viacom knows that the lucrative NIGGER subculture demographic will remain loyal as long as the "E" in B.E.T represents *"Entertainment"* and not *"Education."* Arguably, even if the "E" meant *"Exploitation,"* NIGGERS would still tune in. B.E.T's president (Debra Lee) confirmed their (B.E.T) reluctance to incorporate more non-HoG related content by stating, ***"Our audience always says that they want this kind of***

programming, but they don't show up." In other words, B.E.T is only selling what its audience is buying. B.E.T's lack of positive content reflects the fact that their audience prefers entertainment to education, and fashion shows to financial shows. Therefore, as long as this preference remains, and B.E.T is netting a profit, their programming won't change, even if Neo-Nazi's assumed control of the station.

BET President Responds to Criticism: "We Offer [Positive] Programming, But They Don't Show Up"
clutchmagazineonline.com

(Nielsen Says)

For the year 2010, the Nielsen ratings agency, reported that African-Americans ages 18 to 49 watched television at a record-setting pace; averaging seven hours and twelve minutes per day. With that amount of staggering T.V consumption, it's evident that television is raising children instead of parents; yet, no one blames the parents. If the NIGGER subculture actually utilized schools for their created purposes, so much demand wouldn't be placed on an entertainment channel (B.E.T) for education. They need to limit their child's B.E.T exposure and become B.E.T (T.E.R) parents.

The TV set vs. black families: African-Americans must quit their terrible 7-hour-a-day diet
nydailynews.com

*<u>Usual Suspect</u>: *Hollywood*

African-Americans have a love/hate overview of Hollywood. On one hand, we love when Hollywood ignores the statistical and occupational realities associated with our race, and instead, depicts us as majority holders of credentialed professions. On the other hand, we hate when Hollywood actually acknowledges the statistical realities associated with our race, and illustrates us as criminally prone, hypersexual, non-achievers whose usefulness is limited to non-cerebral endeavors. In other words, we condemn any movie that doesn't fit our historical and ideological perspective of ourselves while endorsing the favorable ones. Furthermore, the grievances are conspicuously absent whenever Hollywood rewrites history for our benefit. For example, no one in the African-American community seem to mind that Morgan Freeman (BLACK man) starred as an innovative doctor/ prosthetist, in the movie *Dolphin Tail* (based on a true story), even though the real-life doctors were two WHITE men. Yup, for diverse appeal, the film merged the contributions of two WHITE doctors (Kevin Carroll and Dan Strzempka) into one BLACK character. Hmmm... now, if Jack Nicholson played the scientist/botanist George Washington Carver or Euro-Americans were cast as the Tuskegee Airmen, NIGGERgeddon would commence.

(Character Placement)

Hollywood has and will continue to make movies in which the African-American character(s) reflect one of the three African-American segments. Understanding the differences between the three classes of African-Americans (BLACKS, NIGGERS, and blacks with NIGGER tendencies), enables me to watch movies with African-American characters and not obsess over positive or negative racial representation. Utilization of this racial reality should also prevent African-Americans from protesting whenever NIGGERS are actually portrayed as NIGGERS. Well, the NIGGERfiliacs would still protest because they're always enraged when others (especially those of another race) attack the NIGGER subculture in any capacity.

(Stop Fighting for NIGGERS)

Logically, BLACKS want to be portrayed authentically and not stereotypically, but the problem is that BLACKS will even fight to re-write any NIGGER or NIGGER subculture portrayals. Although these characters may be undesirable, they're often an accurate illustration of the NIGGER subculture and their continuous bottom feeding. Besides, NIGGERS enjoy any stereotypical and negative characterization that represents their kind, so BLACKS mind your business and let them revel. I'm completely against BLACKS wanting a revisionist narration of any movie that has derogative or stereotypical African-American character(s) or theme. BLACKS need to accept the fact that within the African-American community (like any other community), exists a mixed bag of characters, and unfortunately, NIGGERS are in our bag. Therefore, stop having national temper-tantrums whenever

Hollywood highlights the negative (but true) segment of the African-American community. As an alternative, unleash that anger on the NIGGER subculture. Blaming Hollywood for correctly portraying NIGGERS living a life of exaggerated pride and unapologetic ignorance is misplaced blame, especially when NIGGERS willingly provide continuous material support.

Production halted on reality show starring rapper who fathered eleven children by ten women after public outrage
dailymail.co.uk

[Author's Note: Actually, this "public outrage" was from BLACKS... NIGGERS enjoy the exposure.]

Transformers' Jive-Talking Robots Raise Race Issues
huffingtonpost.com

[Author's Note: The Transformers 2 movie received unfair criticism for having twin robots with NIGGER tendencies.]

(Hollywood Banksters)

NIGGERfiliacs preach that Hollywood execs are racist because they're hesitant to finance quality African-American movies. My rebuttal emphasizes the fact that Hollywood is foremost, a profit driven machine piloted by venture capitalists. Market research, trends, box office receipts, and other factors ultimately determine which movies are financed. The most commonly financed African-American films are those that cater to the most profitable niche segment (Ice Cube and Tyler Perry are testaments to the wealth attaining ability of niche audiences), which unfortunately isn't BLACKS. Moreover, box office receipts consistently reflect the reality that most well-made, morally sound BLACK centered movies don't fare well compared to the low budget, high return, NIGGER subculture-based movies. In other words, with a few exceptions, the African-American community generally doesn't financially support "feel good," inspirational BLACK movies. On the flip side, NIGGERS and blacks (WNT) flock to see HoG-type movies, while BLACKS are the only segment that'll support films that broaden horizons. The Hollywood banksters know that well-written, image positive, BLACK movies are patronized by a small segment (BLACKS), and thus, don't generate returns comparable to NIGGER subculture-slanted movies. I'd even venture to say that more WHITE people patronize well-written, inspirational, BLACK movies than NIGGERS do. Super-producer George Lucas spent upwards of sixty-million dollars to self-finance the inspirational movie *"Red Tails"* (a story highlighting the adversities and triumphs of the Tuskegee Airmen during World War II) after the Hollywood banksters continuously refused. With a resume like Lucas', surely, this pioneer of movie innovation and technology would be able to break the financial curse associated with BLACK pride movies. Right? Well, not quite. His ambitious idea and massive investment yielded the typical, discouraging results, which validated the banksters' premise. Although Lucas did succeed with getting his pet project (Red Tails) to fly, it was quickly grounded at the box office.

George Lucas: Star Wars Director Loses $60 Mil Plus on "Red Tails"
abcnews.go.com

(HoG Movies -vs- BLACK Movies)

In the NIGGER subculture, HoG movies are preferred over stories of redemption and perseverance like *Antwon Fisher,* or *Pursuit of Happyness*. Sequels and trilogies are often made for HoG movies, but I doubt that there will be a second *Akeelah the Bee*. Several years ago, I went to see *"The Great Debaters,"* which was based on a motivational true story and directed by Denzel Washington. While ordering popcorn, I noticed that a comedy titled *"First Sunday"* (starring Ice Cube and Katt Williams) was playing in the adjacent theatre. Midway through my movie, I became curious as to which theatre had the largest audience. So, I peeped inside *First Sunday's theatre* and wasn't shocked that it was packed with all African-Americans, while *Great Debaters* had a modest, racially mixed audience. Unsurprisingly, the domestic total of their theatrical runs was *First Sunday* $37,931,869 and *The Great Debaters* $30,236,407. Unlike HoG movies, stories that celebrate the splendor and strength of BLACK family life, education, and the desire to succeed, simply aren't financial draws.

***Usual Suspect**: *Reality/Talk shows*

Presently, a plethora of reality crime shows narrated from law enforcement's vantage point exists on television. From the long running *"Cops"* series to my current favorite *"First 48,"* there's always a dark commonality...NIGGERS. Why are NIGGERS featured on these shows? Well, it's a no-brainer. If I were to create a crime-based show, I'd simply go where the criminals exist. If I were to create a show about polygamy, I'd go where the polygamists reside. *[Author's Note: NIGGERS are also polygamists, minus the actual marriage and many responsibilities that accompany the lifestyle.]* Naturally, NIGGERfiliacs believe that these types of crime-based reality shows are exploitative and perpetuate stereotypes; but if NIGGERS didn't commit a disproportionate amount of crime, they wouldn't have such a starring role. In other words, don't blame the cigarette for giving the smoker lung cancer; blame the smoker for willing participation. *"First 48"* follows actual homicide detectives through the first forty-eight hours after a homicide, and since NIGGERS don't value life, it isn't surprising that homey-cides are prominently featured. Actually, there's more than enough material for the series to be solely based on homey-cides. Alternatively, it would be a true challenge for any homicide-based series like *First 48* to **not** feature NIGGERS. NIGGERS are to reality crime shows (especially those based on homicides) what Mickey Mouse is to Disney World. Even still, NIGGERfiliacs consider the reoccurring use of African-Americans on these shows as racist ploys. In response, John Langley, the creator of the long-running, syndicated television show "Cops" stated in an interview (5/8/09), ***"What irritates me sometimes is critics will watch Cops and say, 'They misrepresent people of color.' That's not true. Au contraire, I show more white people than is statistically what the truth is in terms of street crime. If you look at the prisons, it's sixty-something percent people of color and thirty-something percent of white people. If you look at Cops, it's sixty percent white and forty percent people of color, it's just the reverse. And I do that intentionally, because I don't want to contribute to negative stereotypes."*** Mr. Langley, despite your effort to appease the NIGGERfiliacs by intentionally underrepresenting NIGGERtivity on your show, they will still target you. They won't be satisfied until the show is NIGGER-free. So I ask, in the spirit of your theme song, ***"Whatchu gon do when dey come fo' you?"*** For what it's worth Mr. Langley, your show doesn't contribute to negative stereotypes... the NIGGER subculture does.

Civil Rights Group Urges Fox to Cancel 'Cops' (Exclusive)
tv.yahoo.com

(Talk Shows)

Talk shows like *Jerry Springer* and *Maury* have made a handsome living from exposing the underclasses. Particularly, *Maury, who* has struck ghetto gold by making "Baby Mama and Baby Daddy" DNA revelations the meat of his show. Thanks to him, the phrases, *"You are the father,"* and *"You are not the father"* are popularly linked to the underclasses. Judging by these shows' longevity, there's a loyal audience that enjoys the subcultures' dysfunction. I still don't understand why these shows are demonized when the potential guests actually call in with their strange stories, hoping to be exploited on national television. Despite NIGGERfiliacs looking down their noses at these exploitative shows, they (programs) truly provide an invaluable service to parents like me. At my disposal, I can show my children the self-defeating consequences of subscribing to the NIGGER subculture's tenets. Therefore, NIGGERfiliacs shouldn't hate the players (Maury, Jerry, et.al), instead, hate the game (the NIGGER subculture's lifestyle).

*Usual Suspect: *News media*

In America, the press is so significant that the United States Constitution granted it the highest level of protection. The First Amendment states in part, ***"Congress shall make no law respecting an establishment of religion, or prohibiting the free exercise thereof; or abridging the freedom of speech, or of the press;"*** Although their job isn't to be judge/ juror or to make declarations determining the guilt or innocence of the accused, the mainstream news media is blamed for villianizing African-Americans. The alleged over-reporting of stories that poorly reflects the African-American community has placed them into a precarious situation. On one hand, they're charged with keeping the public pertinently informed, yet, on the other hand, not expected to accurately report NIGGERtivity because doing so may be deemed racist. Moreover, underreporting crime that occurs within the African-American community is also considered racist. Simply put, it's a lose-lose situation when over reporting, underreporting, and even non-reporting of NIGGERtivity is interpreted as racist.

(The Compromise)

In attempt to avoid the charge of racism, the mainstream media has chosen to downplay NIGGERtivity. In other words, they purposely limit candid reporting of NIGGERtivity as to not offend the African-American community. Not only is NIGGERtivity sometimes belittled, the usage of euphemisms or outright race omission, helps to disguise NIGGERtivity. But by trivializing NIGGERtivity for the sake of political correctness, the citizenry is jeopardized.

Midtown shooter gets life plus 65 years in prison

wsbtv.com

[Author's Note: The national media ignored this story about an Urban Terrorist who claimed that he shot three white women (murdering two, and paralyzing the other) because "slavery was something that had to be answered for." If this guy were a vengeful, White supremacist who mercilessly killed two unsuspecting Black women, the media would have given it national, Trayvon Martin-type coverage instead of local coverage.]

(Hiding Identities)

Once upon a time, when the mainstream media had the community's best interest, headlines and lead stories used to be decided by the simple phrase *"If it bleeds, it leads."* Presently, NIGGERfiliacs have interpreted this mantra as a covert race attack because the African-American community regularly bleeds (like a menstrual cycle). So, to pacify NIGGERfiliacs and race-peddlers, who believe that African-Americans are purposely overrepresented as criminals, the mainstream media will often omit the race of an Af-Am perpetrator. Thomas Sowell noticed the press' lack of courage to racially identify Flashflooders, and subsequently penned an article titled, *"Social Denigration" (lewrockwell.com 8/17/11).* He wrote, ***"Just to identify the rioters and looters as black is a radical departure, when mayors, police chiefs and the media in other cities report on these outbreaks of violence without mentioning the race of those who are doing these things. The Chicago Tribune even made excuses for failing to mention race when reporting on violent attacks by blacks on whites in Chicago."*** Even when video confirms that the perpetrators are African-American, the headlines usually don't reference race.

Instead, generic and politically correct pronouns are used. The mainstream media has become subservient to NIGGERfilacs.

Man attacked by kids at L'Enfant Metro-bystanders watch, film it (video)

tbd.com

[Author's Note: The video shows the "kids" assaulting a man and reveals what the headline wouldn't. Oh, FYI...those "kids" weren't baby goats.]

(Deliberate Neglect)

In a *townhall.com* article (6/22/11) titled *"America's New Racists,"* Walter E. Williams reveals the logic of the typical major newspaper editor. Williams wrote, ***"In many of these brutal attacks, the news media make no mention of the race of the perpetrators. If it were white racist gangs randomly attacking blacks, the mainstream media would have no hesitation reporting the race of the perps. Editors for the Los Angeles Times, the New York Times, and the Chicago Tribune admitted to deliberately censoring information about black crime for political reasons. Chicago Tribune Editor Gerould Kern recently said that the paper's reason for censorship was to 'guard against subjecting an entire group of people to suspicion'."*** Further confirmation of censorship came from Kyle Rogers' *examiner.com* article (10/9/11) titled, *"Should race play a role in how the media reports crime?"* He wrote, ***"In the past year, a multitude of media bosses have publicly confessed to censoring black crime. Some of them proudly confess, and say that the censorship is for the public's benefit. Some of them even call critics 'racists' for asking for accurate news coverage. All of these 'media elites' place political correctness far above public safety."*** Amazingly, even though JuviNIGGERS are nationally terrorizing Euro, Asian, and Latino-Americans via *"Polar Bear Hunting"* and *"Knock-out King,"* somehow they (JuviNIGGERS) escape a race mention. In fact, on June 6, 2007, the LA Times came out the closet and released an official endorsement of censorship by stating, ***"Racial information was once routinely included in news stories about crimes, but in recent decades, newspapers and other media outlets stopped mentioning suspects' or victims' race or ethnicity because of public criticism. Newspapers came to embrace***

the idea that such information is irrelevant to the reporting of crimes, and may unfairly stigmatize racial groups." Learning that the media elites (who yield to the will of NIGGERfiliacs) have placed public safety second to political correctness is frightening and makes no sense; on the other hand, it does makes "cents" for their industry.

Newark Star-Ledger Admits to Censoring Race in Savage Mob Attacks
examiner.com

(Example of a Dangerous "PC" Headline)

As reported by myfoxny.com (5/19/11), ***"Yonkers police are calling suspect Ronnell Jones, 23, the cross-dressing killer. They say he has so far evaded cops by dressing in drag—wearing wigs and women's clothing. It may sound funny, but what he is accused of is anything but. 'We believe he is a vicious criminal,' Yonkers Police Commissioner Ed Hartnett said. 'And we are asking the public to help us capture him.' Hartnett said Jones is wanted for murder, after a bungled burglary in summer 2010 that turned into a bloodbath. Two people were shot and killed and four others were injured, including a 5-year-old boy who was shot in the arm and 17-year-old girl shot in the chest while begging for her life. 'I would certainly classify him as a cold-blooded killer,' Hartnett said. 'And yes, in my 30-plus-year career in law enforcement I have not encountered somebody hiding from law enforcement for a vicious murder wearing women's clothing".*** Despite the merciless murders, attempted murders, assaults, burglaries, cross dressing to evade capture, and classification as a ***"cold-blooded killer"*** by a seasoned 30-plus year veteran police commissioner, the headline ambiguously stated:

Yonkers Police: Male Suspect Now Disguised a Woman
myfoxny.com

[Author's Note: Although this Urban Terrorist was on the loose and had left a trail of blood, this headline was careful not to demonize him.]

(Angry Rant)

The mainstream media's continued protectionism and political correctness through the usage of vague headlines has to halt.

Their typical, sensitive wording approach serves the criminal instead of its readership and community at large. It should be considered unethical to provide this type anonymity to criminals through general descriptions. NIGGERfiliacs believe that mentioning the race of a perpetrator unfairly reinforces stereotypes, and damages the reputation of an entire group. Even so, it's ludicrous to exclude a suspect's race since it's one of the most vital clues. Should we also omit gender descriptions so that the entire male/female species isn't offended? Geesh, I guess, in attempt to not offend anyone, anywhere, at any time, headlines should simply read, *"Homosapien Allegedly Commits Crime"* or *"Someone, Somewhere, Purportedly Committed a Crime."* Perhaps a general, apologetic disclaimer should be placed alongside headlines to assure readers that covering crime isn't intended to be racist. Give me a break!

(Example of a Quality Headline)

The following headline exemplifies an accurate, descriptive headline that serves the public, and not the alleged perpetrator. Although it doesn't go as far as I would've, at least it includes pertinent, identifying information such as the suspects name, age, and race. These details give citizens the maximum opportunity to assist law enforcement or protect themselves. NIGGERfiliacs would look at this headline and yell racism since they believe that any reporting of facts that indicts the NIGGER subculture is racist.

Gabriel Ben Meir: Possible Suspect in MTV Murder Is 35-Year-Old Black Man With Wire Glasses, Gold Jewelry, Shotgun
blogs.laweekly.com

(Pittsburgh)

In Pittsburgh, an odd arrangement exists between the African-American community (26.1% population) and local press. According to the *Post-Gazette*, ***"News directors for the city's three major local news networks are considering signing a joint agreement on coverage policies regarding Pittsburgh's black community as part of an effort to add positive messages to the news as an offset to crime coverage."*** Huh? I expect the press to accurately report current events including NIGGERtivity, and the omission of relevant facts is technically a form of lying. Basically, the Af-Am community wants the Pittsburgh media to fluff their Af-Am coverage beyond crime and sports. Since Pittsburgh is 64.8% Euro-American, and the mainstream media usually has no issue with highlighting Euro-American males as pedophiles, meth dealers, and corporate criminals, should Euro-American demand that the media stop "making them look bad?" The article also mentioned, ***"Many attendees complained the main coverage of black Pittsburghers was at murder scenes or courthouses."*** Again... Huh? BLACKS, unless they're NIGGERfiliacs, need to stop fighting for NIGGERS!! Furthermore, stop expecting the news to show NIGGERS planting Daisies instead of pushing up Daisies! Should the courthouses also be picketed (like the news stations) since the bulk of their violent criminal cases are probably ***"black Pittsburghers***?" Next, these NIGGERfiliacs will demand that the weatherman stop mentioning the possibility of rain because it makes the entire weekly forecast gloomy. Call me crazy, but I expect the constitutionally protected press to effectively do its job, regardless of who is offended.

Media urged to change portrayal of blacks
Summit discusses Pittsburgh news coverage of African-American men and boys
post-gazette.com

(Ratings)

To the media, ratings are the end game. They're the non-discriminatory yardstick used to measure whether a product is attracting viewers, which in turn, draws advertisers. Consequently, news or stories that might negatively affect the media outlet's bottom line may be spun, blocked, or trivialized. Race is such a polarizing issue that the mainstream media usually avoid it, unless it benefits ratings. For instance, *'Af-Am on Af-Am'* violent crime or *'Af-Am on Eu-Am'* violent crime (with the exception of O.J) rarely becomes national news, conversely, most alleged *'Euro on Af-Am'* violent crime is national news (i.e. Trayvon Martin, Tawana Brawley). Although *'Euro on Af-Am' violent* crime statistically occurs less frequently than *'Af-Am on Eu-Am'* violent crime, it typically results in a ratings surge because of its *'hate crime'* marketability. Race-peddlers know the value of the race card, and routinely exploit the historical connotation attached to *'Euro on Af-Am'* situations. Be mindful that the race-hustling occurs with the media's blessing; *'Euro on Af-Am'* crime is good for both (race & media) businesses.

(A Perfect Ratings Monster)

The Duke Lacrosse case, which captivated the nation, is an example of the mainstream media sensationalizing *'Euro on Af-Am'* crime to feed the ratings monster. In March 2006, an African-American female student at North Carolina Central University who worked as a stripper, dancer, and escort, accused three Euro-American Duke University students, members of the Duke Blue Devils men's lacrosse team, of raping her at a party. The media and many people involved with the case, (including prosecutor) immediately called the alleged assault a hate crime or suggested it might be one. The media frenzy surrounding this story lasted a year, and many lives were devastated, even though a verdict wasn't rendered. It wasn't until April 2007 (a year later) that the DNA testing, story, timeline inconsistencies, and lack of credibility vindicated the students, with all charges being dropped. Naturally, once justice prevailed, the story quickly lost its sexiness. It's worth noting that similar to the way BLACKS pay the NIGGER tax, these Euro-American students were punished for assumptions and not evidence.

(BLACK Media)

The yellow journalism spread by BLACK media promotes the misbelief that NIGGERtivity isn't reflective of a criminal subculture; instead, systemic disenfranchisement. Despite the fact that NIGGERS are presently the Ku Klux Klan on steroids, the BLACK media is largely in denial, and routinely trivializes NIGGERtivity. Sure, they occasionally express dissent about it, but usually they're mum; NIGGERtivity is accepted while condemnation is not. Besides, it's always easier to blame the WHITE man and focus on any "White on Black" crime. This tactic always elicits aggressive audience engagement and increased revenue. Even though this form of indoctrination has been a disservice to the community, the BLACK media isn't criticized by African-Americans like the mainstream media.

(Just Sayin')

I argue that since African-Americans have a self-proclaimed patent on the usage of the word NIGGER, the BLACK media should actually use "NIGGER" (as I do) or at least the "N word" to describe the community-destroying degenerates. Heck, NIGGER and NIGGA are already indiscriminately used in the African-American community, so why not use it when it's actually applicable. Moreover, if this unprecedented step was taken, the historical hurt associated with the word might dissipate.

*<u>Usual Suspect:</u> HoG-Centered Advertisements

The goal of any advertisement is to sell, promote, or inform by speaking the language of its target audience. Advertisement firms know that the NIGGER subculture dominates HoGs, so they market there accordingly. Nevertheless, marketing to the NIGGER subculture or overall African-American community is a slippery slope because anything can be misperceived as racism. In the old days, companies commonly used unpolished, African-American caricatures with exaggerated physical features like extremely red lips, charcoal complexion, and bulging eyes on advertising campaigns. Now, in today's race-conscious advertising world, such approach doesn't exist because it's a product killer. Companies understand that racist ads would obstruct their bottom line; therefore, wouldn't purposely offend potential customers. So, the reason why many liquor, cigarette, or any other negatively perceived industry's ads exist in the HoG is because it's where their product sells. Stop blaming the advertisers or malt liquor for NIGGERtivity; NIGGERS knew its effects before they consumed it.

One ad has a racist caricature while the other ad's targeted market actually speaks this way ("Talk to 'Ya mom 'n' em' for less")

*<u>Usual Suspect</u>: *The Internet and Social Network sites*

Just because the NIGGER subculture chooses to nefariously use the internet and social networking sites, these two entities shouldn't be blamed for NIGGERtivity. The internet has become the great equalizer and "all seeing eye" in this information age. Also, it has loosened the corporate media's grip on information, and provides three-dimensional (3-D) sight to news that's purposely delivered in 2-D. Quite simply, the internet has leveled the playing field between traditional (mainstream) and non-traditional (alternate stream) of news stories via blogs and other self-published methods. One of the greatest benefits of the internet is the virtual accessibility to the NIGGER subculture without physically being victimized. Plus, sites such *BLACKSvsNIGGERS.com* can document the daily effects of the NIGGER subculture, NIGGER-Tsunami, and Flashfloods in real time. Those who have had limited personal experience with the NIGGER subculture can now realize the true depth and impact of NIGGERtivity while sipping lattes in their pajamas. The web is releasing the masses from the spell casted by NIGGERfiliacs and promoted by the mainstream media, which blames oppression or racism as catalysts for NIGGERtivity. Eventually, public sympathy for this subculture will be replaced with intolerance.

Suspects Take Selfies Inside Murdered Pastor's Car
myfoxmemphis.com

(Twitter)

Along with Facebook, this social media site really serves as an expose' of the NIGGER subculture, and provides intimate insight into their overwhelmingly self-defeating behavior. According to a Pew study, African-Americans make up approximately twenty-six percent of Twitter's traffic (the NIGGER percentage is unknown), making it their most popular social networking platform along with Instagram. While most people use this median for idle chatter, gossip, entertainment etc., NIGGERS are busy posting their looting spoils (Hurricanes Katrina & Sandy), synchronizing their next Flashflood location, or simply being NIGGERS. Also, these extreme risk takers are purposely using the interacting capability of social networks to connect in ways that law enforcement didn't anticipate and are struggling to prevent. Ironically, JuviNIGGERS are functionally illiterate (except in text or twitter lingo) and struggle to learn effective communication skills in school, yet, communicate effectively via social networking sites. Go figure.

Pew Study: Blacks Over-Index On Twitter; Whites On Pinterest
adage.com

Twitter post leads to teens murder
grio.com

Teen Girl Arrested After Brutal Fight Over Twitter Beef
vibevixen.com

(Video Sharing Sites)

Admittedly, I'm no criminal mastermind, but it doesn't take a genius to know that the first principle of crime is to not be caught. Secondly, this principle is reinforced by planning precisely for a smooth escape. Yet, as evidenced by video sharing sites like YouTube, NIGGERS intentionally and inexplicably violate this universal criminal code. The recording and subsequent posting of irrefutable evidence on public sites are essentially confessions, which expedite any police investigation while debunking the myth that NIGGERtivity is an anomaly or fictional stereotype. These videos publically reveal their sociopathic, destructive behavior, while confirming that *"keepin' it real"* supersedes common sense. Normally, criminals avoid criminality if a camera is present, but NIGGERS love publicity, so they deliberately indulge. Due to the massive amount of NIGGERtivity video clips in cyberspace, chronic xeNIGphobia understandably exists.

Teens arrested after posting YouTube video of beating 13-year-old boy and hanging him from a tree
nydailynews.com

Teen charged in taped CTA attack on elderly man
thegrio.com

Teen Girls in Videotaped Beating of Woman Are Remorseless, Cop Says
abcnews.go.com

(Facebook)

Gone are the days when Facebook's demographic was college students networking amongst each other. Now, gazillion dollars heavier, and open to anyone with internet access, Facebook has become another cyber place where NIGGERtivity is on full display. For attention and increase in *"likes,"* NIGGERS will post lewd pictures, comments, and videos highlighting their degenerative lifestyle, gang affiliations, and overall, fourth world behavior. By expanding Facebook, Mark Zuckerberg has unwittingly "friended" the NIGGER subculture. As a result, Facebook can now add homey-cides, rapes, assaults, and food stamp solicitations to its list of apps.

Cops Catch Alleged Bank Robber Through Facebook Posts

newsone.com

[Author's Note: NIGGERS are their own worst enemy; which is why they are enrolled at HNCUs at such a high rate. Case in point: Forty-seven minutes before committing a bank robbery, this ingenious criminal posted "I Gotta Get That $$$$$ Man!!!"]

Facebook rape suspect, Wayne Smith, charged in 3rd rape

cbsnews.com

Man Charged With Sex Assault; Photos Posted On Facebook

chicago.cbslocal.com

Fights break out at Carson Beach

boston.com

[Article's quote: "Police said the gang members are part of a group of more than 1,000 youths who have used social media sites like Facebook to plan unruly gatherings on the beach on three of the past four nights."]

(Baby Mama Drama on FB)

A Baby Mama posted on her Facebook wall: ***"I will pay somebody a stack to kill my baby father."*** *(Author's Note: A stack is slang for a thousand dollars).* Geesh, her Baby Daddy's life is only worth a stack??? She probably has hair weave worth more than that. LoL. Perhaps she would've offered more money but the devaluation of the dollar on the global market affected her portfolio (I'm just sayin'). Anyway, the story becomes more interesting, yet unsurprising. One of her male Facebook friends ebonically responded to her solicitation by writing, ***"say no more. what he look like. where he be at. need that stack 1st ima mop that bull."*** See, it bears repeating that NIGGERS actually talk in the same manner that they text/tweet; it's as if their thoughts have to be expressed in 160 characters or less (and I'm being generous with 160). Unbelievably, in order to successfully fulfill what is otherwise a meticulous and calculating endeavor (a planned murder), this NIGGER simply needed to know two things: 1) ***"what he look like"*** (Translation) *What does your child's father look like?* 2) ***"where he be at"*** (Translation) *Where does your child's father live or frequent?* Then, he concluded, ***"need that stack 1st ima mop that bull."*** (Translation) *The service will be rendered in lieu of the thousand dollar payment.* Due to the NIGGER subculture's inability to effectively plan, both (Baby Mama & NIGGER hit man) were predictably arrested before the scheme could manifest. However, as fate would have it, the targeted Baby Daddy was still murdered shortly after the scheme was foiled, but the police deemed it ***"unrelated."*** I wonder if that ***"stack"*** bounty was still collectable.

Target in Facebook murder-for-hire case shot dead
philly.com

Brooklyn woman kills brother's girlfriend over $20 following Facebook fight
nypost.com

Shocking moment pregnant woman was shot in the belly over Facebook post – killing her unborn baby
dailymail.co.uk

*<u>Usual Suspect</u>: *Video Games*

Blaming video games for JuviNIGGERtivity is simply a cop-out. I can attest that video games provide one of the few pleasurable escapes to children in the HoG. Let's be honest, JuviNIGGERtivity has existed long before violent video games and game systems. During my youth, the primitive 26-bit Atari produced few games and none were violent, yet, JuviNIGGERtivity existed. In Japan, where top video game systems are made, the negligible violence rate amongst their teens contradicts the following CNN article (11/3/08) titled, "*Violent video games linked to child aggression.*" It states, ***"About 90 percent of U.S. kids ages 8 to 16 play video games, and they spend about 13 hours a week doing so (more if you're a boy). Now a new study suggests***

virtual violence in these games may make kids more aggressive in real life." So, if this study's assessment is accurate, then replacing a popular game such as *"Grand Theft Auto"* with a game called *"Driving Miss Daisy,"* whose objective is to drive to needy communities and perform charitable deeds, would eventually lead to kinder, gentler JuviNIGGERS. For the record, there is no video game called *"Driving Miss Daisy,"* just as there is no kinder, gentler, JuviNIGGER. In an article titled, *"Reality Bytes: Eight Myths About Video Games Debunked,"* MIT Professor Henry Jenkins debunked the *"video games causes violence"* theory. He observed, ***"Researchers find that people serving time for violent crimes typically consume less media before committing their crimes than the average person in the general population. It's true that young offenders who have committed school shootings in America have also been game players. But young people in general are more likely to be gamers — 90 percent of boys and 40 percent of girls play. The overwhelming majority of kids who play do NOT commit antisocial acts. According to a 2001 U.S. Surgeon General's report, the strongest risk factors for school shootings centered on mental stability and the quality of home life, not media exposure."*** Simply put, the NIGGER subculture treats life as if it is a video game, thus, JuviNIGGERtivity is a result.

Man says driving stolen car into group of joggers was 'fun' and 'like Grand Theft Auto'
dailymail.co.uk

[Author's Note: The NIGGERfiliacs would have us believe that the stolen car or video game (but not the NIGGER) are actually responsible for this NIGGERtivity.]

Four Kids Arrested For Beating Elderly Women Over X-Box
newsone.com

[Author's Note: The "kids" assaulted the 77-year-old grandma and held a sixth grader at gunpoint.]

CRIME REPORT: Woman uses three small children to steal video game systems
commercialappeal.com

[Author's Note: If video games influence bad behavior, I wonder which game inspired this mother.]

Video game thief suspect arrested
wistv.com

[Author's Note: The video game forced him to steal game systems from a Charlotte pediatric cancer clinic.]

(Closing Thoughts)

Although I know that O.N.D is the source of NIGGERtivity, I understand why it's easy for others to blame external entities or circumstances. Amongst other pathologies, the NIGGER subculture is mentally shallow, and their lack of horizon is manifested behaviorally. Therefore, to supplement their cerebral shortcoming, they're highly susceptible to having the substance of their thoughts manufactured by external sources. Even still, scapegoating others for exploiting an extremely impressionable people (who love being exploited) is wrong. Interestingly, BLACKS like me and millions of other Americans (Euro, Asian, Latino etc.) have also been subjected to these same cultural influences (Media, Entertainment, Video Games, Guns etc.) blamed for NIGGERtivity, yet have managed to normally function in society. How did we do it?

Chapter X

Abel Kills Cain

"One has not the right to betray even a traitor. Traitors must be fought, not betrayed."- Charles Pierre Peguy

As presented throughout this book, BLACKS and NIGGERS are two different branches from the same African-American tree. Even so, as Zora Neale Hurston assessed, *"All your skin folk ain't your kinfolk."* I frequently equate the relationship of BLACKS and NIGGERS to the twin brothers Cain and Abel from the Old Testament (Genesis Chapter 4). Cain, jealous that his brother Abel was favored because of his work ethic and pride, killed him. When God asked Cain of Abel's whereabouts, he sarcastically answered, ***"Am I my brother's keeper?"*** Consequently, God evicted Cain from the confines of garden, making him a vagabond. As a perpetual wanderer, Cain knew that without God's protection he might be killed. Understanding Cain's plight, God mercifully placed a protection mark upon Cain to ensure that he would not be harmed. The rest is history.

(The Present)

Let's fast forward to the present where the Cain-ites (NIGGERS) are still murdering Abel-ites (BLACKS) and will continue to do so until they are banished from our garden (community). NIGGERS are the evil twin of BLACKS, and like Cain, they need to be called out, exiled, and made into vagabonds. Additionally, like Cain, once outside the safe haven of the garden (African-American community), they're fearful of others. The NIGGER subculture innately knows that no other race will tolerate or make excuses for them as the African-American community has and does. Yes, the Cain-ites still have a protection mark, but it's not from God... it's from the NIGGERfiliacs.

(Grandmomma Starkes)

During my childhood, my great-grandmother often used the word *"Cain"* as a synonym for trouble or hell. She would warn, ***"Stay away from those boys because they're always raising Cain!"*** Whenever she said it, I understood the context, but didn't know that *"Cain"* was a biblical reference. Actually, it wasn't until my teenage years, and repeated encounters with ***"those boys"*** that I fully comprehended this phrase; it was Anti-NIGGER advice. Although she is physically gone, I regret not having the opportunity to hug and thank her for demanding that I stay away from ***"those boys"*** (even though I didn't completely heed her advice). Now, I'm utilizing her sage advice to caution everyone about ***"those boys"*** and their *Cain-causing* subculture. When it comes to ***"those boys,"*** I'm not my brother's keeper.

(P.R Dilemma)

Because of NIGGERS, the BLACK community has a public relations problem. Imagine having a twin that indulges in all kinds of undesirable and criminal activities resulting with an overall negative perception of you. This is the dilemma faced by BLACKS; NIGGERS has become the most visible twin via their characteristically destructive misdeeds. Cain is so busy that BLACKS have conditioned themselves for his usual appearance on the nightly news telecasts. We cross fingers, hold breaths, and then collectively exhale if he isn't featured. There will always be fundamental differences between Abel & Cain's (BLACKS & NIGGERS) cultures. Many of these differences are documented on video at ***www.BLACKSvsNIGGERS.com.*** Here are a few:

1. Abel (BLACKS) wants to benefit from what he has toiled to build, while Cain (NIGGERS) wants equal benefits without equal sweat.

2. Abel (BLACKS) brings "peace" to the community, while Cain (NIGGERS) brings a "piece" to the community.

3. Abel (BLACKS) takes pride in working while the only thing Cain (NIGGERS) has working is pride.

(No Snitch Campaign)

Remember, in the Garden of Eden, God asked Cain ***"Where is Abel thy brother?"*** Cain responded, ***"I know not: Am I my brother's keeper?"*** Although Cain committed the first Biblical homicide, which resulted in a speedy interrogation from God, he still refused to snitch on himself... even to an omniscient being lol. Presently, Cain's subculture is still pushing the "don't snitch" campaign, which demonizes any police cooperation, tipsters, and eyewitnesses. Moreover, in attempt to further their destructive agenda, snitching is equated to "selling out." In reality, NIGGERS are the actual sell-outs! The irony of the "no snitchin" ideology is that NIGGERS are the biggest snitches, and often snitch on each other. Also, their bravado, flashiness, bragging (in person or on social sites), and incriminating videos are forms of snitching on themselves. However, judging by the lack of community intervention in the HoG, Cain's subculture has largely been successful with propagating "no snitching" as a family value. Although a small amount of African-American communities wisely countered the *"Stop Snitching"* campaign with *"Pro-Telling"* slogans, the overall impactful change hasn't occurred. On the other hand, WHITE communities have been successful at preventing subcultures from stealing their neighborhoods because snitching and police cooperation are heavily endorsed.

Which does the HoG support?

(Snitches for Hire)

In Killadelphia (Philadelphia), Pistolvania (Pennsylvania), during halftime at a rec center's basketball game, an Urban Terrorist ran across the basketball court and fired eleven times into the stands, wounding six people. Of course, *"no one saw anything,"* even though an estimated five hundred spectators attended. In other words, none of the estimated five hundred onlookers *saw no evil, heard no evil, spoke no evil* (about the Urban Terrorist). Ultimately, the mayor decided to bribe the many witnesses to "snitch" by offering a taxpayer provided reward of $20,000. It still amazes me that a financial incentive had to be offered in a situation where there were five hundred potential eyewitnesses. The purchasing of witness cooperation to perform a civic duty is an indictment of the African-American community, furthermore, a testament to the power of "no-snitch" mentality. Just think how differently the conclusion of this story would've been if the shooter were Euro-American, he wouldn't have even made it out the gym! This hypocrisy is both hilarious and sad. Killadelphia, like several American cities has a shrinking tax base, yet NIGGERtivity is forcing Philly to raid its rainy day funds to bribe citizens into doing the right thing. In fact, Philly plans to double funds provided to the witness assistance program ($500 for information leading police to an illegal gun, and up to $20,000 for information leading to an arrest in any homicide). Again, in a city like Philly, which is high in NIGGERtivity, this massive bill is forwarded to the remaining taxpayers.

500 witnesses and no one is talking
philly.com

No-snitch case cracked: Witnesses come forward a year after slaying
suntimes.com

[Author's Note: Officers asked the dying 17-year-old to name the gunman. Police said he responded: "I know. But I ain't telling you s---."]

Chapter XI

The "ANTI–NIGGER"

"The best way to solve any problem is to remove its cause."
-Dr. MLK Jr.

I understand that many will interpret the theme of this book as a bleak analysis of the African-American community, indeed, that take is partially true. Nevertheless, being an optimist and believer in the balance of nature, I recognize that every problem has a solution, even if the solution is disagreeable to some. I'm simply saying that wherever a villain exists, surely there's a hero or anti-villain. With so much of this book dedicated to exposing and condemning the NIGGER subculture, it's revitalizing to write this chapter highlighting their arch nemesis; affectionately call the "Anti-NIGGER."

(What is it?)

An Anti-NIGGER in any capacity is essentially NIGGER-bleach that prevents the occurrence of NIGGER-Tsunamis, Flashfloods, or NIGfestations, while offsetting O.N.D. Anti-NIGGERS affect the NIGGER subculture in the same way that sunlight affects vampires. The beautiful aspect of an Anti-NIGGER is that it's three-dimensional; it can be a person, place, or thing. For clarity of said point, I have compiled several Anti-NIGGER examples, but due to the NIGGER subculture's constant regression, this list is not all-inclusive and falls short of completion.

(Anti-NIGGER Personage)

Personified Anti-NIGGERS (like me) are the polar opposite of NIGGERS and won't hesitate to denounce their destructive subculture. Anti-NIGGERS know that major differences exist between themselves and NIGGERS. While NIGGERS aspire to be perpetual antagonists, the Anti-NIGGER strives to maximize his/her potential and become societal assets. Moreover, they're determined to contribute to the community through charity, volunteerism, activism, public servitude, etc. while embracing education, and accountability. The victimhood mentality isn't incorporated into their ideology, therefore, alleged systemic racism and institutional biases aren't used as crutches; instead, all experiences are used to build strength. They don't worship the streets, and possess attributes that transcend the confines of the HoG mentality. Although many may excel in academia and others may not, overall, they still counter the NIGGER philosophy that education is secondary to street credibility. Being the opposite of NIGGERS, they purposely sidestep the regressive NIGGER subculture wherever it exists, and consciously distance themselves from any NIGative cultural indicators that may mislabel or stereotype them. They embrace exposure to the world outside the HoG and ultimately strive to blend into larger society with the understanding that the HoG is a place to escape, not personify. Their adaptability allows them to dress appropriately for any situation and adjust their language to suit any circumstance. The increase of Anti-NIGGERS will eventually marginalize the NIGGER subculture.

(More Anti-NIGGER Attributes)

The Anti-NIGGER knows that NIGGERS are inherently unhappy, which is why they (NIGGERS) degrade others that don't subscribe to their degenerative lifestyle. In other words, hurt people will hurt people. Anti-NIGGERS personify the mantra that society doesn't take on the characteristics of its exceptions. Indeed, NIGGERS aren't the African-American standard; they're the exception. Furthermore, the Anti-NIGGER dispels the notion perpetuated by the NIGGER subculture that "BLACKness" equals dysfunction, poverty, and lack of academic achievement. Even though Anti-NIGGERS associate with like minds, and purposely avoid any interaction with NIGGERS, they may associate with blacks (W.N.T) to help them exorcise their NIGGER propensities.

(Anti-NIGGER Places)

An Anti-NIGGER place is one that deters the NIGGER subculture. Whether these places are located in rural areas or inner-cities, they're essentially "NIGGER-free" retreats. While many places strive to create Anti-NIGGER environments, others are naturally Anti-NIGGER by virtue of their themes. The NIGGER subculture is naturally disconnected from resourceful places whose themes promote cultural achievement, societal advancement, science/technology, arts, mental/physical health, well-being, etc. Unsurprisingly, these places never have to take precautionary measures against NIGGERtivity, Flashfloods, or NIGGER-Tsunamis. Listed below are several examples of Anti-NIGGER places, and the reason(s) for their status.

Libraries or Bookstores – NIGGERS avoid these serene and cerebral places because they're congregated by readers. NIGGER patronage is further dissuaded by the mere fact that libraries and bookstores offer Anti-NIGGER things (books) as marque products. However, blacks (WNT) may frequent libraries because of the additional available resources and activities (DVD rentals, internet, etc.).

Organic food stores or Farmer's Market – Of course they don't patronize these health conscious places; especially since Kentucky Fried Chicken, Popeye's, and many other fast food places now accept EBT cards.

Museums – For obvious reasons, museums are Anti-NIGGER places, even African-American museums.

Broadway Musicals/Shows - They're simply dismissed as WHITE people stuff.

Science Exhibits – NIGGERS aren't concerned about the origin of things, only the benefits.

Yoga Studios – The mere fact that Anti-NIGGER principals such as meditation and self-reflection are part of the process is a turnoff.

Ivy League Colleges – NIGGERS never make it to the collegiate level unless it's via athletic scholarship. By far, Ivy League colleges are the biggest Anti-NIGGER places (as far as colleges) because academics (not athletics) define them.

Comedy Shows with Non-Af-Am Comedians – NIGGERS aren't receptive to any comedy that lacks vulgarity, profanity, or black people/white people contrasts. In other words, the content has to be HoG based.

Charity Events – As explained in the ***NIGGERnomics*** chapter, "giving" is a foreign concept to the NIGGER subculture because their culture is based on receiving. Moreover, they intentionally practice selfishness instead of selflessness.

Community Gardens – The words "community" and "garden" in the same sentence automatically makes this an Anti-NIGGER place.

(Anti-NIGGER Things)

Characteristically, NIGGERS routinely fight and kill over inanimate objects and other expendables (sneakers, cell phones, clothing etc.) yet, will never kill or hurt anyone over Anti-NIGGER items such as academic scholarships or books. Since NIGGERS avoid places that promote educational endeavors, by association, any instrument used to promote such interests is also shunned. Listed below are several examples of Anti-NIGGER things, and the reason for their status.

Microscope/Telescope – NIGGERS believe that nothing of importance needs a microscope or telescope to be seen. According to their superficial logic, if they can't see it, then it doesn't exist.

Dictionary - Well, first off, it's a book... duh! Secondly, it's a double deterrent because it teaches "diction" coupled with definitions. Learning how to properly pronounce, enunciate, and define words isn't beneficial in the HoG or HNCUs.

Educational Channels – There is no need to watch educational channels when B.E.T and ESPN keeps them pertinently informed.

Birth Control/Contraception – These are Anti-NIGGER things because their usage would cut the Baby Mama's income stream; thus, jeopardizing a financial pillar of their subculture.

Conscious Hip Hop – NIGGERS hate this genre of Hip Hop because it lacks violence, drug dealing, and misogyny.

Hybrid Vehicles – NIGGERS believe that environment-friendly cars (actually, environment-friendly anything) is WHITE people's stuff. Besides, caring for the environment is always considered someone else's job.

(Anti-NIGGER Activities)

Hiking – Actually, running (from law enforcement) is their version of hiking.

Reading/Studying- These two pastimes are the quintessential Anti-NIGGER activities. Although mind-stimulation via reading or studying may broaden one's horizon, "broadening horizons" is sacrilegious in their subculture; "keepin it real" is their way of life, and recreational reading violates that tenet. Oddly, the only way a NIGGER can openly indulge in such a shameful pastime (without reprisals) is if it occurs in a HNCU dorm room.

Recycling – There's no concern about saving the planet or any other forward thinking agendas because they live in the moment. In fact, throwing trash from moving vehicles is their method of recycling. In their subculture, the only thing that's actively recycled is Baby Mamas.

Speaking Correct Grammar – While enslaved, it was illegal for African-Americans to learn how to read or write, but today, NIGGERS purposely act as if it's still illegal. Speaking correct Grammar entails thinking before speaking, which clashes with their "react first" ideology.

Camping – Although camping offers NIGGERS the opportunity to bond with nature, the great outdoors would actually expose the limitations of their so-called "street smarts." The HoG keeps them urbanized and alienated from nature. As a result, outside the HoG, they're fish out of water. The extent of NIGGERS bonding with nature is generally confined to barbeques at local Public Parks.

Community Service– The only community service that they're familiar with is court-ordered community service. Don't hold your breath for anything more.

Blood Donation- The only donation that NIGGERS provide is sperm to Baby Mamas. Ironically, NIGGERS rely heavily on donated blood (due to NIGGERtivity), yet, won't donate blood. My son often donates blood, and since we live in a predominately African-American city, a victimized NIGGER is statistically likely to receive his blood. This is another societal aspect where the NIGGER subculture disproportionally benefits without contributing.

Chapter XII

What do NIGGERS Fear?

"The one permanent emotion of the inferior man is fear – fear of the unknown, the complex, the inexplicable. What he wants above everything else is safety."- Henry Louis Mencken

Because NIGGERtivity is unabatedly spreading across America at warped speed, a logical question is... what do NIGGERS fear? Firstly, society has to recognize that although their (NIGGERS) "keepin' it real" hardcore persona perpetuates an image of fearlessness, it's really a facade. Secondly, in addition to registered mail and child support court, NIGGERS are actually afraid of numerous things, some of which are detailed in this chapter.

(Exposure)

Like roaches that scatter when the light switch is flipped on, NIGGERS react similarly when exposed. Since, they're community agitators and not community assimilators, vigilant, intolerant neighborhoods are a detriment to their subculture. NIGGERS fear attentive neighbors and active town watches dedicated to community upkeep. In communities where the spirit is high, responsibility is delegated, and laws are enforced, they cannot thrive. In other words, they fear Anti-NIGGER communities.

(Austerity Measures)

Although NIGGERS don't know or even care to know the meaning or impact of austerity measures, they'll learn as soon as that EBT card is rejected. Hopefully, it stops working at the exact moment a Baby Mama is at the checkout register with her usual cartful of non-nutritional, non-essential groceries. Undoubtedly, in this age of pending austerity, Sugar Daddy will have to stop sprinkling monthly candy from the sky. Be warned that once it occurs, the NIGGER subculture will quickly collapse and NIGGERgeddon will commence. Many states are struggling to subsidize this dysfunctional subculture, which has shown no propensity for self-reliance or assimilation. In fact, as reported by *nbcchicago.com*, ***"The state of Illinois has reached a new level of broke. Come Monday, it won't have enough cash to bury its indigent dead. Illinois officials sent a letter to more than 600 funeral directors around the state to let them know there's no money for funerals for individuals on public assistance."*** Due to the unrelenting homey-cides, NIGGERS disproportionately rely on this particular state service more than any other group, and this is only the beginning of unwelcoming news. NIGGERS fear austerity measures, but don't know it yet.

Why Illinois Can't Afford its Poor Dead
nbcchicago.com

(Strict Welfare Reform)

The problem occurring in many American cities is that NIGGERS are over-utilizing local services without contribution. This subculture remains super-dependent on these services despite dwindling tax bases. Consequently, the curtailing of subsidized support systems and strict welfare reform will crush them. Welfare dependency is addictive like drugs, and like most drugs, it's a temporary fix. Even so, Quadruplers remain addicted to welfare while many cities struggle to sustain the Ponzi scheme that subsidizes their subculture.

Congress Mulls Cuts to Food Stamps Program Amid Record Number of Recipients
abcnews.com

(Travelling Abroad)

It bears repeating, NIGGERS don't broaden their horizons because they simply aren't interested in anything outside of the HoG. Uprooting themselves from familiar circumstances and comfort zones forces them to think outside the HoG, which is a frightening prospect. Therefore, they purposely travel to the typical places that other NIGGERS or African-Americans migrate (N.B.A All-Star weekend, Daytona Bike week, Hair shows, etc.). In the rare event that they travel internationally, it's usually to familiar places like Jamaica, Bahamas, or Cancun. Travelling abroad to experience and learn different cultures is Anti-NIGGER behavior.

(The Anti-NIGGER)

In the personage, Anti-NIGGERS progress on paths that NIGGERS cannot venture. Niggers fear and hate Anti-NiGGERS; the hate is comparable to the way a liar hates the truth. NIGGERS know that Anti-NIGGERS represents a form of thinking that (if practiced everywhere) would ostracize the NIGGER-subculture.

(Af-Am Abandonment /Segregation)

The NIGGER subculture would suffer immensely from withdrawal symptoms if rejected by the African-American community. Without the cover of the African-American community, their subculture would be a virus without a host. The African-American community has consistently provided a safe haven, while sheltering them from the consequences of their dysfunction. Across America, WHITES have created numerous Whitopias that are void of their underclass; BLACKS need to mimic that concept.

(Gentrification)

The bold act of gentrifying a HoG defies conventional wisdom. WHITES with the financial means usually avoid anything that's HoG-related, yet many are actually investing and renovating "written off" HoG landscapes. Despite the horrid HoG conditions created by the NIGGER subculture, and the apparent inability of the Af-Am natives to change them, the transformative power of gentrification makes the impossible, possible. NIGGERS know that it disrupts the flow of NIGGERtivity and will eventually displace them. Through gentrification, effective and active town watch associations are established, along with other Anti-NIGGER activities such as "snitching" and testifying in court.

(The WHITE Power Structure)

NIGGERS inherently fear the WHITE power structure. Yes, it's true! Ignore their misleadingly hardcore, anti-society, rebellious appearance. Sure, NIGGERS commit crimes against individual Euro-Americans, but rarely against the power structure. They know that (unlike the African-American community) Euro-Americans will mobilize against NIGGERtivity and continuously fight to remove it from their midst. If nothing else, NIGGERS respect overwhelming force.

(Green Zones)

I don't mean Green Zones in the environmental sense, but in the military sense. These Green Zones are safe havens found within cities that are plagued by NIGGERtivity. The visitors, residents, employees etc. inside these bubbles are insulated and secured from the NIGGERtivity that surrounds them. Their sense of security exists because of the heavy-handed and quick response by the power structure to any NIGGERtivity that happens within the Green Zone's perimeter. Years ago, I took my children to a Green Zone in Orlando, Florida, popularly known as Disney World. While watching Orlando's local news, I was surprised to learn that it (Orlando) was experiencing homicides and other violent NIGGERtivity at a record pace. Of course, I immediately knew that NIGGERS were responsible for that sad benchmark, then realized that Disney World (which is located in this same bloody city) seemed far removed from NIGGERtivity. It was as if Disney World and Orlando were located in two different cities. One part was hell, while the other part was heaven. Even so, with the massive influx of Disney tourists, I assumed that at the very least, NIGGERS were feasting on tourists in the same manner that predators (in the wild) feast during migrations. But such wasn't the case. As stated in the previous paragraph, NIGGERS fear the WHITE power structure, which is why they keep the NIGGERtivity confined to the HoG. The HoG is the opposite of a Green Zone... it's a Red Zone. NIGGERS understand that Disney World is a certified Green Zone, so Orlando's NIGGERtivity rarely breaches its borders. They know the ramifications of disrupting Disney's tourism; therefore, they keep it in-house (Red Zone) where it's tolerated. Meanwhile, as a Disney World tourist, I was happy to know that Mickey Mouse and crew had my back.

Chapter XIII

Memorandum to BLACK People

"I think that it is time for concerned African-Americans to march, galvanize and raise the awareness about this epidemic to transform our helplessness, frustration and righteous indignation into a sense of shared responsibility and action." - **Dr. William H. Cosby, Ed.D**

Contrary to popular belief, African-Americans do not think or move monolithically on every issue. Moreover, as far as internal differences, we're no different from any other community. But honestly, our foremost distinguishing feature is the tolerance and lack of unilateral movement to combat our subculture. Other groups have been able to prevent a takeover from their subcultures because they separate from them; we coddle ours. White Trash has been effectively ostracized by Whites, and is repeatedly referenced as living examples of failure. Conversely, in our community, "black trash" (NIGGER) is harbored, and accepted as examples of racism. I agree with John Ridley's assessment (*The Manifesto of Ascendancy for the Modern American Nigger, 11/30/06*) ***"It's time for ascended blacks to wish niggers good luck. Just as whites may be concerned with the good of all citizens but don't travel their days worrying specifically about the well-being of hillbillies from Appalachia, we need to send niggers on their way".***

As consistently stated throughout this book, all races have an underclass; but shockingly, only in the African-American community can continuous, underclass-sponsored travesties occur without aggressive reaction. We desperately need to replace the reactionary candle light vigils with assertive "shock and awe" campaigns. Our silence has not protected us. Furthermore, BLACKS can no longer internalize the NIGGER problem because we believe that acknowledgment makes our community "look bad." Well, I hate to be the bearer of bad news, but we need to fire our self-appointed public relations (P.R) people because our image couldn't be any worse. This nightmare of a reality exists because we've allowed the inmates to run the asylum; they must be confronted, or we risk the continued declined of schools, neighborhoods and cities.

Communities Struggle to Break a Grim Cycle of Killing
wsj.com

Black-on-black victims could fill our stadiums
suntimes.com

(Willing Hostages)

The general perception regarding our lack of action is accurate. In fact, we're essentially aiding and abetting this subculture while severely suffering from Stockholm syndrome. As explained by Wikipedia, ***"Stockholm syndrome is a term used to describe a paradoxical psychological phenomenon wherein hostages express adulation and have positive feelings towards their captors that appear irrational in light of the danger or risk endured by the victims, essentially mistaking a lack of abuse from their captors as an act of kindness."*** As a result of us sitting on our hands in silence, our neighborhoods have become our captor's playground. How much more incalculable communal damage has to occur before changes are implemented? Is there a certain level of anger that has to be reached before we rebel? We'll collectively "snap" whenever statistically rare Trayvon-type murders occur, meanwhile, we "nap" when the intra-racial murders occur. This acute form of Stockholm syndrome is specific to the African-American community.

(Misplaced Priorities)

Isolating this virus from our community should be the highest priority. It seems almost futile to address education, health, and other pertinent issues affecting our community without first ensuring that we aren't extinguished by NIGGERtivity. The opposite of courage isn't cowardice, but conformity; and many of us have certainly conformed to cowardice, except when race-baited. When race-baited, our collective strength goes on full display, while simultaneously (and contradictorily) refusing any mobilization to confront Urban Terrorism. Time after time, the BLACK race-peddlers go out of their way to get offended by others to justify a national temper-tantrum. Expectedly, these race-peddlers' agenda isn't new; Booker T. Washington exposed them long ago. ***"There is a class of colored people who make a business of keeping the troubles, the wrongs, and the hardships of the Negro race before the public. Some of these people do not want the Negro to lose his grievances, because they do not want to lose their jobs. There is a certain class of race-problem solvers who don't want the patient to get well."*** Again, our predictable outrage over any perceived racism has become fashionable while contradictorily ignoring the direct NIGGER threat. Understanding the NIGGER subculture's damaging impact, columnist Juan Williams wrote (*Ghetto Culture is Killing Civil Rights, 8/22/06*), ***"If systemic racism remains a reality, there is also a far more sinister obstacle facing African-American young people today: a culture steeped in bitterness and nihilism, a culture that is a virtual blueprint for failure".*** Even still, as evidenced by the following headlines, the race-peddlers would rather fight the lesser battles.

Racist Hallmark Card? NAACP Says Yes
theroot.com

The NAACP Believes "You Mad Bro?" Is Racial Intimidation
buzzfeed.com

[Article's Quote: "After a high school football game, fans of the winning team held up a sign saying, "You Mad Bro?"]

TEXAS COUNTY OFFICIAL SEES RACE IN TERM 'BLACK HOLE'
foxnews.com

'Black' hurricane names brewing swirl of dissent
wnd.com

[Author's Note: An African-American congresswoman wanted to incorporate "Black names" for hurricanes.]

Anger rises over proposed Mpls. dog park
startribune.com

[Author's Note: Af-Ams angrily attended community meetings singing "We Shall Overcome" while arguing that creating a dog park in MLK Park would desecrate his legacy. Unmentioned by the protestors, were the daily prostitution, drug dealing, and other NIGGERtivity that occurs in the park. I guess those things aren't desecrations.]

(Ghettopoly)

Another example of a misplaced, ferociously waged, cherry-picked battle was one waged against a board game titled Ghettopoly. Although the game was a parody of the HoG and NIGGER subculture's tenets, the BLACK Clergy, NAACP, and other NIGGERfilacs considered it racist. Soon after, the race-peddlers and NIGGERfiliacs boycotted the game, and stores quickly stopped selling it. The hypocrisy of this *"Ghettopoly"* boycott was accurately captured in a Chicago Sun-Times article by columnist Mary Mitchell (*"Ghettopoly' Is What Happens When Hip-Hop Is Celebrated 10/5/03)."* She wrote, ***"The symbols found in Ghettopoly are an accurate reflection of what hip-hop heroes are selling ... Ironically, people are outraged about Urban Outfitters' selling a foul board game, but few people of influence seem to care that every record store in America is selling music that glorifies the very stereotypes the game promotes. How can black people be outraged over a board game when black superstars have gotten rich by promoting those same stereotypes? These performers aren't boycotted. They are worshipped."***

Black leaders outraged at 'Ghettopoly' game at Urban Outfitters
usatoday.com

Game's street theme upsets NAACP
sptimes.com

(The Boiling Frog)

Even an unbiased, untrained eye can see that NIGGERS are a clear and present danger in any community, yet, our misplaced attention and complacency has likened our situation to the *"boiling frog"* story. The boiling frog story is a widespread anecdote describing a frog slowly being boiled alive. The premise is that if a frog is placed in boiling water, it will jump out, but if it is placed into cold, slowly heated, water, it will not perceive the danger; consequently, cooking to death. The story is often used as a metaphor for the inability of people to react to significant changes that occur gradually. We are the boiling frog.

(S.O.S)

Although marginalizing the NIGGER subculture is primarily a community endeavor, outside assistance from BLACK based groups (National Association of BLACK Journalists, NAACP, BLACK Caucus, etc.) is desperately needed. Ironically, these groups characteristically focus on everything "BLACK-related" except this menacing subculture. Sure, there have been a few articles, symposiums, and even a Million Man March addressing the dysfunction, but these limited efforts are simply symbolic side shows. The BLACK front group for political interests aka the Congressional Black Caucus has been in existence for more than four decades, yet, the newcomer Tea Party movement has been more effective at pushing agendas. The BLACK Caucus, or more accurately, the Black Carcass, describes its goals as ***"positively influencing the course of events pertinent to African-Americans and others of similar experience and situation,"*** and ***"achieving greater equity for persons of African descent in the design and content of domestic and international programs and services."*** I understand that legislation alone won't remove the NIGGER subculture, but if the CBC's goal of ***"positively influencing the course of events pertinent to African-Americans"*** is accurate, the least they can do is pretend to care about this Un-Civil War. Like clockwork, Urban Terrorists have ensured that annually, African-Americans have the nation's highest victimization/perpetrator rates for murder, assault, and other crimes. Yet, even with this statistical evidence, most BLACK legislators lack the fortitude and/or desire to address these types of unflattering issues. Even still, to solve this crisis, we also need more than prayer from the BLACK church, BLACK mosque, BLACK synagogue, Black temple etc. because NIGGERS are fighting with something more tangible. Let me be clear, I'm not suggesting that we fight fire with fire; instead, let's fight fire with water.

Black America's #1 Civil Rights Issue: Violence
politic365.com

(BLAXODUS)

Realizing the misery of co-existing with the NIGGER subculture, many BLACKS (who could afford to do so) physically and mentally flee the HoG. Thus, giving rise to the terms *"Black*

Exodus" or *"Black flight."* Wikipedia explains the initial BLACK exodus, ***"Following the emergence of anti-discrimination policies in housing and labor sparked by the civil rights movement, members of the BLACK middle class moved out of the ghetto. Urban sociologists frequently title this historical event as "black middle class exodus" (also see black flight). Elijah Anderson describes a process by which members of the black middle class begin to distance themselves socially and culturally from ghetto residents during the later half of the twentieth century, "eventually expressing this distance by literally moving away". This is followed by the exodus of black working class families. As a result, the ghetto becomes primarily occupied by what sociologists and journalists of the 1980s and 1990s frequently title the "underclass". William Julius Wilson suggests this exodus worsens the isolation of the black underclass – not only are they socially and physically distanced from whites, they are also isolated from the black middle class."*** Regardless of race, no principled person wants to live amongst a people where family values, community standards, and personal responsibility are absent. Unfortunately, those who are unable to leave the HoG must vigilantly unite or suffer in silence. In other words, fight, flight, or agonize.

(Closure)

The helping hand that we're looking for is at the end of our collective arm, but seemingly, we're waiting for Captain America to save us. Utilizing proactivity and reactivity is how menacing subcultures are marginalized. I don't want to hear any more rhetoric about a so-called BLACK agenda, unless, that agenda addresses this Un-Civil War.

Chapter XIV

Memorandum to NIGGERS

"He who makes a beast of himself gets rid of the pain of being a man." -Samuel Johnson

The above referenced quote concisely captures my feeling about your kind. Grandmomma Starkes used to say, ***"The best way to avoid looking "bad" is by not doing "bad" things."*** Well... you look horrible! While writing this memo, I had a moment of clarity and realized the futility of actually writing to a subculture that despises reading. So, in attempt to make this memo appealing to your kind, I actually considered writing it in Ebonics or text message vernacular lol. However, I eventually decided against dumbing down because I'm not accommodating your subculture as the NIGGERfiliacs do. Ultimately, whether you read this memo or not, I won't lose any sleep.

Growing up in the HoG, specifically the projects, I partially assimilated into your subculture. I used to think that you deserved pity over scorn, but I was wrong; my pity is now reserved for victims (of NIGGERtivity) and taxpayers (who subsidize your culture). Amazingly, in this age of information and technology, you still choose to believe that there is no equity in education (unless the education furthers NIGGERtivity). Instead, you promote ignorance as a viable alternative. Moreover, you reject higher educational quests, and disregard universal values because you think, *"street knowledge"* is *"supreme knowledge."* Also, you willingly embrace a narrow worldview while encouraging NIGGERtivity as a legitimate path to success; meanwhile, responsibility and accountability are punted to society. Although your subculture purposely promotes every conceivable extremity (talk, dress, lifestyle, etc.) to be distinguished from the mainstream, you contradictorily expect mainstream parity, and then yell racism when shunned by the mainstream. As a student of life, I recognize that in many cases, non-conformity has actually led to the rise of great ideas, music, art, inventions etc.

in history; yet, your non-conformist subculture only produces rebels without causes. Honestly, I'm not asking you to subscribe to learning a positive cultural standard; clearly, you have chosen to be a multigenerational underclass, defined by dysfunction, violence, and dependency. Furthermore, I want to be clear; this book wasn't written to assert superiority over you. Instead, it addresses the quality of life issues that you pose, and emphasizes our voluminous differences. In fact, our foremost difference is that NIGGERS benefit from BLACKS, whereas BLACKS suffer because of NIGGERS.

Mistaken Identity and the NIGGER tax exist because your subculture is undoubtedly responsible for a massive amount of the negative pathologies (crime, prison inmates, welfare, violence rates, sexually transmitted diseases, high school dropout rates, Baby Mamas/Daddies, illegitimate birth rates etc.) associated with the entire African-American community. In all fairness, I don't blame you for all the deficiencies in the African-American community, but the general belief that a high concentration of African-Americans detrimentally transforms any environment is a result of your kind.

In closing, I've accepted the irrationality of your subculture. A culture that blames the "WHITE" man for failures, bleeds the system, avoids social responsibility, and education, while claiming to "keeping it real." Quite simply, you are feral blacks with sociopathic tendencies, and **N**egro **I**ndividuals **G**enerating **G**rief **E**verywhere **R**outinely. Unquestionably, your disagreeable traits distinguish you from us. You're unconcerned about the sacrifices (including lives) and investments made to help African-Americans obtain equal footing in America. Instead, you intentionally squander the yielded opportunities in favor of O.N.D. I'm perplexed as to why you don't embrace alienation whenever it's practiced against your kind, especially since you've already decided against civil, societal participation. Time is running out for your subculture; the taxpayers' patience is thinning and the country (with the exception of NIGGERfiliacs) no longer believes that your behavior is a manifestation of despair caused by centuries of racism and oppression. If pioneers like Frederick Douglass and Booker T. Washington (who were actually enslaved) didn't suffer from Post Traumatic Slavery Disorder, then how dare you use slavery as a cop-out! The only positive aspect of your existence is that it provides continuous teachable moments for BLACK children to learn how not to be. And for that, I thank you.

Chapter XV

Memorandum to blacks With NIGGER Tendencies

"Accountability breeds response-ability" - Stephen R. Covey

Unlike NIGGERS, I believe that most blacks (WNT) are capable of evolving into productive BLACKS. Several prominent BLACKS that were once blacks (WNT) have successfully progressed in to societal assets. As repeatedly revealed throughout the book, I spent a large portion of my life as a black (W.N.T) before realizing that it was a dead end path.

Thousands of American lives from multiple ethnicities were lost pre/post-civil war, and during the Civil Rights era to give African-Americans a legitimate chance at assimilation and equality. In fact, the *Tuskegee Institute* documented that 1,294 Euro-Americans were lynched between the years 1882-1968. Undoubtedly, they were lynched for aiding and abetting African-Americans. Additionally, the creation of the *"Great Society"* was in essence, an effort to eliminate poverty and racial injustice; both conditions disproportionately affected African-Americans. Nonetheless, while BLACKS looked to capitalize and build from the paved foundation, NIGGERS chose to become professional victims. Not only did they intentionally opt out of productive participation in society, they've disrespected the very legacies of those who fought for them to have that freedom of choice. Incalculable amounts of taxpayer's money, social services, job training, and educational opportunities have been dedicated to transitioning African-Americans into the mainstream, yet the NIGGER subculture thrives. Overall, these benevolent endeavors have largely been fruitless.

Although NIGGERS blame everyone else for their failures, as evidenced by their chosen behavior, chosen speech, chosen dress, and chosen lifestyle, they've actually chosen to be their own worst enemy. As this Un-Civil War continues, and circumstances worsen, new recruits will be needed on both sides. Therefore, you blacks (WNT) will eventually have to decide between BLACKS or NIGGERS.

I believe that all blacks (WNT) eventually come to a fork in the road, which forces them to either retain or forfeit their NIGGER tendencies. The problem is that you falsely believe that these NIGGER tendencies are a form of BLACK cultural identity, and the absence of these tendencies means "selling out." No, you will not be a sellout! NIGGER tendencies don't define BLACK culture! Actually, these tendencies are specific to the NIGGER subculture! Again, that NIGGER-promoted belief of "selling out" is an outright lie! This is simply their way of making evil appear fair-seeming. Here's the truth; NIGGERS are inherently miserable, and since misery loves company, they'll make absurd, illogical, and contradictory statements as an attempt to keep you in the crab barrel. If you have the desire to expel your NIGGER tendencies, become surrounded with Anti-NIGGERS and indulge in Anti-NIGGER activities. Remember, you can't soar with the eagles if you are walking with Dodo birds.

19 Questions posed to *TALEEB STARKES*

1. What qualifies you to write a book exposing the African-American community's "dirty laundry"?

Answer: *In reality, one doesn't have to be "qualified" to communicate the truth. But since my 'eyes' have witnessed massive NIGGERtivity, 'ears' have heard massive NIGGERtivity, and overall being has been massively impacted by NIGGERtivity, I'm massively overqualified to write this book. Contrary to the typical* ***"hear no evil, see no evil, speak no evil"*** *coping mechanism used in our community (which has allowed NIGGERS to continue their guerilla warfare without restraint), I will not deliberately deny the existence of this subculture just to protect the image of the African-American community or NIGGER interests... I'm no NIGGERfiliac. Denial is another reason why our so-called* ***"dirty laundry,"*** *is destroying the fabric of our community.*

2. Taleeb, are you a self-hating BLACK?

Answer: *No, and as stated in the book's intro, this battle is actually being waged because I'm a self-loving BLACK. Moreover, these feelings aren't simply based on emotion; instead, they're based on past/present happenings, logic, experience, and common sense. As a kid, I can remember one Sunday evening watching the mini-series* ***"Roots,"*** *and then attending school the next day violently angry at all Euro-Americans; I was upset for what their ancestors did to my ancestors. Not only was I upset, but seemingly, the entire housing project. The Roots mini-series was the talk of the HoG, and our collective anger seemed* *justified. Yet, even though Roots also showed Africans actively selling other Africans, no one was moved by that instrumental detail. In fact, no one even acknowledged it. To this day, every time Af-Ams cast a blind eye to any black on black infliction, I'm reminded of that communal, "mum's the word" dynamic, which is only abandoned when the inflictor is white. The statistics consistently confirm that slavery, racism, or poverty, aren't the reasons why African-American males are an endangered species; NIGGERS are the blame! My loathing towards them is because they have more blood on their hands than Al Qaeda, Ku Klux Klan, and the other terrorist groups combined. So, instead of inaccurately labeling me as a "self-hater," call me what I am..."prejudiced." My prejudice against NIGGERS and their subculture is based on up-close and personal experiences. I estimate that thousands of innocent lives could've been saved and will be saved if more people become prejudiced towards NIGGERS.*

3. Do you fear criticism for exposing the NIGGER subculture?

Answer: *No! Properly labeling and exposing our internal nemesis is a critical first step in reclaiming communities. Certainly, NIGGERS will not rebuke this book because they love attention of any kind. To them, this book is actually a promotional on how NIGGERS "Keep it real." They probably hope that it's adapted into a movie lol. The old adage still holds true:* ***"If you want to hide something from a NIGGER, put it in a book!"*** *Predictably, the loudest condemnation will be from the NIGGERfiliacs. These self-appointed gatekeepers of the African-American image (but not communities) will probably say many* *nasty things to assassinate my character while ignoring the facts. It's always easier to attack the messenger instead of the message, especially when the message is substantiated by statistics, headlines, and other evidence. Some will claim that I've created a demonic caricature of a disenfranchised segment of African-Americans, and others will infer that I'm a "House NIGGER" slandering the "Field NIGGER" just to pander to Euro-Americans. Since NIGGERfiliacs preach that NIGGERS aren't truly responsible for their misbehavior because they're disadvantaged minorities raised in broken, poverty-stricken environments crafted by institutionalized racism, I've realized that the only possible way to escape their criticisms is to write NIGGER-apologist books (which will never happen). At the end of the day, their anticipated criticisms aren't unique. Audre Lorde succinctly observed,* ***"Black writers, of whatever quality, who step outside the pale of what black writers are supposed to write about, or who black writers are supposed to be, are condemned to silences in black literary circles that are as total and as destructive as any imposed by racism."*** *If a WHITE person wrote a book condemning a violent, Neo-Nazi subculture that was destroying Euro-American communities, assuredly, the backlash would mostly come from the Neo-Nazi group, not the WHITE community (that the book serves). Contrarily, in the African-American community, Anti-NIGGERS like me are chastised while NIGGERS are given asylum. Go figure.*

4. Why does crime seem to follow African-Americans, and why is it that places with a large concentration of African-Americans have more murder and other forms of criminality?

Answer: *Because lurking within that African-American community is the parasitic NIGGER subculture, creating its usual* *havoc; but publically, the culpability falls onto the entire African-American population. This pattern will continue until the NIGGER subculture is exposed and ostracized.*

5. Why are African-Americans hesitant to publically acknowledge this problematic subculture?

Answer: *A large segment of the African-American population is NIGGERfiliacs. Additionally, several African-Americans have NIGGER or blacks (WNT) relatives that they love in spite of their dysfunctional/criminal ways. Oftentimes, love makes you see a person, as you want to perceive them instead of whom they really are. This illusory type of love is comparable to domestic abuse situations where the continuously battered woman repeatedly justifies the spousal abuse, and remains in the relationship. She believes that the abuser really isn't a "bad person." The worst kept secret in the African-American community is our pretending that everything is under control. Publicly discussing the bloody and destructive footprint that NIGGERtivity leaves on any environment breaks the unspoken oath of silence seemingly pledged by all African-Americans at birth. My city has a majority African-American population; including a BLACK mayor, BLACK District Attorney, BLACK Police Chief, BLACK Fire chief, BLACK School superintendent, and a majority BLACK city council with a BLACK president, yet, NIGGERtivity runs unchecked. As stated in* ***Memo to BLACK People****, we fight the wrong battles, and predictably mobilize for cherry picked causes. It's time to re-direct that energy into eradicating the virus within our community. My frustration forced me to become a whistleblower and go public with this book.*

6. Is poverty an excuse for violent crime?

Answer: *No!!! To further their personal agendas, NIGGERfiliacs construct disingenuous talking points to shield NIGGERS from justified criticisms. NIGGERfiliac explanations for NIGGERtivity such as,* ***"African-Americans resort to crime out of desperation and when the effects of racism and discrimination have denied them all other means of making a living, criminal behavior is the only way of survival,"*** *should be considered insults to those victimized by NIGGERtivity. Refer to the* ***NIGGERnomics*** *chapter.*

7. Is institutionalized racism the blame for their criminality?

Answer: *No, it bears repeating that being a NIGGER is a choice! So, whenever one chooses to be a NIGGER or behave like a NIGGER then the associated consequences are warranted. NIGGERS are a walking paradox; on one hand, "institutionalized" racism is the source of their tribulations, yet they wear their "institutionalized" HNCU background as a badge of honor. It's only a matter of time before NIGGERS blame Affirmative Action for their high HNCU rate. Another NIGGERfiliac method of pardoning NIGGERtivity is to fault the so-called oppressive sociological state of affairs stemming from slavery; in other words, Post Traumatic Slavery Disorder (PTSD). I say, stop using history to justify NIGGERtivity! The reality is that "institutionalized racism" is not perpetrating a disproportionate amount of murdering, raping, robberies etc. inside and outside the African-American community... NIGGERS are.*

8. Is the lack of quality education the reason for their condition?

Answer: *No. This is another sermon preached from the NIGGERfiliacs' false gospel. For decades, society has believed that improving the quality and access to educational opportunities would erase the NIGGER subculture. But attempting to educate those who adore ignorance is mission impossible. Even still, a lack of quality education doesn't excuse the lack of morality. In the* ***"JuviNIGGER"*** *chapter, I discuss some of the accomplishments of BLACK trailblazers who persevered without any of the "free" resources available to today's students. Even the NIGGERfiliacs will have to concede that there are bad apples in every bunch, but the massive amount of NIGGERtivity confirms that it's far more than just a few of bad apples in the African-American bunch... it's an entire subculture.*

9. Do you agree with the notion that increased funding for outreach programs and recreational facilities will reduce or prevent Af-Am teen crime?

Answer: *Not necessarily. JuviNIGGERtivity can't be prevented, only postponed. Social programs only work if the intended beneficiary wants to be helped. The fact is that JuviNIGGERS enjoy being NIGGERS with little intention of changing. For that reason, these repeated outreach/prevention efforts to get orange juice from apples are simply a waste of taxpayer's money. With all the opportunities and organizations that are specific to African-Americans, why spend another cent to reform those who chose not to be reformed? Instead, let's help those who want to be helped. In an article titled, "The color of murder and gun violence in New York (11/10/10)," Washington Post's Jonathan Capehart correctly observed,* ***"People have railed against black-on-black crime for decades. And yet it persists. Yes, there are a host of factors that push someone to a life of crime, but not all of them have to do with the limitations or failures of***

society. Some folks are just plain evil, and no amount of social intervention will stop them from preying on people, especially people who look like them." *It's time to accept the reality that a substantial portion of our populace has chosen to be NIGGERS and damaged beyond repair. In other words, brass will never be gold, regardless of how often it's polished. Don't accept the NIGGERfiliacs' dogma that society has failed this subculture; society hasn't failed them. Contrarily, NIGGERS have consciously chosen O.N.D as their path; too much taxpayer money has already been spent on this failed investment.*

10. Is a NIGGER born a NIGGER?

Answer: *Although NIGGERfiliacs rationalize the NIGGER subculture by blaming everyone and everything under the sun (except NIGGERS), I repeat, being a NIGGER is ultimately a choice. A child's first teacher is his/her parents, and if the kid is raised in an environment where the NIGGER subculture's tenets are prevalent, the child is predisposed to becoming a NIGGER (or black [WNT] at the very least). Quite simply, NIGGERS aren't born... they're nurtured. Even so, remaining a NIGGER is ultimately a choice.*

11. Is "NIGGER" and "NIGGA" the same?

Answer: *Disclaimer... I'm not the definitive source for either word; therefore, it depends on the user's intent. With that, I view "NIGGER" as a term that's specific to the dysfunctional, criminal, and self-depreciating, splinter group existing within the African-American community. Whereas, "NIGGA" is generally used as a term of endearment and even crosses racial lines. Also, it's often liberally used and interpreted without negative connotations. Language evolves, which is why dictionaries are routinely updated* *to reflect such changes. Rapper Tupac Shakur stated that "NIGGA" was an acronym for "Never Ignorant Getting Goals Accomplished (N.I.G.G.A)." I say that "NIGGER" is also an acronym, which stands for "Negro Individual Generating Grief Everywhere Routinely." The difference becomes obvious whenever a N.I.G.G.A starts behaving like a N.I.G.G.E.R.*

12. Is it O.K for other races to call them NIGGERS?

Answer: *Grandmomma Starkes always reiterated,* ***"It's not what you're called, it's what you answer to."*** *And so, if an African-American is called a NIGGER based solely on race, I think that it's an undeserving racial jab. However, if that African-American is exhibiting NIGGER tendencies, indulging in NIGGERtivity, or is actually a NIGGER, then yes, regardless of the speaker's race, I fully support such usage. As creators of chaos, NIGGERS deserved to be rebuked. Furthermore, in this context, it really isn't a racial epithet... it's a fact. Despite who utters the word, remember that NIGGERS have done incalculable damage to all communities. Thus, I won't defend them in any capacity. In fact, if an alien species landed on Earth, I'd introduce this segment of African-Americans for who they were... NIGGERS! On many occasions, BLACKS have expressed their support for my mission, but not usage of the "N-Word." I argue that calling NIGGERS anything besides NIGGERS still won't erase their status as feral blacks with sociopathic tendencies. In other words, a change of name will not change their standing or behavior. But, OK... if people desire that I not refer to NIGGERS by that name, I'll stop...as soon as they stop behaving like NIGGERS! We live in an age where the word 'NIGGER' is treated as if it's more dangerous than the actual beings who intentionally personify it. African-Americans need to concern themselves with patenting and* *trademarking S.T.E.M ideas instead of protecting this pseudo-patent of the "N-Word." As a BLACK man, I naturally understand the historical hurt associated with the term, but again, language changes over time and the word NIGGER hasn't escaped this reality. Still, African-Americans cannot fight for equality on all fronts, and then contradictorily claim exclusively of "NIGGER or Nigga." So, if "NIGGER" cannot be said by Euro-Americans, then it's only fair that "wigger" or "cracker" cannot be said by African-Americans. Actor Alec Baldwin felt the hypocritical wrath of the NIGGERfiliacs when he audaciously tweeted the actual name of song that he enjoyed (How dare he!!!). He tweeted,* ***"I love that song Niggas in Paris!!! I love Kanye!!"*** *Apparently, the self-appointed gatekeepers would've preferred he said,* ***"I love that song-- Two black rappers in Paris!"*** *If African-Americans policed their communities with the same passion as is done with policing the "N-word," the NIGGER subculture would've been marginalized decades ago; ultimately, ending this Un-Civil War.*

Minorities Represent Largest Sector Not Interested In Pursuing STEM Careers
prnewswire.com

[Article's Quote: "The largest group contributing to this percentage is African-Americans, with 61 percent of respondents declaring that they are not interested in pursuing careers in healthcare and the sciences."]

13. Is the term "REDNECK" equivalent to NIGGER?

Answer: *Great question. Many try to parallel these two groups, but rednecks simply don't create the vast amount of violent crime as NIGGERS. Clearly, every race has an underclass, but being an underclass is not a license for maniacal behavior. For generations, rednecks have been marginalized and stereotyped, yet, aren't committing astounding amounts of "redneck on redneck" homicides. Another major difference between the two groups is that rednecks usually love America, and are patriotic,* *whereas NIGGERS despise America, and are chaotic. Professor Thomas Sowell provided his analysis on the subject in the Wall Street Journal (April 26, 2005):* ***"The redneck culture proved to be a major handicap for both whites and blacks who absorbed it. Today, the last remnants of that culture can still be found in the worst of the black ghettos, whether in the North or the South, for the ghettos of the North were settled by blacks from the South. The counterproductive and self-destructive culture of black rednecks in today's ghettos is regarded by many as the only 'authentic' black culture—and, for that reason, something not to be tampered with. Their talk, their attitudes, and their behavior are regarded as sacrosanct."*** *If the NIGGER subculture is a byproduct of the redneck culture, as Professor Sowell asserts, why aren't redneck infested trailer parks suffering from violent crime like NIGfested housing projects? Therefore, my final answer is no.*

14. According to the latest U.S Census, African-Americans are approximately 13% of the population. Of that 13%, how many are NIGGERS?

Answer: *This is another good question that's worthy of debate. This rogue splinter group has and continues to create so much hell that they seem larger than their actual count. The African-American community has allowed NIGGERS to hijack their image without penalties; consequently, others sometimes have difficulty differentiating between BLACKS and NIGGERS. BLACKS have to separate themselves to a point where NIGGERS are recognized as easily as a drunken person is to a sober person. Although I don't know the NIGGERS' true count, I know that they're still a minority within a minority, despite the fact that they unfathomably commit crimes proportionate to a majority.*

15. Are there NIGGERS outside the United States?

Answer: *Absolutely! The internet corroborates that their destructive and chaotic existence will extend to any environment if left unchecked. Globally, their only contribution to the world is to bring pain and suffering. This book focuses on American NIGGERS because unfortunately, I'm most familiar with them.*

"Black men 'to blame for most violent city crime'... but they're also the victims"
dailymail.co.uk

16. Throughout the book, you mentioned that there are blacks with NIGGER tendencies; conversely, can NIGGERS have tendencies of responsible BLACKS?

Answer: *Not really. The only time that a NIGGER appears to be a responsible is when it is advantageous. During those times, they suppress their true nature and use any positive BLACK imagery whenever/wherever their NIGGER identity is a detriment. This technique has been extremely effective in getting NIGGERfiliacs, to rally for the NIGGER subculture. As the poet Maya Angelou eloquently recommends,* ***"When people show you who they are, believe them."***

17. Can you further explain the differences between Obsessive NIGGER Disorder (O.N.D) and NIGGER tendencies?

Answer: *As stated in* ***Why Write this Book*** *(Chapter I), O.N.D is a pattern of behavior exclusive to NIGGERS. However, O.N.D has many attributes, and blacks (WNT) may exhibit one or several symptoms of the disorder. I liken O.N.D to A.I.D.S (Acquired Immune Deficiency Syndrome), and NIGGER tendencies to H.I.V (Human Immunodeficiency Virus). A person can live with HIV without developing full-blown AIDS. Similarly, a black (WNT) can live with these NIGGER tendencies without developing full-*

blown OND. HIV weakens the immune system, and if left untreated may develop into AIDS. Similarly, if the NIGGER tendencies are left untreated, they may eventually develop into OND. In other words, there is a high probability that blacks (WNT) will become NIGGERS if they don't take Anti-NIGGER medicine.

18. Can blacks with NIGGER tendencies become productive BLACKS?

Answer: *Yes, they typically have the potential to change. However, a horse can only be lead to water; it can't be made to drink. Quite simply, blacks with NIGGER tendencies need to indulge in Anti-NIGGER activities while disassociating themselves from the NIGGER subculture. Booker T. Washington articulated,* ***"Associate yourself with people of good quality, for it is better to be alone than in bad company."***

19. How were you able to make the transition from being a black (W.N.T) to a BLACK man?

Answer: *The short answer is that I decided to R.A.T. (Read and Travel). Both aspects have broadened my horizon and allowed me to see the myopia of the HoG and NIGGER subculture. Those experiences are the reason why I was able to evolve from the projects to this project.*

ACKNOWLEDGEMENTS

I want to publicly salute the following talented visionaries and realists. Realizing that this unique endeavor is both polarizing and controversial, you still lent your support, and placed principles over everything.

Firstly, my ***Beautiful Wife***: For every successful man, there's a resilient woman beside him. Undoubtedly, you're that woman. I want to thank you for riding this roller coaster, tolerating my spontaneous vents along with the seemingly endless writing/researching, and all the other book-related activity that interfered with our quality time. Because of you, I am better in so many ways, and eagerly anticipate marrying you... again :*

Secondly, my fellow ***Un-Civil War Soldiers***, who diligently use mentorship to deter the youth from joining the other side. ***Sixx King, Marlon Williams, Jhonn Puente***, *and* ***Yusef Keith,***

Thirdly, my **Sister**: You've always given more than you've received. In fact, many people have mistaken your kindness for weakness. However, it's not a weakness; it's actually a strength that many don't possess (especially from where we came). Keep growing and shining. I love you.

Last but not least, my wonderful family and friends. Although we may not regularly talk, and some of you may even disagree with the book's premise, I still draw inspiration: **Jim (who always keeps a balanced viewpoint)** ***Ike & Kim C., Grandpa Jack, Tia & Aunt Cookie, ZuBe, K. Story, Jay Berry, Day Neal, and Mother/Sister Abiona.***

*Can't forget the graphic artists who lent their talents: **Joonaria Photography** (Rear cover photo credit), ***YJK Design USA, JDLP Photography, Leonartist, John***

Allen Photography, and ***Lawless Law at Badd Kompany***.

Eternal respect for these underappreciated staff who work with me in the trenches: ***Big Momma Pam*, ***Baby "D" Edwards***, ***Nina F.***, ***Pam C.***, and **Gary H.**

Special Shout outs to ***Dr. K.W. Cosby, DeVone Holt, Clay Calloway, Laura Jean*, ***George Galatis, Tyrone Steels II, Frank Gennaro,*** and ***Paula Webber*** for their undying support.

RIP: ***Grand matriarch Alice Starkes, Uncle Al, J.T Mull, Genevieve Corley, Ahmad Curry, Burnell Harrington, Uncle Larry, and Lil John Berry.***

Twitter: ***@TaleebStarkes***

Email: ***Taleeb@blacksvsniggers.com***

*********Thanks For Listening*********

BILL COSBY and TALEEB STARKES

21231589R00147

Made in the USA
Middletown, DE
22 June 2015